CALIFORNIA STUDIES IN URBANIZATION
AND ENVIRONMENTAL DESIGN

MANAGED INTEGRATION

HARVEY
LUSKIN
MOLOTCH

Managed Integration
Dilemmas
of Doing
Good
in the
City

BERKELEY
LOS ANGELES
LONDON
UNIVERSITY OF CALIFORNIA PRESS

University of California Press
Berkeley and Los Angeles, California
University of California Press, Ltd.
London, England
Copyright © 1972, by
The Regents of the University of California
ISBN: 0–520–01889–3
Library of Congress Catalog Card Number: 74–142049
Designed by W. H. Snyder
Printed in the United States of America

For Linda

Contents

Preface

LIKE many students of contemporary issues in the middle 1960's, I believed that most of "our urban problems" could be ameliorated if only the expertise of the social scientist could be applied to their solution. This justified my choice of vocation and shaped my intellectual work and political life while I was a graduate student at the University of Chicago.

This book is the product of that belief as it was played out in the context of sociology graduate work and in the context of local and national events between 1965 and 1967. Given the interest of local scholars and citizens in the apparent success of urban redevelopment and racial integration in the Hyde Park-Kenwood Community adjacent to the campus, the feeling was that the next problem was to discover means by which this success could be achieved in other more typical urban communities. That was to be my task and South Shore my turf.

I was uneasy with the project from the start. It did not, I thought, promise to be profound enough to lead to general sociological insights. Nor did it seem to hold promise for a rich learning experience—especially in regard to sophisticated technique, theoretical depth, or involvement with the more exotic cutting-edge subfields of the discipline. Finally, and this feeling grew as time passed, I became skeptical of residential racial integration as a goal, and particularly of the means used to achieve it. Given the environments with which I had to contend (the university and the study area), this proved to be a blasphemy difficult to live with and one which undermined much of the rationale for my work. What results is a compromise between that first vague study design and the misgivings picked up along the way.

My first research act was to embark upon a series of walks through the community to get the feel of the area. I decided to keep walking until something serendipitous finally happened. In a number of preliterate North American societies, as the puberty rite of

ix

passage, the young males are sent into the wilderness to listen for certain words from the spirits. If they are able to return and report the proper message they are men; if they cannot return with the sacred words, they perish in the wild. Miraculously, they come back with the guiding words from the gods. And so did I.

The gods of the wilderness were helpful all along, but not alone. Morris Janowitz provided enough threats to keep things moving as well as an informed critique. David Street and Gerald Suttles (who joined the department as I finished up) commented in detail on a first draft. Brian J. L. Berry, Eugene Smolensky, R. Joyce Whitley, and Jack Meltzer of the Center for Urban Studies were frequently on hand to make helpful suggestions. Financial support was provided through successive fellowship grants from the Bowman C. Lingle Foundation, Marshall Field Foundation and NIMH. My multi-disciplinaried student colleagues, besides offering strategic advice on how to deal with the above, also provided warmth and analysis. I thank Stephan Barsky (who shared the interviewing), C. Nirmahla Devi, John Dyckman (who assisted in data collection), Peter Goheen, Charles Goldsmid, Saundra Parsons, Patricia Peery, Robert Stauffer, Suzanne Roffler Tarlov, and Linda Wolf. The Sociology Department at the University of California, Santa Barbara, has provided me with the best of working environments and my colleagues there have done more to my head than they know. Because their influence came so late in the game, I have not been able to do justice to the many insights they have given me. In particular, I thank Aaron Cicourel, Lloyd Fitts, Richard Flacks, Milton Mankoff, Tomatsu Shibutani, and Don Zimmerman. The influence of my wife Linda, as always my most astute collaborator and demanding critic, is in everything I have written here.

Much of my work rests on the comments and behavior of my South Shore "subjects"; most of them will probably never read this book, but I am nevertheless in their debt. I don't think they would have had me in South Shore and cooperated so fully had they envisioned the final product, and so my debt to them is doubly great and the source of some anxiety. There is no more presumptuous activity than to record, analyze, and—at least implicitly—pass judgment on the lives of other people, especially people who are known only casually, who have no opportunity for reciprocal investigation, and for whom one has no lasting responsibility. Life is too complicated for me to have been anything more than a little bit right.

There is almost no passage in this book about which I have not had second thoughts, and in some cases the reader will find here third and fourth thoughts. Disturbing as it may seem for our discipline and its "knowledge base," as well as for the feelings of my respondents reading this, it likely would only take more time and more drafts to revise and perhaps reverse many of my conclusions. I hope to be gracious enough to appreciate those who, after reading this book, are able to do it for me.

Portions of Chapter Eight have appeared under the title "Racial Change in a Stable Community," *American Journal of Sociology,* Vol. 75, No. 2, September 1969. Much of Chapter Nine is being reprinted from "Racial Integration in a Transition Community," *American Sociologoical Review,* Vol. 34, No. 6, December 1969. Chapter Ten contains materials which first appeared in "Toward a More Human Human Ecology: An Urban Research Strategy," *Land Economics,* Vol. 43, No. 3, August 1967.

The following organizations and agencies provided data and assistance: City of Chicago Departments of Police, Urban Renewal, Planning and Development, Maps and Plats, Human Relations Commission and Board of Education; Cook County Recorder of Deeds and Department of Welfare; Chicago Real Estate Board, Hyde Park-Kenwood Community Conference; Southeast Chicago Commission; Real Estate Research Corporation; Hospital Planning Council for Metropolitan Chicago; Chicago Urban League; South Shore Commission; South Shore Organization for Human Rights; Archdiocese of Chicago; South Shore Hospital; and South Shore Open Housing Center.

Santa Barbara
July, 1971

Part I

The Racial Change Process

1
Introduction:
Community
Action and
Ecological
Structure

For most middle-class Americans, residential racial change is a public issue with impact. On most matters of "public concern," even persons routinely interested in politics and their community are generally detached observers who somehow choose to care about matters of no real personal importance. Compared to concerns of family, job, and health, "issues" are not usually sources of felt personal troubles,[1] and they tend to enter the life space only at parties and on other occasions when material is needed for less than important talk.

But racial change in one's own neighborhood is different. For a white caught up in neighborhood change, the pattern of his or her mental and physical existence is disrupted; to the extent that milieu is important to one's identity and round of daily movements, neighborhood racial change can take on as much significance as a job lay-off or an offspring's unwise marriage. Perhaps this is why it occupies so much of the talk of white urban dwellers, is so salient a "problem" to their leaders, and is so widespread a source of investigative material for white sociologists.

This study thus rests upon a past rich with lay speculation and social-science analysis. It is an attempt to evaluate, in light of the actual determinants of racial change, the potential for community action to prevent the resegregation of urban communities.

One changing community was the center of attention. I examined the interactions between ecological forces which make for racial change and the techniques used by community organizations to

1. See C. Wright Mills, *The Sociological Imagination* (New York: Oxford University Press, 1959).

intervene in that change. We thus study matters of rather broad significance: first, the mechanisms which set in motion and which sustain urban ecological change; second, an attempt by citizens to take on forces beyond their ordinary powers to control and to collectively expend energy to effect a goal which is linked to both a public issue and a private trouble. The combination of these broad concerns into a single research focus was made possible by an ambitious attempt by an indigenous community group, operating without massive support from external civic and governmental bodies, to intervene in the ecological forces which underlie racial change in order to replace racial transition with racial integration.

BACKGROUND CONCERNS

Since World War II American cities have undergone a transition of many neighborhoods from white to black occupancy, and an increase in the number and scope of active neighborhood improvement groups. These were not two independent phenomena. The organizations, often called "improvement associations" or "community development" associations, typically consist of residents of an urban area working to effect what they regard as the betterment of their community. Their representatives are seen often at civic hearings, they meet often with local political leaders, and they have generally become ubiquitous on the urban scene. As seen by city officials and civic "boosters," an important value of such groups (at least when they are in white neighborhoods) is in their usefulness in creating and maintaining communities capable of attracting middle-class whites to city areas. Indeed, as past investigations have shown, the existence and vigor of such organizations tends to be a function of the prospect or reality of racial change in or near the community.[2]

Racial segregation in the United States rests, in many ways, upon *residential* segregation, which generates separation of races within schools, recreation and social centers, places of work, and retail shopping facilities. One locale in which racial integration occurs, at least in some form and at least for a short time, is the changing neighborhood on the ghetto's edge. But any integration occurring in

2. See Zorita Wise Mikva, "The Neighborhood Improvement Association: A Counter-Force to the Expansion of Chicago's Negro Population" (unpublished Master's thesis, Department of Sociology, University of Chicago, 1951).

such areas is short-lived. Although many hundreds of such neighborhoods have experienced transition since the war years, the amount
of residential segregation in American cities remained virtually un-
changed from 1940 to 1960.[3] Thus the process by which blacks
come to occupy housing in white areas continues to result in a
"resegregation" of the races, although with the consequence that
newly drawn boundary lines increase the size of the housing supply
available to the growing black population.

PATTERNS OF NEIGHBORHOOD CHANGE

The process of residential succession and various aspects
of the transition pattern have been described in numerous studies.[4]
We have found a classic pattern of block-by-block replacement of
whites by blacks in areas contiguous to the constantly expanding
black residential area. By a process of push and pull, upwardly
mobile whites are replaced by upwardly mobile blacks.

A comprehensive demographic view of the racial succession
process has been set forth by Duncan and Duncan,[5] who deduced

3. Karl Taeuber and Alma Taeuber, *Negroes in Cities* (Chicago: Aldine, 1965),
p. 44.
4. Case studies of particular changing communities include: Robert L. Fulton,
"Russel Woods: A Study of a Neighborhood's Initial Response to Negro Invasion"
(unpublished Ph.D. dissertation, Department of Sociology, Wayne State University,
1960); Ruth M. McIntyre, "The Organizational Nature of an Urban Residential
Neighborhood in Transition: Homewood-Brushton of Pittsburgh" (unpublished
Ph.D. dissertation, Department of Sociology, University of Pittsburgh, 1963);
Paul F. Cressey, "Succession of Cultural Groups in the City of Chicago" (un-
published Ph.D. dissertation, Department of Sociology, University of Chicago,
1930); Frederick Burgess Lindstrom, "The Negro Invasion of the Washington
Park Subdivision" (unpublished Master's dissertation, Department of Sociology,
University of Chicago, 1941); Fay Lee Robertson, "A Study of Some Aspects
of Racial Succession in the Woodlawn Area" (unpublished Master's dissertation,
Department of Sociology, University of Chicago, 1957); Kathryn Meadow,
"Negro-White Differences Among Newcomers to a Transitional Urban Area,"
Journal of Intergroup Relations, III (Autumn 1962), 322–330; Alvin Winder,
"White Attitudes Towards Negro-White Interaction in an Area of Changing
Racial Composition" (unpublished Ph.D. dissertation, Department of Sociology,
University of Chicago, 1952); Herbert Gamberg, "White Perceptions of Negro
Race and Class as Factors in the Racial Residential Process" (unpublished Ph.D.
dissertation, Sociology Department, Princeton University, 1964).
5. Otis Dudley Duncan and Beverly Duncan, *The Negro Population of Chicago*
(Chicago: University of Chicago Press, 1957). For other general discussions of
succession, see: Taeuber and Taeuber, *Negroes in Cities, passim;* Charles Tilly
et al., Race and Residence in Wilmington, Delaware (New York: Columbia University Press, 1965).

from their studies of black migration in Chicago a four-stage process of racial change: "penetration" marks the initial entry of blacks into an all-white area; "invasion" occurs as a substantial number of blacks follow; "consolidation" indicates a continuing increase in the number and proportion of blacks, leading to complete replacement of whites by blacks; "piling-up" occurs as the number of blacks exceeds the original number of whites. The Duncans' analysis, although based on the crudely racist terminology of the times, is usefully sensitive to the fact that neighborhoods do not "turn overnight," and as their analysis of mobility data makes clear, an area's transition may take several months, several years, or more than a decade.

Taking a perspective not inconsistent with that of the Duncans, Morrill [6] has proposed a model of neighborhood racial change based on a process of "spatial diffusion," by which larger and larger amounts of city area come to be occupied by blacks. Again, diffusion is not an immediate turnover of population in a white community contiguous to the ghetto, but an increasing *probability* in that community that units will become occupied by blacks rather than by whites with decreasing proximity to the already existing black residential area. In the Duncans' terms, a community or tract undergoing penetration, invasion, or even consolidation may still have within it housing units which are being purchased or newly rented by whites (especially at points most distant from the original point of black entry).

Rapkin and Grigsby[7] have provided empirical support for this view with their discovery that white purchasing is not uncommon after black in-migration has begun, although the proportion of purchasers who are white decreases almost to the vanishing point with increasing propinquity to blocks which are largely black. Thus succession should not be viewed as a process in which whites cease to buy or rent in a changing community, but one in which, to use Morrill's words, "the rate (of white in-migration) is insufficient, the net flow clear-cut, and the transition inevitable." An increasing number of blacks, in search of better housing near existing black areas, attempt to locate within the changing community. The "pres-

6. Richard Morrill, "The Negro Ghetto: Problems and Alternatives," *Geographical Review,* LV (July 1965), 339–361.
7. Chester Rapkin and William G. Grigsby, *The Demand for Housing in Racially Mixed Areas* (Berkeley and Los Angeles: University of California Press, 1960).

sure" of the growing black population is the "push" of the succession process—a push which determines that an ever-increasing proportion of new residents in a transition area will be black.

Succession theory and the empirical research based on it are less clear in explaining the "pull"—the response of indigenous whites in an area undergoing change or where change is imminent. Often it is held that whites leave a community before and during the change process for reasons having nothing to do with issues of race; they are simply translating upward social mobility into geographical mobility. More commonly, however, it is assumed that contiguity to blacks is at least part of the reason why whites leave a changing area. Such a response is often held to reflect not "pure" anti-Negro bigotry but rather the concern of white residents for their social status,[8] for the education of their children in the public schools,[9] or for other matters related to, but not intrinsic in, the race of their neighbors.

Another characteristic often ascribed to the succession process is resistance on the part of the indigenous group. At least some form of resistance was included in Burgess' notion of racial succession;[10] the Duncans believe the question of resistance requires empirical verification. We have studies that document instances of violent resistance to black in-migration and cases of neighborhood change without violence.[11] Resistance can take forms other than violence, but little attention has been given them in the literature of changing neighborhoods.

In some communities that are contiguous to all-black residential areas and otherwise ripe for black occupancy, community improvement associations more subtly strive to maintain an all-white neighborhood by building community "morale," pressuring local real estate firms to resist making sales to blacks, or by repurchasing homes from blacks.[12] From the limited number of studies of such attempts, we may assume that these efforts are not likely to succeed

8. See Gamberg, "White Perceptions."

9. See Eleanor P. Wolf, "The Baxter Area, 1960–1962: A New Trend in Neighborhood Change?" *Phylon*, XXVI (Winter 1965), 348–361.

10. Ernest Burgess, "Residential Segregation in American Cities," *Annals of the American Academy of Political and Social Science*, CXL (November 1928), 105–115.

11. See studies cited in note 4.

12. See, for example, Fulton, "Russel Woods"; The Divinity School, University of Chicago, *The Edge of the Ghetto* (Chicago: University of Chicago Divinity School, 1965).

except perhaps when coupled with violence or intimidation of black in-migrants.[13]

Another form of resistance—and one most relevant for this study —is the attempt to inhibit succession through the creation of a racially integrated community. A community organization attempts to preserve, at least in part, the character of an area by maintaining white residency concomitant with the assimilation of significant numbers of black residents. What ultimately comes to be actively resisted is thus not black in-migration per se, but rather the complete replacement of one population group in the area by another. Thus, through a combination of necessity and desire, the goal is to create a new kind of community—one different from the community as it was previous to black in-migration, but also different from what would result if succession were to run its course.

The Hyde Park case described by Rossi and Dentler[14] and by Abrahamson[15] is the best known example of what can result. In this instance success in achieving a biracial community after black in-migration began was due to the work of the Hyde Park–Kenwood Community Conference (a local voluntary organization) and to the commitment of funds and personnel by the area's dominant institution, the University of Chicago. In addition, the community received support from a large federally financed urban renewal grant. Despite the widespread attention which Hyde Park has received, it remains difficult to determine the relative significance of each of the three components (community organization, institutional support, urban renewal) in achieving the community's continued bi-raciality.

THE SOUTH SHORE CASE

The Chicago community of South Shore, the area on which this research is based, was regarded as worthy of special attention because its community organization was operating with-

13. See Fred Hoehler, "Community Action by United Packinghouse Workers of America" (unpublished Master's dissertation, Department of Political Science, University of Chicago, 1947).

14. Peter Rossi and Robert Dentler, *The Politics of Urban Renewal* (New York: The Free Press, 1961).

15. Julia Abrahamson, *A Neighborhood Finds Itself* (New York: Harper, 1959).

out such external supports yet attempting to achieve what Hyde Park had accomplished. In its South Shore Commission, the area had perhaps the largest community organization in the United States. It was founded in *advance* of racial change and developed an array of programs probably as great in depth and scope as that of any other comparable area in the country. In addition, South Shore had a middle-class, relatively educated population—persons who presumably would be willing to accept black neighbors rather than give up the sound housing and other amenities characteristic of the community. Moreover, South Shore residents might be expected to be influenced by the "demonstration" in Hyde Park (a neighborhood only a few miles to the north) of the possibilities for, and benefits of, racial integration.

But in the main, South Shore's major asset was its community organization. Unlike Hyde Park, it could not rely on a great university, a major renewal program, or any other massive form of outside intervention. The resources available in South Shore, it seemed, were probably not very different from those accessible to the citizens of many other changing areas. Thus South Shore seemed typical enough of the "grey areas" where racial change is likely to occur, so that findings would be generalizable to many other communities.

South Shore possessed the attributes which, as other studies have suggested, are characteristic of areas likely to undergo racial change —a high proportion of renter-occupied housing, a relatively educated population, an old age structure, a large Jewish population, and dwellings which were predominantly basically sound but obsolete.[16] Most important, however, was the fact that South Shore was contiguous to black residential areas; and given the block-by-block expansion pattern of the black ghetto characteristic of Chicago and other cities, this is perhaps the crucial common characteristic which South Shore shared with other changing areas.[17] A success in South Shore, it might be assumed, would thus imply that many other communities bordering the black ghetto, similarly subject to intense pressure from blacks in search of good housing, could

16. See Annette Fishbein, "The Expansion of Negro Residential Areas in Chicago" (unpublished Master's dissertation, Department of Sociology, University of Chicago, 1962); Taeuber and Taeuber, *Negroes in Cities,* pp. 155–158.

17. For documentation of the block-by-block "propinquity pattern" of neighborhood racial change, see: Chicago Urban League, "Negro Migration in Chicago, 1950–1960–1964" (Chicago: The Chicago Urban League, 1965); Duncan and Duncan, *The Negro Population of Chicago*; Morrill, "The Negro Ghetto."

achieve a similar goal, and so significantly reduce racial segregation in American cities.

ACTIONS AND IMPEDIMENTS

Given the validity of this assumption—one which will be examined in greater detail later on—it followed that the techniques and strategies used by the South Shore Commission should be recorded and analyzed so that they could be used by other communities. In addition to describing the various programs and policies of the commission, I tried to determine their effectiveness in influencing neighborhood racial patterns. For this purpose, I examined in some detail larger ecological forces as they manifest themselves in the real estate market of a changing area. For example, I have tried to determine how real estate dealers perceive their interests to be affected by the prospect and reality of racial change. How and why are decisions made to rent an apartment or to sell a home to blacks where in the past they have been excluded? I have tried to answer such questions in order to point out some of the obstacles to achieving racial integration and the relevance of specific community programs and techniques to overcoming those obstacles.

I also call attention to organizational factors likely to influence the ability of a voluntary association, such as the South Shore Commission, to achieve its goals. How, for example, are goals formulated? What organizational resources are available in such a residential community and how can they be mobilized effectively? How can a large voluntary association effectively overcome tendencies which create internal controversy and dissension?

Finally, I have tried to assess the degree to which the South Shore Commission achieved its ultimate goal. That is, to what extent and in what ways was South Shore emerging as a stable, integrated community at the close of the study period? In what ways was South Shore different from a community experiencing racial succession in the classic pattern? I have tried to determine the degree to which community action can be expected to alter the larger ecological system.

An organizational effort like that put forth by the South Shore Commission has effects on community life not directly related to the attempt to influence racial patterns. For example, how does the existence of such an organization affect the lives of its leaders, of less active residents, and those whose behavior or residence in the area is regarded as harmful to the community? What styles of interaction develop between members of different races in such settings? In the face of inevitable periodic defeats, how is enough *esprit* maintained to guarantee continued organizational functioning? What are the kinds of rewards which keep organizational leaders working without pay or other tangible benefits? How can an organization like the South Shore Commission continually generate willingness among its members to sacrifice time and effort for communal gains? How does a "self-help" organization differ in these regards from more militant protest-oriented community groups? Is the dynamic of organizational energy found in South Shore transferable to other communities—especially low-income areas where attempts based on the self-help doctrine so often seem to fail?

Finally, what are the general implications, for the metropolitan area as a whole, of successful intervention in the ecological process such as that attempted by the South Shore Commission? What would be the consequences for urban growth and change if there were many "South Shore Commissions" operating in an urban area, each attempting to intervene in the processes by which various social groups are deployed over urban space? In plant and animal ecology, certain unanticipated consequences are assumed to follow any intervention in the natural ecological system; what are the analogous results of intervention in the human sphere? What are the goals of such interventions likely to be, and if they are met, what general results for the larger human habitat can be expected?

These are large questions, and I can offer only tentative answers for them. I hoped that by examining an organization that was attemping to influence the racial change process, while at the same time investigating the secular forces which constitute that process, additional light could be shed on two important issues which have been the subject of much sociological investigation and speculation:

community organization and contemporary urban ecology. The general setting of the study thus provides an opportunity to examine the dynamics and limitations of voluntarism—the mechanisms of successful community intervention and the consequences, foreseen and unforeseen, which surrounding ecological and demographic forces come to create.

RESEARCH STRATEGY

I have closely observed community life, particularly the meetings, special events, and day-to-day operations of the South Shore Commission. From July 1965 to July 1967, I attended approximately one hundred community meetings, conducted sixty semi-structured interviews with community leaders, and had countless informal discussions with other residents and commission leaders. I always tried to learn how the residents perceived what was happening to their community and how they thought its problems could be solved. In addition, I used these contacts to gather specific information on the history and effectiveness of the commission and its various programs and policies.

In the process, I became personally known to most community leaders, but I played no part in organizational decision making and gave no advice and few opinions; only occasionally did I provide technical information on the community and city, and make available certain city planning source materials. After the initial interviewing and intensive observation in the summer of 1966, my presence at community meetings became accepted as routine. I took notes during meetings and after informal discussions with local residents.

I read all issues of the community newspaper which serves South Shore, *The Southeast Economist,* during the study period and the relevant reports which appeared in two metropolitan newspapers, the *Chicago Sun-Times* and the *Chicago Daily News.* I kept a clipping file of publicized events and statements on South Shore that provided useful substantive information and a record of the stimuli which residents received about their community. Reports of crime, racial "incidents," and changing racial composition of local schools I saw as important factors affecting the "mood" of the community and thus perhaps the racial change process as well.

I studied other appropriate documents: census data, school board reports, deed transfer records, local hospital records, and reports of various civic groups relevant to population movements in the Chicago area. I investigated the reports issued by the South Shore Commission and those of other important community groups. When possible I compared South Shore with other Chicago communities in an attempt to make findings more meaningful.

I tried to use hard data to temper and inform the more subjective judgments I derived from impressionistic observations, including the use of certain unobtrusive measures of community behavior. For example, I counted "for sale" signs in front of area homes, and made racial head-counts in various community institutions and specific locales.

Another source of important information was an interview survey of real estate dealers doing business in the South Shore area and in other districts of metropolitan Chicago. Real estate dealers are perhaps closest to the process through which housing is allocated to diverse social groups in city areas; their viewpoints are significant because they know the workings of the market and influence those workings by the ways in which they act upon their opinions. Thus in order to learn of the cognitive set with which such businessmen approach the prospect and reality of a racially changing neighborhood, I asked dealers what they thought happens to rents, maintenance costs, and other business conditions when a neighborhood comes to experience racial transition. A detailed statement of my survey methods is presented in the Appendix.

My methods and various research focuses were not chosen with reference to a worked-out study design; I developed procedures as opportunities, financial and intellectual, arose. My foremost methodological concern was to come up with something significant or interesting, and so I did whatever I could to increase the possibility of that happening. Gradually my somewhat disparate activities came to yield results that I saw as connected, or connectible, into a single story line.

PLAN OF PRESENTATION

In the pages that follow I have tried to hide the chaos, the ad hoc procedures, and the personal opportunism through which this research (like perhaps all research) was carried out; whatever its failings, my presentation is more orderly than the activities which led up to it.

Chapters One and Two in Part I are a general introduction to the subject of community racial change and its underlying issues. Real estate market mechanisms of changing areas are described through the results of the landlord survey presented in Chapter Two.

Part II is an account of the intervention attempted in South Shore. Chapter Three describes the study area and the causes and consequences of community boundary formation. Chapter Four examines the South Shore Commission's base of support, organizational make-up, methods of operation, and history of growth. Chapter Five deals with the tactics and strategies used to improve South Shore as a home area for middle-class whites. Chapter Six describes South Shore's most ambitious intervention program, a tenant referral service.

Part III contains the evaluation and analysis of the intervention. Within the context of the general market mechanisms set forth in Chapter Two, Chapter Seven describes the speed of racial change in South Shore and Chapter Eight the amount of property turnover there. In Chapter Nine I try to evaluate the extent, patterns, and quality of biracial social life accompanying the entry of blacks into the community. Chapter Ten offers my conclusions and some final speculations prompted by the findings.

2
The Dual Market

Because of the segregated housing patterns characteristic of all large American cities, there are two different housing
markets in urban areas—one for whites and one for blacks.[1] A
neighborhood in transition, like South Shore, is a setting in which
housing is being transferred from the white market to the Negro
market. Taeuber and Taeuber have written:

> It can be assumed that the supply of housing for non-whites is re-
> stricted in terms of both number of units and quality of units. For
> non-whites, then, demand is high relative to supply, and this situation
> is aggravated by the rapidly increasing urban Negro populations. Housing
> within Negro areas can command higher prices than comparable housing
> in white residential areas. Furthermore, there has been continual need
> for Negro housing, which has been met by transferring property at the
> periphery of Negro areas from the white housing market to the Negro
> housing market. The high demand among Negroes for housing, com-
> bined with a relatively low demand among whites for housing in many
> of these peripheral areas makes the transfer of housing from whites to
> Negroes profitable.[2]

An implicit assumption of the Taeuber model is that blacks pay
more for comparable housing than whites—at least in a transition
zone. Indirect evidence, provided by census data, indicates that
blacks generally pay about a third more for housing, at a given

1. For documentation of how segregation is only insignificantly determined by
differences in the economic status of the two racial groups, see Karl Taeuber and
Alma Taeuber, *Negroes in Cities* (Chicago: Aldine, 1965), pp. 28–37.
2. *Ibid.,* p. 25.

income level, than whites.[3] Richard Muth points out that at least
part of this difference may be due to blacks purchasing additional
services, such as utilities and furniture, which may be more likely to
be included in rentals to blacks than to whites.[4] Studies which compare housing values in the white and Negro markets offer more
direct evidence. At least with regard to single-family units, it seems
clear that blacks do pay more than whites. Muth, who compared
changes in housing value in Chicago South Side tracts over a ten-
year period, concluded that average values in tracts which changed
from white to black occupany rose by 18 percent *more* than the
value rise in tracts remaining white.[5]

In the case of apartment rental levels, the evidence is less clear.
Muth compares apartment rentals in the same way he compares
changes in single-family house values; he concludes that the black
rental premium is slight, if it exists at all. The methodological problem here is that it is reasonable to expect that buildings in black-
occupied tracts received lower levels of maintenance than did those
in white tracts; thus equal rents were paid for unequal facilities,
implying that blacks may actually have paid substantially more.
Muth attempts to control for this possible difference by including
census judgments of "substandard" and "dilapidated" in his regression analysis. Unfortunately, these variables are too crude to catch
maintenance differences such as deterioration in landscape, frequency
in painting, tuckpointing, and cleaning which are important in determining housing quality. As I will argue later, it is routine practice
for landlords to decrease maintenance levels concomitant with increasing black occupancy. If this is correct, there is no way of
controlling for this variable without finding measures refined enough
to tap subtle condition changes over relatively brief periods. I would
interpret Muth's differential findings in regard to houses and apartments as owing to the fact that single-family homes tend to remain
under the control of the user and thus do not suffer the maintenance
decline associated with landlord control. Thus single-family house
prices rise while apartment rents appear (but only appear) to
remain almost constant.

3. Richard Muth, *Cities and Housing: The Spatial Pattern of Urban Residential
Land Use* (University of Chicago Press, 1969), p. 12.
    4. *Ibid.*, p. 12.
    5. *Ibid.*, Chapter 11. Muth's conclusions are somewhat different from mine. He
distrusts his findings on houses, but trusts his data on apartments. I have done the
reverse.

In any event, these differences involve general comparisons of the black population with the white, or general comparisons of housing in white tracts with those in "turned" black tracts. The Taeuber model, however, rests not upon differences between the two markets in general, but only upon a disparity at the point of racial transition. There are important reasons to suppose that changing communities are precisely those in which black demand is likely to be strongest relative to white demand. First is the fact that such areas are likely to have become increasingly inferior, because of age and obsolescence, to other communities in which whites (but not blacks) have the opportunity to move. Further, contiguity to existing black areas is, in itself, perhaps a reason for a decline in white demand. Black demand, on the other hand, increases with such propinquity. Blacks can locate in such areas without losing contact with existing black institutions and old friends; in a more general way, proximity presents intervening opportunities[6] which inhibit a search for housing in white areas further distant. Finally, blacks perceive (often along with local real estate firms), that there is a trend [7] in which the contiguous area is next in the path of the expanding black residential area. Blacks will thus believe that it is *possible* to buy or rent in such an area and will more often attempt to do so. We thus have good reasons to suppose that the differences between the two housing markets will be exacerbated in areas of racial transition.

Studies of single-family house values in changing areas support the Taeuber model. Housing values seldom decline, and often rise, as blacks move into white areas.[8] Other, somewhat outdated studies, indicate that blacks pay more than whites for comparable houses in

6. See: Samuel Stouffer, "Intervening Opportunities: A Theory of Relating Mobility and Distance," *American Sociological Review*, V (February 1940), 845–867.

7. For a description of the ideology of real estate dealers regarding racial change and the conceptual framework with which they interpret neighborhood change processes, see Rose Helper, "The Racial Practices of Real Estate Institutions in Selected Areas of Chicago" (unpublished Ph.D. dissertation, Department of Sociology, University of Chicago, 1958).

8. Studies which have indicated that housing values rise or remain constant following Negro in-migration include: Luigi Laurentin, *Property Values and Race* (Berkeley: University of California Press, 1961); E. F. Schietinger, "Racial Succession and Value of Small Residential Properties," *American Journal of Sociology*, LVII (May, 1951), 832–835; Chester Rapkin and William Grigsby, *The Demand for Housing in Racially Mixed Areas* (Berkeley: University of California Press); Hugh Nourse, "The Effect of Public Housing on Property Values in St. Louis" (unpublished Ph.D. dissertation, University of Chicago, 1962).

changing areas.[9] Data on apartment rental levels in changing areas is not available; we can only infer that because similar processes are probably at work, the results would be comparable. Given the general quality of housing typical of transition neighborhoods, it is likely that the Negro market (whether for houses or apartments) is relatively starved for supply.[10] Thus prices are bid high enough to compensate for any fall in white demand. It should be noted that if this were not the case—if the Negro market was not characterized by short supply—the transferral of properties from the white to the Negro market would be more likely to result in a drop in property values. Indeed this has occasionally occurred,[11] but given continuing discrimination against blacks by white landlords, sales agents, and

9. See, for example, Robert Harding Brown, "A Study of the Living Arrangements of the Washington Park Subdivision Family" (unpublished Master's dissertation, Department of Sociology, University of Chicago, 1957); Paul Cressey, "Succession of Cultural Groups in the City of Chicago" (unpublished Ph.D. dissertation, University of Chicago, 1930); and Frederick B. Lindstrom, "The Negro Invasion of the Washington Park Subdivision" (unpublished Master's dissertation, Department of Sociology, University of Chicago, 1941).

10. Martin Bailey has taken issue with this kind of argument. He reports that for a "selected" Chicago neighborhood, "values in slum and Negro areas . . . seem to have fallen below the values of comparable housing" (p. 220), and that "there is no indication that Negroes, as such, pay more for housing than do other people of similar density" (p. 218). These conclusions rest, however, on methodological errors. For example, Bailey's first conclusion rests primarily on his finding that the higher the proportion of black blocks *surrounding*, but not including, the block of a sold house, the lower will be the selling price of that house. Bailey does not report (and likely does not know) the race of the house seller, the house buyer, or the racial composition of the block in question. He does not report the number of cases involved in his regression analysis. Most significantly, he fails to mention that his "selected" area is Hyde Park, adjacent to the University of Chicago, a celebrated case because of the peculiar nature of racial change processes in that student-populated, liberal-intellectual, urban-renewed, institutionally manipulated community. Compounding the mischief, Edward Banfield argues on the basis of Bailey's work that "in Chicago, at least, the statistical Negro pays about the same rent and lives at about the same density as the white." Bailey's argument is much more limited, though, and such a "finding" can emerge from Bailey's article only through misunderstnding or fabrication. Banfield's treatment of Muth's work is somewhat less distorted, but he ignores Muth's important findings which are at variance with his (Banfield's) hypothesis. See Martin Bailey, "Effects of Race and of Other Demographic Factors on the Values of Single-Family Homes," *Land Economics*, 42 (May 1966), 215–219; Edward Banfield, *The Unheavenly City* (Boston: Little, Brown, 1970), p. 71.

11. See Erdman Palmore and John Howe, "Residential Integration and Property Values," *Social Problems*, 10 (July 1962), pp. 52–55; Raymond Wheeler, "The Relationship between Negro Invasion and Property Prices in Grand Rapids, Michigan" (unpublished Ph.D. dissertation, University of Michigan, 1962).

developers (a fact to be documented in this chapter) black-white parity is likely to remain uncommon.

My informal observations in South Shore seem consistent with this dual market model of the racial change process, whether for apartments or houses. First, blacks did appear to be paying more for homes and higher rents for apartments than whites. For certain types of housing in South Shore, such as the large, luxury houses in Jackson Park Highlands, values seem to have declined, perhaps due to a quick saturation of the black market for such extraordinarily expensive dwellings.[12] But for most other kinds of homes and apartments, prices paid by blacks seem to have been higher than those paid by South Shore whites and certainly not below the going rates for similar housing in other parts of the city.

South Shore residents who were in any way familiar with what both blacks and whites were paying for housing were virtually unanimous in their opinion that blacks paid more. Clergymen, in particular, were often shocked to discover the differences in rents charged to their white and black parishioners. Similarly, some University of Chicago graduate students moving into the area remarked that their rents were significantly lower than those paid by black neighbors—even neighbors living in the same building. Similar observations of rental and price differentials were made by officials of the South Shore Commission—including those involved in the work of its real estate committee and those who were familiar with real estate through their professional and business activities (for example, a mortgage banker, a building manager, and two real estate attorneys).

My informants generally thought that blacks paid a "color tax" of approximately 20 percent on rentals and home purchases. This was considered to be less than what once characterized changing neighborhoods, but still high enough to influence real estate dealers to rent to blacks rather than to search for whites.[13] Regardless of the

12. This judgment is based on impressionistic comparisons of Jackson Park Highlands prices with selling prices of similar housing in other Chicago areas. It is consistent with comments made by most residents on the subject; stories of dramatic price declines almost always were for Highlands homes.

13. This differential demand in South Shore led a Commission leader to remark: "If there are 200 vacancies in South Shore today, this means there are about 2,000 Negroes and maybe 250 whites who want them. So it's easier to rent to Negroes but possible to rent to whites. We've got to get the real estate people to search out the whites." The respondent failed to percive that the inevitable effect of the difference in demand would be different rent levels.

specific amount of the differential, *the key economic fact of a transition neighborhood is that housing on the market is worth more to blacks than to whites.* At a certain point, then, as white demand continues to fall as neighborhood conditions deteriorate (physically and socially) and as black demand increases, the racial price differential grows, thereby inducing larger numbers of whites to rent apartments or sell their homes to blacks. This process does *not* depend upon panic by whites who flee hysterically under the pressure of "block-busters" and "speculators." Panic behavior would probably accelerate the process of course, but it is not a necessary part of neighborhood racial change.

A SURVEY OF CHICAGO AREA LANDLORDS

To determine whether or not this dual-market, disequilibrium model is descriptive of what occurs in transition areas, it is necessary to document whether or not real estate dealers' perceptions are consistent with it; that is, dealers must really think there is a dual market and, at least in an area contiguous to black communities, that blacks will pay more for housing than whites. If such attitudes are not held, a transfer of properties from one market to the other would not take place, regardless of the actual costs involved to exclusionist landlords. The reality, which we are most interested in at this point, is what landlords *think* happens, not what actually happens.

Evidence gathered as part of a survey of Chicago area real estate dealers can be used to determine the profit-loss "cognitive set" with which landlords are likely to confront the prospect and reality of racial change in a neighborhood in which they do business. During the winter and spring of 1966–1967, owners or high-ranking officials of all firms which operated multiple-dwelling units and who maintained offices in South Shore—as well as groups of real estate dealers in other areas of metropolitan Chicago—were interviewed in order to determine their perceptions of how various phases of neighborhood change were thought to affect a real estate man's business. The universe consisted of members of firms which were engaged in professional management of apartment buildings which were either owned by the firm in question or managed by that firm for another party (hereafter referred to collectively as "landlords"). The sample was limited to managers and/or owners of apartment buildings. Of a total sample of 260, successful interviews were held with 177 (68 percent). The procedures followed in drawing this sample as well as other methodological details are described in Appendix I.

The Sample Areas

In addition to South Shore, I tried to interview officials of all firms engaged in professional apartment management in the following areas of metropolitan Chicago:

Northeast Chicago. A predominantly white area, consisting of the middle-class Community Areas of Rogers Park, West Ridge (West Rogers Park), Lincoln Square, and the working-class area of Uptown. The whole region is several miles from any black residential area and was thus not generally considered to lie in the path of the expanding black population.

Oak Park. A middle-class suburb located on the western edge of Chicago. It was virtually all white in 1966, although a few recent Negro migrants were said to be living in its westernmost portion.

Evanston. A middle-class suburb (and location of Northwestern University) located on the northern edge of the city. The 12 percent of its population which was black in 1960 continued to live almost exclusively within a delimited "ghetto" area in the west-central part of town.

Hyde Park. This is the one Chicago neighborhood generally considered to be racially integrated. It abuts the University of Chicago, located in the southeastern part of the city.

Southeast Chicago. Areas sampled within this large region included the working-class black Community Areas of Woodlawn, Greater Grand Crossing, Washington Park, Kenwood, Oakland, as well as the black middle-class area of Chatham.

Loop. Eight interviews were held with "city-wide" landlords who, because they managed properties in many Chicago areas (including one or more of those listed above), carried out their business operations from offices located in the central business district.

The Survey Instrument

I used an interview schedule to investigate the cognitive set with which real estate dealers anticipate racial change. I attempted to learn what a landlord *thinks* happens as a building and neighborhood experience various racial conditions. Questions were asked in a general way; with the exception of the last two questions, the focus was not upon the actual practices or experiences of those men interviewed. With various items we probed expectations regarding rentals, maintenance expenses, and net profits. Information was also gathered regarding the current racial composition of a respondent's buildings, experiences with local community organizations and other matters considered relevant to the purposes of a larger study of which this survey was a part.[14] Respondents were encouraged to elaborate upon answers to forced-choice questions; their statements were recorded in detail and served as the basis for some of the more impressionistic conclusions which follow.

Findings

In general, the survey results are consistent with the model of racial change set forth in this chapter. First, for virtually all real estate dealers, an assumption of two separate housing markets—one for blacks and one for whites—is the underlying element of the conceptualization and vocabulary used in discussing neighborhood change. In trial interviews, in early discussions with real estate industry informants, and in the course of the survey itself, real estate dealers (whether in South Shore or elsewhere) seldom spoke of racial change in any other terms. Thus, for example, landlords spontaneously spoke of "Negro (colored) buildings" or "white buildings"; they talked about "the Negro market" and "the white market"; they spoke of when one "turns" a building and when one does not. Two separate housing supplies with two separate housing demands were the pervading assumptions. In holding such views, respondents were describing a long established housing pattern in urban residential housing, one which has been explicitly supported in the most commonly used real estate textbooks and one which has, in the recent past, been endorsed by the National Association of Real Estate Boards as well as by local realty groups throughout the country.[15]

It is significant, in this regard, that when respondents were asked to specify the conditions under which they would rent to Negroes,

14. See Eugene Smolensky *et al.*, "The Economics of Anti-poverty Programs Involving Income-In-Kind, Phase 1: The Public Housing Case" (a report of the Center for Urban Studies, University of Chicago, 1967).

15. Rose Helper, "The Racial Practices of Real Estate Institutions in Selected Areas of Chicago" (unpublished Ph.D. dissertation, Department of Sociology, University of Chicago, 1958).

few gave the only legal (in light of the Chicago Fair Housing Ordinance) response: that they would rent to Negroes anywhere at any time regardless of local market conditions or existing racial composition of building or neighborhood. Thus only 29 percent of all respondents chose to answer in this way and of these fifty-two persons, twenty-eight were black and the others were operating in all-black areas or, in a few instances, were the managers of luxury housing on the Chicago "gold coast"—a location where few blacks can afford to live. Among the respondents for whom it was a meaningful issue, virtually all indicated policies which were not "color-blind." [16] The response pattern indicates that one of the key conditions of a dual market is present in Chicago: there are two different "supply" stocks of housing. It cannot be doubted that Chicago landlords were well aware of this fact.

Anticipated rental levels. Given the dual market as a part of the world view of landlords, the question remains whether the two markets were perceived to be in disequilibrium in a changing area. To answer this question, respondents were asked to specify the rent levels which could be anticipated for a hypothetical apartment located in an area experiencing various stages of racial transition. Each respondent was asked to choose among four possible rent levels the one which would most likely be collected for a four-room apartment (exactly like one renting for $100 per month in an all-white "unthreatened" area) as the building and neighborhood moved through three major stages of racial change: all-white, "threatened";[17] mixed occupancy; all-Negro status. Respondents were also asked to indicate what they thought generally occurs to

16. Respondents were asked this last interview question: "What criteria does your firm use in deciding when it is appropriate to rent to Negroes in a building which has previously been all-white?" Responses were as follows: 29 percent would rent to Negroes anywhere at any time; 7 percent after one Negro is already on the block, 11 percent when the block is less than one-fourth Negro but at least two Negro families were already in residence; another 10 percent would rent to a Negro if the block population was between 25 and 50 percent Negro; 6 percent indicated they would rent to Negroes only if over half the block was already Negro; 3 percent indicated they would not rent to Negroes under any circumstances. Ten percent of respondents refused to specify a policy, indicating that the decision was made by the owner, not the agent; 22 percent of respondents either evaded answering or offered another kind of response.

17. The term "threatened" neighborhood was used in the interview schedule because it was consistent with the vocabulary and ideology of respondents despite the fact that the interviewer found the phrase distasteful.

a manager or owner of such property in terms of maintenance costs and operating profits.

From the responses to such questions, it was clear that the existence of a dual market was assumed by respondents. Although there were objections that neighborhoods were different and that, for example, middle-class Negroes made more profitable tenants than "welfare types," it is unlikely that any respondents, in any area, thought there was one rather than two Chicago real estate markets.

The dual market model set forth depends for its validity on a perception of a specific market disequilibrium—that is, blacks pay more than whites in a transition area. There are actually two questions implicit in a test of this hypothesis: Do landlords *perceive* rentals to be higher for blacks than whites? Are rentals actually higher for blacks than for whites? If rentals to blacks are seen as higher, transfer of housing from the white to the black market could occur *regardless* of the actualities involved. It is also true (at least theoretically) that if such rent disparities are actually present, but not perceived to be present, properties would *not* be transferred from one market to the other.

It is more likely, however, that reality and perceptions of reality would tend to be more or less congruent. For example, if blacks did not pay more, transfers based on this assumption would decrease in frequency as reality came to impose itself upon the landlord's definition of his profit-loss situation. It seems that a proper test of the dual-market model of racial change would involve presentation of evidence that there is both a perception and a reality of higher rents to blacks—especially under optimal conditions of full information to landlords. This study provides direct evidence on the *perceptions* of landlords and thereby indirect evidence on the reality upon which such perceptions are likely to be based.

In general, respondents did consider *rents* to rise with black occupancy. For example, almost two-thirds of Chicago area respondents considered it generally true that *entering* blacks would pay higher rents than would be paid by a white for a similar unit in an all-white, "unthreatened" neighborhood. Table 1 presents the rent levels expected of blacks renting "a $100 apartment" by real estate dealers located in various Chicago areas.

In a more advanced state of transition, approximately the same percentage of respondents (60 percent) considered blacks likely to be paying *higher rents than whites*. Table 2 depicts rent *differentials*

TABLE 1

PERCENT OF LANDLORDS, BY AREA, PERCEIVING VARIOUS RENTAL LEVELS PAID BY ENTERING BLACKS IN A TRANSITION AREA FOR AN APARTMENT VALUED AT $100

Expected Black Rental Level (in dollars)	Location of Respondent's Office							All Respondents
	NE Chicago (White)	Oak Park (White)	Evanston (88% White)	South Shore (Transition)	Hyde Park (Integrated)	SE Chicago (Black)	Loop (City-Wide)	
Below 90	1.7	6.3	5.9	0	0	0	0	1.7
90–99	8.5	18.8	0	3.2	12.5	0	0	5.6
100	33.9	43.8	5.9	32.3	12.5	15.4	14.3	26.0
101–110	28.8	12.5	23.5	35.5	62.5	38.5	71.4	33.3
Over 110	23.7	12.5	64.7	22.6	12.5	46.2	14.3	30.5
Don't know	3.4	6.3	0	6.5	0	0	0	2.8
Blacks pay More than 100	52.5	25.0	88.2	58.1	75.0	84.6	85.7	63.8
N =	(59)	(16)	(17)	(31)	(8)	(39)	(7)	(177)

QUESTION: Now let's say a few Negro families have moved into the area. How much rent do you think the first families will pay for the kind of unit we've been talking about? One that would ordinarily go for $100 a month in an unthreatened all-white area? (R shown card listing rents as in stub of table).

TABLE 2

PERCENT OF LANDLORDS, BY AREA, PERCEIVING VARIOUS RENT DIFFERENTIALS BETWEEN BLACKS AND WHITES FOR A $100 APARTMENT IN AN ADVANCED TRANSITION NEIGHBORHOOD

Expected Racial Rent Difference	Location of Respondent's Office							
	NE Chicago (White)	Oak Park (White)	Evanston (88% White)	South Shore (Transition)	Hyde Park (Integrated)	SE Chicago (Black)	Loop (City-Wide)	All Respondents
No difference	39.0	43.8	11.8	32.3	37.5	28.2	42.9	33.3
Blacks pay 1 level higher[a]	15.3	6.3	23.5	32.3	25.0	15.4	28.6	19.2
Blacks pay 2 levels higher	22.0	18.8	29.4	22.6	25.0	33.3	28.6	25.4
Blacks pay 3 levels higher	15.3	12.5	35.3	6.5	12.5	18.0	0	15.2
Other[b]	8.5	18.8	0	6.5	0	5.1	0	6.8
Blacks pay more	52.5	37.5	88.2	61.3	62.5	66.6	57.1	59.9
N =	(59)	(16)	(17)	(31)	(8)	(39)	(7)	(177)

[a] One "level difference" approximates a $10 monthly rent discrepancy. Levels are as set forth in the stub of Table 1.
[b] This category included respondents who did not provide answers to all three questions on which classification is based.

QUESTIONS: Now let's say there are many more Negroes living in the neighborhood although it is still heavily white. There will be many buildings which are all white and some which are mixed. How much would new white tenants pay in an all-white building? (R shown card) How much would Negroes pay in a mixed building? (R shown card).

anticipated for a neighborhood in which racial change is well under way.

Tables 1 and 2 show that the South Shore responses were similar to aggregate totals for the entire sample. There were, however, certain striking variations among sampled areas. Except for the Evanston respondents, the landlords with firms located in heavily black areas were most likely to perceive the dual market in a manner consistent with the major hypotheses. Thus, as shown in Tables 1 and 2, the greater the proportion of an area's population which was black, the more likely it was that a rent increase for blacks and a rent discrepancy between blacks and whites would be perceived. For example, 65 percent of southeast Chicago respondents thought blacks would pay more, whereas in predominantly white Oak Park the analogous figure was 37 percent and in northeast Chicago it was 52 percent.

The Evanston exception requires additional attention. Blacks are a small minority in Evanston (12 percent of the population), yet nine of the fifteen respondents providing information on the subject reported that they managed at least some structures in which blacks lived. It seems reasonable to suppose that in a small city like Evanston, where realtors are organized in their own independent real estate board, the lessons learned from the widespread experience with the Negro market would spread even to landlords without direct experience themselves, thus causing the Evanston responses to resemble those given in predominantly black areas. Indeed, it is striking that this widespread experience with the black housing market is unique to Evanston among white areas sampled; in predominantly white Oak Park, for example, only two of fifteen respondents who answered the relevant question indicated that blacks were served by their firms.[18]

A more critical hypothesis suggested by the Evanston case is that landlords with *experience* in the black housing market are more likely to perceive blacks paying more than whites. The relevance of this hypothesis is great: if it is true that an *actual* disequilibrium between the two markets leads to a *perception* of such a disequilibrium, then those respondents who have had experience in the black market (and hence "full" information) should be most likely

18. The small number of Evanston cases precludes any attempt to determine whether landlords with experience in the Negro market are more likely to perceive rental discrepancies than those landlords who rent only to whites.

TABLE 3

PERCENT OF LANDLORDS WITH EXPERIENCE IN THE NEGRO MARKET,
PERCEIVING VARIOUS RENTAL LEVELS PAID BY BLACKS DURING
NEIGHBORHOOD TRANSITION FOR AN APARTMENT VALUED AT $100

Expected Black Rental Level	Black[a]	Whites Who Rent to Blacks	Whites Who Do Not Rent to Blacks	All Respondents
Below $90	0	0	5.2	1.9
90–99	0	4.0	10.3	5.6
100	0	34.2	24.4	24.8
101–110	28.0	39.5	25.9	33.5
Over 110	68.0	21.1	29.3	31.1
Don't know[b]	4.0	1.3	5.2	3.1
N =	(25)	(76)	(58)	(159)

[a] All blacks in the sample rented some or all of their units to blacks.
[b] Includes respondents who did not provide answers to all of the three questions upon which classification was based.

to perceive that disequilibrium. This proposition was tested and found to be valid when comparing landlords who were renting to blacks with those who were renting only to whites.[19]

This finding may be spurious, however, because black landlords were much more likely to see a rental increase than were other respondents. When I controlled for race of respondent, the relationship between the two variables was not great, although among white landlords those with experience are more likely to perceive higher black rents than those without experience. Among inexperienced white landlords, 16 percent thought blacks paid below market prices, whereas only 4 percent of the experienced ones held such an opinion. These results, however, are based on a very small number of cases, as is indicated by the data in Table 3.

Long-term expectations. The responses recorded so far were to questions regarding rents *during* two different stages of the transition itself; that is, my concern was with short-term effects of renting to blacks. Such short-term effects, however, may be less important determinants of landlord behavior than perceptions of long-term effects. Some respondents, for example, who perceived a rent increase for blacks thought this was a temporary phenomenon, with rents returning to, or even falling below, their original level in a

19. A landlord was defined as one renting to Negroes if 25 or more of his housing units were occupied by Negro households.

white neighborhood. To determine whether this was the general case, the rent expectations of all respondents for three successive stages of neighborhood change—"threatened" all-white, during transition, and when area all-Negro—were classified according to the perceived long-run effect which was indicated about rental levels. There were three possible categories: (1) rents up over the long-term (i.e., stage 3 higher than stage 1); (2) rents down over the long-term (i.e., stage 3 lower than stage 1); and (3) rents the same over the long-term (i.e., stages 1 and 3 equal).

The finding was that 30 percent of Chicago area landlords considered rents to fall over the long-term from their levels in a "threatened" neighborhood and 55 percent anticipated a long-term rise in rental levels. The hypothesized relationship between experience in the Negro market and perceived rent increases with black occupancy was confirmed more strikingly for *long-term* rent change than for short-term change. Thus, for example, 61 percent of *white* respondents who rented units to blacks perceived a long-term rise in rents, whereas only 35 percent of white respondents not renting to blacks considered such an increase likely. The difference between white landlords with experience and those without experience is that the experienced landlord thinks that high black rent levels persist over the long-term (or at least beyond the transition period), whereas the inexperienced landlord thinks that such rent increases are temporary. Table 4 presents the findings in detail.

Owners' and managers' profits. Levels of rent and levels of profit are two different things. Similarly, profits to *owners* of property and profits to *managers* (or agents) of property are two different things. Rent increases affect the profits of a building manager more directly than the profits of a building owner. Almost all interview respondents (phone-book listed real estate landlords) were officers of firms involved in the *management* of buildings for nonresident owners (although most owned some structures themselves). Except for one firm in the sample, all collected flat-rate management fees of 6 percent of the total building gross rent; expenses for maintenance or improvements were borne by the owner. Thus under conditions of rising rents accompanying black occupancy, managers were clearly in a position to make financial gains. These gains could be decreased if transition brought increased vacancies or delinquent tenants who did not pay their rent. Respondents in this study frequently expressed concern that such developments often accom-

TABLE 4

PERCENT OF LANDLORDS WHO PERCEIVE LONG-TERM RENT INCREASE,
DECREASE, OR NO CHANGE DURING NEIGHBORHOOD TRANSITION
BY RACE AND RACIAL MARKET EXPERIENCE

Anticipated Long-Term Direction of Rents	Black[a]	Whites Who Rent to Blacks	Whites Who Do Not Rent to Blacks	All Respondents
Rents rise	88.0	60.5	34.5	55.4
Rents decline	0	7.9	10.3	7.5
No change	8.0	27.6	41.4	29.6
Don't know[b]	4.0	4.0	13.8	7.5
N =	(26)	(76)	(58)	(159)

[a] All blacks in the sample who were actively engaged in the rental business rented some or all their units to blacks.
[b] Includes respondents who did not provide answers to *all* three questions upon which classification was based.

QUESTIONS (in addition to those noted in tables 1 and 2): How about rents at this stage—when the area is all-Negro? How much total rent do you think the landlord would be getting from those same four rooms that would be $100 a month if they were in an all-white area? (R shown card). So then, would you say that the rent collected from an apartment building is more before it becomes Negro or after it has been all-Negro for a while?

panied racial change, but still considered renting to blacks the most profitable long-term option available to an *agent* operating in a "threatened" area. Again, black landlords were most optimistic about gain accruing to agents renting to blacks, and whites renting to blacks were slightly more optimistic than were whites renting to whites only. Table 5 shows these findings. Respondents saw very different profit prospects for owners, however. The great majority of respondents (74 percent) considered maintenance costs to rise with black occupancy and to be highest in an all-black building in an all-black neighborhood. Almost all white respondents, with and without experience in the Negro market, considered increased maintenance to be an extra cost of doing business in the Negro market. Respondents cited such reasons as increased numbers of children, vandalism, and "lack of respect for property" as important factors in causing costs to rise. Some felt blacks cause higher heating bills.

Such problems were considered great enough to offset increased

TABLE 5

PERCENT OF LANDLORDS ANTICIPATING MAXIMUM PROFITS
TO BUILDING AGENTS UNDER VARIOUS RACIAL CONDITIONS

Racial Condition	Black	Whites Who Rent to Blacks	Whites Who Do Not Rent to Blacks	All Respondents
Stable all-white area	4.0	49.4	58.6	45.6
Unstable all-white area	0	0	0	0
All-white bldg. in black or mixed area	0	1.3	0	.6
Mixed bldg. in mixed or white area	4.0	6.5	3.4	5.0
Black bldg. in black area	72.0	23.4	17.2	28.8
No difference	12.0	11.7	7.0	10.0
Don't know	8.0	7.8	13.8	10.0
N =	(25)	(77)	(58)	(160)

QUESTION: How about the agent's profits on a building which he doesn't own, but only manages? What situation will bring him maximum profits? (R shown card listing conditions as in stub of table).

rents, and to result in lower profits to building owners expending funds necessary to keep their property in good condition. When respondents were asked to specify the racial condition under which a building would bring *least* profits to an owner, the circumstance chosen most frequently by white respondents was that of an all-black building in an all-black neighborhood. Consistent with other findings of the survey, black respondents were more apt to consider that lowest profits occurred in white areas where, it was said, tenants' demands were more exacting and expensive. Among white respondents, there appears to be no difference between those who do and do not rent to blacks in terms of profits expected for owners of buildings which are in all-black areas. Virtually all white respondents were pessimistic about long-term profits for owners of buildings destined for racial change. When respondents were asked to specify the condition under which a building would bring *maximum* profits to an owner, black buildings in black areas were seldom seen to portend high profits. Tables 6 and 7 show the expectations of landlords of the racial conditions likely to bring least and most profits, respectively, to owners.

TABLE 6

PERCENT OF LANDLORDS ANTICIPATING LEAST PROFITS
TO BUILDING OWNERS UNDER VARIOUS RACIAL CONDITIONS

Racial Condition	Black	Whites Who Rent to Blacks	Whites Who Do Not Rent to Blacks	All Respondents
Stable all-white area	36.0	1.32	6.90	8.8
Unstable all-white area	4.0	10.53	12.07	10.06
All-white bldg. in black or mixed area	8.0	10.52	3.45	7.54
Mixed bldg. in mixed or white area	4.0	18.42	20.69	16.98
Black bldg. in black area	28.0	47.37	39.66	41.50
Other	20.0	11.85	17.24	15.09
N =	(25)	(76)	(58)	(159)

QUESTION: At what point is it least profitable to operate? (R shown card).

TABLE 7

PERCENT OF LANDLORDS ANTICIPATING MAXIMUM PROFITS
TO BUILDING OWNERS UNDER VARIOUS RACIAL CONDITIONS

Racial Condition	Black	Whites Who Rent to Blacks	Whites Who Do Not Rent to Blacks	All Respondents
Stable all-white area	12.0	68.8	62.1	57.5
Unstable all-white area	4.0	2.6	0	1.9
All-white bldg. in black or mixed area	0	1.3	0	.6
Mixed bldg. in mixed or white area	8.0	5.2	5.2	5.6
Black bldg. in black area	52.0	3.9	10.3	13.8
No difference	16.0	10.4	5.2	9.4
Don't know	8.0	7.8	17.2	11.3
N =	(25)	(77)	(58)	(160)

QUESTION: Now, taking all things into consideration like total rental income, costs of maintenance and everything else involved—at what point in the process would you say a building is MOST profitable to operate for an OWNER who had the building all along from the time it was all white? (R shown card). (This question preceded those listed in tables 5 and 6.)

There were certain other additional problems, for both owners and agents which were thought to accompany black occupancy. One was discomfort or even physical danger felt by some white respondents to accompany involvement in the black housing market. There was also concern that management of such buildings could mean a possible scandal should a code violation be publicized or a tenant union be formed. Especially among officials of large, prestigious Chicago firms, there was an intense desire to run no risk of publicly linking the company name to any structure bearing the stigma of a slum. Finally, some landlords mentioned that they could not bear the thought of ever doing business with blacks; the idea was personally repulsive. They would move their business elsewhere, voluntarily giving up management of structures bound to "go colored," rather than enter the Negro market.

Among the South Shore respondents, such firms had been in the area for many years and their business depended upon a network of slowly built-up personal contacts. The owners of such firms had outspoken concern to "protect" the community by excluding blacks in order to preserve the social networks upon which one's business rested. For almost all established real estate firms, neighborhood change endangers the good will which, in the real estate business, is considered an all-important asset.

For these reasons white landlords, especially owners and those dependent upon local ties for their livelihood, perceive important reasons to resist renting to blacks and to induce others not to admit blacks. (This explains, in part, what some economists take to be the mystery of how housing can be arbitrarily held off the Negro market when there appears to be an immediate "economic incentive" to do otherwise.)[20] Yet the data implies that when in a difficult business position due to decreased white demand (that is, depressed rents and high vacancies), landlords are aware that blacks will pay more. *Agents* see it as a clear opportunity to increase profits for themselves, as well as to show at least short-term results for their owner-clients. For an absentee owner, an agent's advice is extremely important, and considered (at least by respondents in the present sample) advice which is likely to be taken.[21]

20. See Richard Muth, *Cities and Housing*, p. 11.
21. Respondents were asked: "How frequently do you think owners take the advice of agents on important decisions involving management of a building?"

For owners, however, renting to blacks is more likely to be seen as a risk to long-term profits—especially if structures are to be maintained at a constant quality level. But even here, if maintenance standards are lowered, it may be possible to increase profits—at least to a point above the levels of a white neighborhood near to a black area.

THE DECISION TO RENT TO BLACKS

Again and again in the more extensive South Shore interviews, real estate dealers state that they rented to blacks in a particular white building because "there was no choice, it's all economics." In each case in which firsthand information was gained of what were occasionally described as heartbreaking decisions to "turn" a building, a change in racial policy was prompted by a crisis of excess vacancies. Such vacancies exist, of course, because rent levels demanded of whites are above the level appropriate to the supply-demand relationship of comparable housing on the white market. Not a single landlord in South Shore who rented to blacks in a building which he previously operated on an all-white basis explained his actions in terms of the Chicago Fair Housing Ordinance (although white landlords who dealt *exclusively* in the black market often cited the ordinance as the basis of their racial policy). The answer was always in terms of rents and vacancies.

Thus, even for white *owners* who perceive eventual long-term profit decline, and who also have a "moral commitment" to the idea, there comes a point where a continued whites-only policy becomes financially untenable. For agents, of course, the gains of admitting blacks are more obvious and become manifest earlier in the game. Especially in an area which is already changing, an area which has been defined as "going Negro" according to the trend perceived by local real estate dealers, prospects for profitable long- or short-term white occupancy come to be seen as having ceased to exist. Thus whatever long-term difficulties are perceived by and for owners, and

---

Sixty percent of the respondents answered "always" or "almost always"; 32 percent answered "sometimes," and only 12 percent indicated "less than half the time" or "never." When asked, "On what kinds of decisions do owners generally resist the advice of their agents?" only 3 percent of the respondents mentioned anything connected with the race of tenants. The questions were asked before race was mentioned in the course of the interview.

regardless of the psychic distresses in store for agents, both agents and owners eventually come to feel what landlords term a pressure which can no longer be withstood. The presence of vacancies and ready availability of blacks offering premium rents become sufficient to overcome the exigencies of civic morality, personal bigotry, or private taste which served as the vocabulary of motive[22] for previous rental policy.

Besides the emergency created by increasing numbers of vacancies, two additional forces are probably at work which accelerate the transfer of buildings from the white to the Negro market in a changing area. The first is that, as the survey findings imply, real estate dealers with experience in the Negro market are more optimistic about rent levels than those without the experience. Presuming this difference among respondents to be due to a reality in which the black market *does* yield higher rentals than generally anticipated by inexperienced real estate dealers, we gain an additional insight into the dynamics of the racial change process. That is, transition may be facilitated as more and more landlords in a changing area come to perceive this rental disparity as they themselves rent to blacks in *some* buildings—including buildings in sub-areas which have become virtually all-black. In addition, those without direct experience may learn from colleagues with such experience of the long-term increase in rents available in the Negro market. In a manner somewhat similar (although perhaps with very different social-psychological dynamics) to the process of attitude change wrought by biracial interaction in housing projects[23] and in military units,[24] experience with blacks might ameliorate some of the unwarranted pessimism which whites hold regarding biracial contact—in this case, biracial tenant-landlord relationships.[25] As this process con-

22. See C. Wright Mills, "Situated Actions and Vocabularies of Motive," *American Sociological Review*, V (6 December, 1940), 904–913.

23. See Morton Deutsch and Mary Collins, *Interracial Housing* (Minneapolis: University of Minnesota Press, 1951).

24. See Shirley Starr, Robin M. Williams, Jr., and Samuel A. Stouffer, "Negro Soldiers," in Samuel A. Stouffer *et al.*, *The American Soldier: Adjustment During Army Life, Studies in Social Psychology in World War II* (Princeton: Princeton University Press, 1949), I, 486–559.

25. Evidence on the "contact hypothesis" is mixed. For a general discussion summarizing results of many studies, see: Daniel Wilner, Rosabelle Walkley, and Stuart Cook, *Human Relations in Interracial Housing: A Study of the Contact Hypothesis* (Minneapolis: University of Minnesota Press, 1955).

tinues over time, increasing numbers of white landlords may be prompted to open up to blacks.

The other force is that for some landlords, especially blacks, profits to be had from the Negro market are seen as dramatically higher than those from the white market. For example, 61 percent of black respondents considered the Negro market to be the most profitable over the long term for *owners,* and 71 percent considered this to be the case for agents. These firms, moreover, are generally excluded from the white market either because they are owned by blacks or because they are small and newly established or have gained notoriety as companies which open up buildings to blacks. These companies are the marginal operators of the real estate industry; they are also the leaders in a transition area. Change permits them entry into areas from which, either because of their race or their lack of "good reputation," they had been excluded. Their tactics of direct solicitation for business in changing areas lead to their being labeled block-busters or panic peddlers. They are the firms despised by community organizations such as the South Shore Commission precisely because they have the effect, by deed and by example, of accelerating the transfer of properties from the white to the Negro market. In doing so, they perform a service for many other firms as well—landlords who, financially pressed by the falling rentals and increasing vacancies of the local white market, become free to reluctantly transfer their properties to the Negro market, once the block has already been "broken" by their "unscrupulous" colleagues.

In summary, the following factors appear to be at work in the neighborhood racial change process: a dual market with rents generally higher to blacks than to whites, especially in a transition area; a perception by real estate dealers of this dual market condition which increases with experience in that market; and an appreciation of the rewards of the Negro market (especially to agents); the existence of real estate "specialists" who, being most convinced of the profitability of the Negro market and being excluded from the white, lead their competitors in the transfer of properties to the Negro market.

Taken together, these factors constitute the institutional mechanisms which implement racial transition. They reflect ecological phenomena external to the world or the real estate business—e.g. black urban migration rates, racially differentiated rates of natural increase, and interest rate fluctuations affecting the housing stock available to whites. These concerns lay beyond the scope of this study. But we are interested in these factors insofar as their manifestations at the community level impinge upon attempts to manipulate processes of racial change. We turn now to a detailed examination of South Shore as an instance of such attempted intervention, with sensitivity to those forces of the real estate market which lay beyond the control of local residents.

Part II

Intervention for Integration in South Shore

3
The Study Area:

Definition and
Characteristics

THE processes of racial change we discussed in abstract terms of housing markets do happen at real places in real time. In South Shore, Chicago, the forces described in Chapter Two are perceived in varying degrees of clarity by the residents who feel the consequences of racial change and by the activists who hope to intervene for integration. The locale of this drama thus becomes the subject of the following several chapters. The present chapter is primarily descriptive—a brief statement of the region's history and present social status[1] and gives an account of the procedures used to establish area boundaries for the purpose of community analysis.

HISTORY

South Shore is named for its location on the Chicago lakefront about ten miles south of the city's central business district (the Loop). A much larger region is, generically, "the south shore," but over the years the remainder of the territory received other designations—usually first applied by early land speculators and subdividers (for example, Hyde Park, Woodlawn, Kenwood). South Shore was the name of the area which remained after all the naming had been done. Although the area gained its name by default, the words "South Shore" have for almost its entire history conveyed the image of a desirable middle-class residential area with comfortable families living in substantial homes and apartments lining pleasant streets and boulevards.

1. The term "present" here as elsewhere in the book implies the study period, 1965–1967.

In 1881, South Shore's first village settlement was stimulated by the construction of Bryn Mawr railroad station by the Illinois Central Railroad at what is now the corner of 71st Street and Jeffrey Boulevard.[2] With the exception of this small village, South Shore was largely open land when the old Hyde Park township of which it was a part was annexed by the city of Chicago in 1889.

Extensive development began at the turn of the century, partially in response to the opening of the Columbian Exposition just to the north in Jackson Park. A high-income apartment district began to spring up around the Bryn Mawr station of the Illinois Central Railroad and large, costly single family homes were constructed in the subdivision known as "Jackson Park Highlands." In 1906 many residents of "The Highlands" together with other prominent Chicagoans founded the South Shore Country Club, located, as today, on the lakefront between 67th and 71st Streets. The country club with its golf course, private beach, stables and tracks, and imposing buildings, was to serve as the focal point for the social life of the South Side's elite for many years to come.

During the great building boom of the 1920–1930 decade, enough new apartments and homes were constructed to double the area's population to 78,755—a population size slightly larger than that of 1960. The building boom brought with it not only new structures, but also a modification of the ethnic composition of the area which had always been heavily English and Swedish. Into the newly developed areas such as "Windsor Park" in the southeast, as well as into the older Bryn Mawr area, came large numbers of Irish Catholics and Jews. They gave an ethnic heterogeneity to South Shore which was perhaps unusual among high-status residential areas of large cities. With a spurt of new apartment construction along the lakefront in the immediate postwar period, South Shore gained still larger numbers of Jewish residents.

Taking stock of these developments in 1930, a South Side booster

2. This fact and much of the following historical information which follows is derived from the *Local Community Fact Book.* See the three successive editions: Louis Wirth and Eleanor H. Bernert (eds.), *Local Community Fact Book of Chicago* (Chicago Community Inventory, University of Chicago, 1949); Philip M. Hauser and Evelyn M. Kitagawa (eds.), *Local Community Fact Book for Chicago, 1950* (Chicago Community Inventory, University of Chicago, 1953); and Evelyn M. Kitagawa and Karl Taeuber (eds.), *Local Community Fact Book, Chicago Metropolitan Area, 1960* (Chicago Community Inventory, University of Chicago, 1963).

wrote enthusiastically of South Shore as: "the home of Health and plenty, of culture and refinement . . . this beautiful center of domestic felicity." [3] Visitors to the area were said to consider it "the last word in residential and social perfection," characterized by a maintenance of "unified and harmonized architectural development in both residence and shopping districts." [4]

Writing approximately ten years later, in 1942, Homer Hoyt, at that time Director of Research for the Chicago Plan Commission, described South Shore as: "One of the best examples of a so-called 'stable area' which has several remaining generations of useful economic life. The proximity to the park, to the lake, and to the South Shore Country Club, its excellent shopping centers along Stony Island, 71st Street, and 79th Street, its fine schools and fast transportation are advantages that cannot be duplicated in any other community." Hoyt went on to argue that the area should be preserved by means of conservation plans designed far in advance "so that any idea of abandoning this choice residential location in favor of what might appear to be greener pastures in the suburbs will never be seriously entertained." [5]

RECENT DEVELOPMENTS

Although South Shore's economic life was by no means over in 1960, the prestige and "social perfection" for which Hoyt's phrase "useful economic life" was perhaps an adept euphemism, was very much on the decline. The perfection of 1942 was seen as deterioration in the 1960's. A generation in the increasingly sooty air of Chicago's South Side had given much of the area's brick and concrete exterior a dingy cast appropriate to what is frequently called a grey area. The shopping strips, once considered modern and architecturally "harmonized," struck the contemporary witness as a jumble of neon and false commercial fronts obscuring any limited architectural merit the original structures might have had. Shoppers seeking scarce parking spaces on the congested streets faced the additional strains imposed by the always unsightly and dangerous

3. John C. Spray (ed.), *Chicago's Great South Shore* (Chicago: South Shore Publishing Co., 1930), p. 33.

4. *Ibid.*

5. *Forty-Four Cities in the City of Chicago* (Chicago: The Chicago Plan Commission, 1942), p. 43.

Illinois Central railroad tracks which now were considered a blight upon the very business strips whose prosperity they had created in a previous era. Seventy-five percent of South Shore's housing stock came to consist of apartments, many in old walkup buildings, which, although once "the last word," had become a poor second to the suburban split-levels and ranch homes which most young families seemed to prefer in the postwar period. Most important, the physical attributes of South Shore came to connote a life style not characteristic of persons with significant means and high social prestige.

The all-black residential area of Chicago (the black belt) had expanded south and east, impinging upon South Shore's western border. The first black families are said to have moved into the extreme northwest corner of South Shore at 67th and Stony Island in 1958, although most residents dated the onset of racial change with 1960. By 1965, when this present study began, South Shore had a large number of black residents—close to a fourth of the area's total population.[6] They were concentrated in the northwestern portions of the community, although the racial "line" was conceived by most white residents as continuously moving to the south and east. Residents frequently viewed this process as unstoppable and likened it in their conversations with one another to the growth of a cancer or, in the words of a prominent local rabbi, to a "spreading ink blot." The frequent casting of racial change in negative terms is perhaps indicative of the fact that black migration, perceived as a threat by local residents, could only have the effect of adding to the increasingly declassé image which white Chicagoans generally had of the area.[7]

At the 1960 census, South Shore was by no means a slum. The income of its residents was well above the city median ($7,888 vs. $6,738 for the city as a whole); only 2 percent of the housing stock was considered to be in substandard condition. The residential streets were still generally pleasant; there was virtually no "blighting" industry within the area. South Shore was still on the lake, and the country club was still there—although falling in membership level to the point where consideration was given to broadening the

6. More precise estimates of the area's black population for the year 1966 are presented in Chapter Seven. The community boundaries used in these observations are set forth in Figure 2.

7. This image was perhaps dramatized by a conversation I overheard in a swank Loop restaurant in which a Chicago North Side resident asked a long-time resident of South Shore: "When are you moving to America?"

membership base by accepting Jews. (No consideration was ever given to admitting blacks.) But changes in the tastes of the middle and upper-middle class, together with inevitable symptoms of physical deterioration and racial transition, were bringing the area into social decline. South Shore was no longer a prime area; it was the old neighborhood for larger and larger numbers of Chicagoans who moved on to the suburbs to raise families or to the lakefront highrises, the symbols of a life which was to be "swinging" for the young, elegant for the middle-aged, quiet and dignified for the old. The other pastures indeed looked greener for those with the means and freedom to graze wherever their preferences might lead them.

BOUNDARIES OF SOUTH SHORE

The exact location of South Shore's boundaries, the degree to which they are agreed upon and the significance to residents of the territory they enclose, are of special importance in an area experiencing racial change. People's response to racial change can reasonably be expected to be dependent on whether they perceive a community as changing and whether they place themselves within the boundaries of that changing community. It must be *their* community that is changing if they are to *act* (either as individuals or in unison) in response to the change.

A community exists only insofar as it exists in people's minds. Demarcations on maps may describe territorial units useful for logistical convenience, but they do not, in themselves, bespeak of the shared identity which differentiates mere territory from a geographical community. There must be some shared conception, however rough, of a demarcated place providing common identification and shared interest. Such a consensus not only *facilitates* a community study, it is a necessary (although not sufficient) justification for it.

I have thus tried to begin a definition of South Shore by an inventory of the notions which regional residents have about the location and boundaries of something called "South Shore" and, more generally, the methods which people seemed to use to establish such boundaries. Some assumptions were of course made of where South Shore generally was located—there was no attempt to locate the community in Akron, Ohio, or the North Side of Chicago or in the middle of Lake Michigan. There was thus a tacit beginning point

—a point located in the researcher's general conception, derived from study and his own residency in Chicago, of where one should look.

Within the general region south of Jackson Park, below the community of Woodlawn, but north of the steel mills and in the residential areas adjacent to the Lake, I conducted fifty brief interviews with local people. The method was informal; interviews took place under a variety of conditions: some were on street corners (especially the main business crossing under the sign of the South Shore National Bank); others were in stores or offices; three were at gas stations. I asked various bystanders and service personnel such questions as: "What part of town is this?" "How far over does South Shore go?" [8] I considered these and similar probes appropriate to determine the respondent's notion of local neighborhoods and their boundaries. My questions were those of an ordinary person seeking orientation.

The most basic finding is that something called a "South Shore," as a distinct Chicago area, does exist. The term never draws a blank stare when used in appropriate contexts. For example, "I thought this was South Shore here?" "No, I think South Shore starts at 67th." The *boundaries* of South Shore are not unanimously viewed, but there is widespread agreement—especially on three of the four boundary lines.

The clearest South Shore boundary is Lake Michigan on the east; on this, agreement is unanimous. The western boundary of Stony Island Avenue—a wide, congested boulevard—is the line chosen by almost every respondent who ventures a reply. (See Figure 1.) The seven respondents living west of Stony Island Avenue ("out" of South Shore) also considered this street to divide the area from contiguous communities. Similarly, long-time residents could recall no point at which the boundary was ever farther west. Real estate advertisements in Chicago newspapers did not list vacancies west of Stony Island Avenue as "South Shore" as they did the properties on the east. Shops on streets other than Stony Island Avenue did not use the term South Shore in their names, nor did the few churches and clubs in the tracts west of Stony Island. Further evidence that Stony Island Avenue has in fact always been the

8. The methods generally follow Lynch. See Kevin Lynch, *The Image of the City* (Cambridge: MIT Press, 1960).

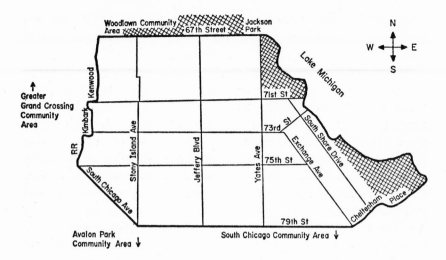

Key:
Parks and recreation ▨▨▨▨

FIGURE 1: Community Area of South Shore as Defined by *Local Community Fact Book*

western boundary of the area is provided by the editor of *Chicago's Great South Shore* (a publication sponsored by South Side boosters) who, in 1930, described the "South Shore District" as comprising the neighborhoods *west of Stony Island Avenue* as far as the Lake.[9]

This same document placed South Shore's northern boundary at 67th Street. Contemporary informants seem to be in consensus that the area's northern boundary is in fact 67th Street—a major roadway bordering an extensive regional park (Jackson Park) to the north. When not mentioning 67th Street as the northern boundary, residents gave a variety of other streets as the northern line such as the business strips of 71st Street and, less frequently 75th Street.

Residents expressed the greatest diversity of opinion on the southern boundary of the area. For many it was 83rd Street, but other residents frequently chose 79th Street. Still other replies gave 75th Street or even 87th Street as the southern boundary of the area. *Chicago's Great South Shore* is of little use in eliminating the ambiguity. It specifies as the southern boundary South Chicago Avenue—a thoroughfare which runs diagonally through the south

9. John C. Spray, *Chicago's Great South Shore*, p. 33.

side of the city and which, if used, would incorporate into South Shore a vast industrial region as far south as 106th Street.

In order to "close" the ambiguous southern boundary of South Shore and to test the tentative conclusions concerning other demarcations, I examined other boundary evidence. As an unanticipated result of the survey I learned that almost all respondents acted as if there were real and official boundaries around South Shore—lines drawn by some political or other legitimate public authority—even though respondents sometimes did not know where such lines were or have any idea what body had set up the demarcations. (Frequently, however, the appropriate source was given as "the city.") In several instances, my questions set off heated arguments among a group of respondents as to just where the "official" boundaries of South Shore really were. The implication is that residents are "ripe" for "official boundaries" and thus it would seem reasonable that actions by public and quasi-public bodies might help create them. (There are no legal or official community boundaries in Chicago, although the city is divided into differing administrative units by various welfare, political, and religious institutions and governmental agencies.)

One famous system of Chicago community demarcation, begun several generations ago by Ernest Burgess and continued by his successors at the University of Chicago, is depicted in the Chicago *Local Community Fact Book*. The *Fact Book* divides the city into seventy-five sub-units conceived by the authors as natural and homogeneous regions. These Local Community Areas, as derived originally from 1930 census data, have been retained in all succeeding editions of the *Fact Book*. Figure 1 shows South Shore's boundaries as set forth in the *Fact Book*. The northern boundary at 67th Street is identical to presently understood boundaries as is the eastern boundary of Lake Michigan. The *Fact Book* places the southern boundary at 79th Street, coinciding with at least some contemporary local opinion; the western boundary is placed, quite surprisingly, west of Stony Island Avenue. The *Fact Book* western boundary would bring into South Shore certain areas which virtually all local residents consider to be outside of South Shore.

Other "official" sources of boundaries indicate still different demarcations. The South Shore Commission uses the same northern and eastern boundaries as the *Local Community Fact Book,* but draws the western boundary at Stony Island Avenue, thus reducing

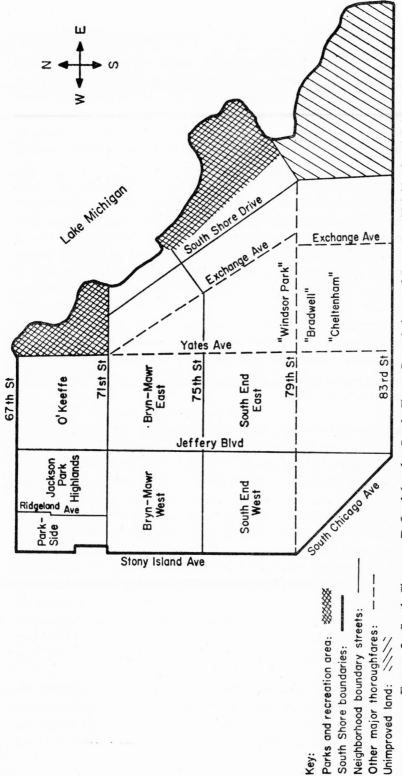

FIGURE 2: South Shore as Defined by the South Shore Commission and Important Neighborhood Sub-Areas

Key:

Parks and recreation area: ▨

South Shore boundaries: ▬▬

Neighborhood boundary streets: ———

Other major thoroughfares: – – –

Unimproved land: ⧄

Lake Michigan

South Shore Drive

Exchange Ave

Exchange Ave

"Windsor Park"

"Bradwell"

"Cheltenham"

Yates Ave

67th St

O'Keeffe

71st St

Bryn–Mawr East

75th St

South End East

79th St

83rd St

Jackson Park Highlands

Ridgeland Ave

Jeffery Blvd

Bryn–Mawr West

South End West

Park-Side

South Chicago Ave

Stony Island Ave

N E S W

South Shore's territory to the west but extending it to the south as far as 83rd Street (see Figure 2). The Chicago public school authorities, in planning a school integration scheme for the area, have adopted the boundaries offered by the commission for a South Shore school district (District 22) which came into existence with the 1965 school year. Commission leaders felt quite strongly that these are the "real" boundaries of South Shore.

Compared to *Fact Book* demarcations, commission boundaries serve to reduce the number of blacks in the area by eliminating the predominantly black tracts west of Stony Island Avenue, while increasing the number of whites by adding portions of mostly white tracts below 79th Street. Although a possible interpretation is that commission boundaries are themselves part of a strategy aimed at maximizing the whiteness of South Shore's image, the fact remains that the commission's boundaries conform, overall, most closely with people's perceptions, the demarcations of other institutions (for example, churches, schools) and the historical record of the perceptions of previous generations.

The commission boundaries were adopted for this study, and unless otherwise specified, the term "South Shore" will be used to denote the area located within the territory depicted in Figure 2.[10] There is ambiguity regarding the southern boundary, but for present purposes as in the case of the mundane purposes of the man on the street, the boundaries have to be placed *somewhere*. All things considered, the commission boundaries seem the most reasonable.

Using the commission boundaries makes additional sense because one of the study's goals is to measure the degree to which commission programs were effective. It is thus appropriate to adopt as the present unit of analysis the same territory as the commission's own target area. I adopted the boundaries before the study design was developed and before I gathered data for the ecological and demographic analyses which follow.[11]

10. For some statistical purposes, however, I have used *Fact Book* boundaries, in which case I refer to the area as the "Community Area (CA)" of South Shore.

11. Harvey Molotch, "Urban Community Boundaries," Working Paper No. 60, Center for Social Organization Studies, University of Chicago, January 1966, mimeo. A small controversy on this point is contained in Avery Guest and James Zuiches, "Another Look at Residential Turnover in Urban Neighborhoods" and Harvey Molotch, "Reply to Guest and Zuiches," both in *American Journal of Sociology*, 77 (November 1971), 457–471.

THE NEIGHBORHOODS OF SOUTH SHORE

Although local residents are aware that they live in a place called "South Shore" there are smaller places within the area which function as communities for many residents. The sub-areas, or "neighborhoods" as they will henceforth be called, are depicted in Figure 2. They are referred to by name by respondents when interviewed and by residents engaged in casual conversation with one another. In the interviews, I attempted to determine the degree to which the existence and precise boundaries of the neighborhoods are known to residents. The existence of the neighborhoods, with their varying physical and social characteristics, facilitates an examination (albeit a cursory one) of the possible effects of such variables upon the racial change process and upon support for a voluntary organization which seeks to speak and act in the name of the entire community. There thus follows a description of the boundaries of these neighborhoods, a brief characterization of the physical and social conditions found in each and an account of their residents' differing levels of identification with South Shore as a community and the South Shore Commission as their voice.

Jackson Park Highlands

Boundaries: 67th Street on the north, Jeffery Boulevard on the east, Ridgeland Avenue on the west, and 71st Street on the south. This neighborhood is the most clearly delineated in South Shore and highly differentiated from surrounding areas in terms of social and physical circumstance. It is the highest status residential area of South Shore, consisting of large, well-maintained brick and stone homes on elaborate grounds. Other South Shore people think of Highlands residents as uniformly "rich"—sometimes speaking of residents as "millionaires." Highlands homes were in the cost range of the upper middle-class, selling in the general area of $35,000 to $70,000.

Jackson Park Highlands functions as a symbol of elegance for all of South Shore; community leaders presumed that because so few blacks could afford housing in the Highlands, this part of South Shore would always be predominently white. Indeed, black migration had jumped over the Highlands; the neighborhoods west and east of the area had become heavily black during the study period, while the Highlands remained predominantly white (although racially mixed). The Highlands contained a smaller population than any other South Shore neighborhood, at most of only 2 percent of South Shore's population.

A neighborhood group, the Jackson Park Highlands Association, had long existed, but was not active in any important way during the study period. Highlands residents appeared to think of themselves as living in South Shore, occasionally participated in commission functions, and generally contributed financially to the organization. Perhaps because there were so few of them, Highlands residents were not prominent among the commission's most active leaders.

Parkside

Boundaries: Stony Island on the west, 71st Street on the south, Ridgeland Avenue on the east, 67th Street on the north. This neighborhood was considered by respondents, including leaders of the commission, to have been virtually all black since 1963—the only all-black neighborhood in South Shore. The area has been considered a "Negro residential area" since 1964, according to a survey by the Chicago Urban League.[12] Parkside is occupied almost exclusively by apartment dwellings with six and twelve flat walk-ups predominating. At the beginning of the study period, virtually all white South Shore residents considered Parkside "gone." No efforts were made by the commission to locate whites in Parkside. Several black Parkside residents came to be very active in commission affairs; local block groups contained enthusiastic commission supporters. That Parkside was a part of South Shore was a source of gratification to these participants. Chicago real estate dealers routinely advertised Parkside apartment vacancies as located in "South Shore."

O'Keeffe

Boundaries: Jeffery Boulevard on the east, Lake Michigan on the west, 71st Street on the south, 67th Street on the north. O'Keeffe

12. "Negro Migration in Chicago, 1950–1960–1964" (The Chicago Urban League, 1965).

is an area of well-maintained middle-class apartment buildings, mostly of the three and six flat variety. At the time of the study period, O'Keeffe was regarded as an important testing ground of South Shore's intervention efforts. Blacks were rapidly becoming a neighborhood majority and the commission saw the "preservation" of O'Keeffe as a middle-class heavily white area as central to the successful rejuvenation of South Shore as a whole. Many commission activists were drawn from the O'Keeffe area. It is likely that the great majority of neighborhood residents (both black and white) considered O'Keeffe to be a part of South Shore and the commission as the legitimate voice of their larger community.

Bryn Mawr East

Boundaries: Seventy-first Street on the north, Lake Michigan on the east, Jeffery Boulevard on the west and 75th Street on the south. If and when Bryn Mawr East becomes predominantly black, South Shore whites will probably stop talking about "preserving South Shore." For Bryn Mawr is the "heartland" of South Shore, and the frequently used phrase is meant to imply more than the geographical centrality of the neighborhood. Although Bryn Mawr East does contain a large number of walk-up apartments, its visual impact derives from the pleasant single-family homes on both sides of most blocks. The families of the middle middle-class are raised here and it produces the greatest proportion of South Shore's leaders —including leadership of the South Shore Commission. Bryn Mawr was biracial, with blacks a minority, throughout the study period.

Bryn Mawr West

Boundaries: Jeffery Boulevard on the east, Stony Island Avenue on the west, 71st Street on the north and 75th Street on the south. It consists of small apartment buildings and single-family bungalows with 18 percent of its housing stock owner-occupied in 1960. The Chicago Urban League considered it an area of Negro residence at the time of its 1964 demarcation of Negro residential areas in Chicago. It was racially mixed to some degree throughout the study period; blacks had become the predominate racial group by spring, 1967. Despite the fact that Bryn Mawr West was clearly within South Shore, the area provided a smaller number of active participants in commission affairs than Bryn Mawr East.

South End

Boundaries: Indefinite. This area lies south of Bryn Mawr and is sometimes vaguely split along Jeffery Boulevard into "South End East" and "South End West." The South Shore Commission has defined South End as the territory from 75th Street south to 83rd Street and from Stony Island on the west to Lake Michigan on the east. The area from 75th to 79th was described in 1930 as the neighborhood of "Windsor Park"—a name which derived from the defunct "Windsor Park Golf Club" on whose land the present neighborhood stands. The term "Windsor Park" is still heard in South Shore to refer to the general area. The eastern part of the general South End area is often referred to by residents as "Bradwell"—a name taken from the elementary school which serves the immediate neighborhood. The eastern portion of the area below 79th Street, but above 83rd Street, is often called "Cheltenham"; the combined Windsor Park-Cheltenham region occasionally is called "Chel-Win." In this area small bungalows, some of frame construction, are mixed with walk-up apartments. Unlike the racially mixed area to the west, eastern South End (for example, Cheltenham, Windsor Park, Bradwell) remained virtually all-white throughout the study period. Especially in the Bradwell area, the presence of Jews is less marked than in the rest of white South Shore.

The residents of this area seem to identify least with South Shore, and from them came the greatest opposition to the South Shore Commission. A neighborhood organization was formed, known as the "Chel-Win Association," which sporadically opposed the commission.

South Shore Drive

Although South Shore Drive forms the eastern boundary of O'Keeffe, Bryn Mawr East and South End, "the Drive," is often spoken of as though it were a distinct area—because it includes a large number of luxury high-rise buildings and because its well-kept shade trees (maintained by the County Forestry Department) lend an air of elegance to the thoroughfare which distinguishes it from nearby streets. Throughout the study period, "the Drive" remained predominantly white.

Its residents, said to be mostly older people, seldom participated in commission activities, although an identification with the area is perhaps indicated by the fact that membership and fund drives aimed at the high-rise residents were generally successful. This was not the case in door-to-door appeals in the Bradwell area.

DETERMINANTS AND CONSEQUENCES OF COMMUNITY
AND NEIGHBORHOOD BOUNDARIES

There was thus in South Shore a great divergence in the degree to which its neighborhoods functioned as an integral part of the community. Schemes to stabilize a racially changing area must cover the entire area and depend on an ability to mobilize all area resources for a common goal. The resources include money, political influence on governmental decision-makers, and above all white bodies (especially middle-class white children) to distribute and re-distribute so that a reasonable number of whites are integrated into most community institutions and scenes. Those neighborhood sub-areas which resist making common cause for the good of the whole pose a genuine threat to many efforts aimed at "doing something" about racial change.

The existence of Bradwell as a separate neighborhood (facilitated by the 79th Street business corridor on Bradwell's northern bound-ary) provided the requisite condition for holding back full identifica-tion with the whole of South Shore. As a result, there was a concomitant tendency to hold back the resources that ordinarily might have accompanied such identification. For example, Brad-well contained a large number of the increasingly scarce white children who could be transferred to other South Shore schools in order to integrate them; the reluctance of Bradwell parents to con-tribute to the cause became the stumbling block to the execution of a major commission program. Bradwell lay in the corner of South Shore most distant from the moving line of black migration; its long-standing existence as something not-the-same-as the neigh-borhoods to the north (South End, Bryn Mawr) meant that its residents could consider racial change to be a phenomenon hap-pening elsewhere (South Shore, the rest of South Shore or Bryn Mawr) but not in Bradwell. There was a feeling, at least among some area residents, that all would be well if, in the words of one neighborhood leader, "they would leave us alone." Residents tended to see the different racial circumstance of Bradwell, compared to much of the rest of South Shore, as determined by a difference in

degree of commitment to neighborhood, rather than to accident of
geography. They widely believed that, unlike those to the north and
west, Bradwell people would not flee. There was therefore no reason
to help those living to the north.

While some behavior of Bradwell residents can be explained
by their social differences from other South Shore residents (for
example, fewer Jews), additional explanatory weight is being
assigned to the fact that the rather clear-cut boundaries inclosing
the rest of South Shore into a single unit were not present in the
Bradwell case. The uniqueness of Bradwell can perhaps be made
clearer by a consideration of the elements which, based upon the
South Shore case, seem to effectively create community and sub-
community boundaries. The following is not meant as an exhaustive list of these elements, but rather as a description of those
that operated in one urban community.

Paths and Edges

The most obvious factor at work in South Shore is what Lynch
has called the clarity of paths and edges—roadways, commercial
strips, or other physical features which naturally divide one area
from another.[13] South Shore itself has clearcut edges on three sides:
a large park on the north, Lake Michigan on the east, and the very
broad path of Stony Island Avenue on the west.

The same variable also serves well to explain most divisions
within South Shore. Three streets make up seven of the eight boundaries which divide the neighborhoods from one another. These
streets, 71st, 75th, and Jeffery Boulevard are the major thoroughfares of South Shore—the busiest, widest, most difficult to cross, and
most heavily developed commercially. They are thus easily dis-
tinguished from other streets within South Shore. The eighth edge,
however, which divides Jackson Park Highlands from Parkside is
not a major street at all (Ridgeland Avenue) and thus constitutes
an exception to the pattern.

Social Class, Physical Structure Variation

Although not a major thoroughfare, Ridgeland Avenue marks
the meeting place of South Shore's highest and lowest income areas
and similarly divides an area of large single-family homes from a

13. Kevin Lynch, *The Image of the City*.

neighborhood of densely built-up apartment structures. Structure type and social class variation can similarly explain the delineation of South Shore Drive as a separate neighborhood—high-rent, highrise structures distinguish the drive from its environs.

Race

Residents' perception of Stony Island Avenue as the western boundary of South Shore may be due, in part, to the fact that Stony Island Avenue served until five years ago to differentiate the white and black populations in this part of the city. White respondents generally dated black entry into South Shore from the period when blacks "crossed Stony Island." There is a slight possibility that the area west of Stony Island was "defined out" of South Shore over the period 1940–1965 by the indigenous white population because of its changing color composition, although the early writings of South Side boosters suggest that Stony Island was always considered the western boundary.

School Boundary Lines

The creation of school attendance boundary lines is one of several public actions that can contribute to community boundary formation. Public schools, unlike some other neighborhood institutions (like Protestant churches and synagogues), are typically territorially based. Identifications (academic, social or athletic) which bind residents to a particular school are thus shared by persons who are linked by geographical ties as well. To the extent that other institutions draw their constituencies from the same geographical base, a piling up of allegiances can occur, further strengthening the significance of the areal unit as a locus for community feeling and action.

The high school which serves South Shore, called "South Shore High," had district boundaries which coincided with commission boundaries. Some South Shore residents expressed bitterness that those portions of South Shore north of 71st Street were a part of a different school district until 1965, thus in their view, "weakening the community."

The three most clear-cut neighborhoods (Parkside, O'Keeffe, and Bryn Mawr) share their names with the elementary schools which serve them, and their boundaries generally coincide with the attendance zones of the schools. In the rather amorphous South

End area, it is the Bradwell School, with its relatively stable attendance boundaries that serves as a primary source of community identification.

The significance of the elementary schools for neighborhood definition goes beyond the mere fact that the school may provide a name for the geographical area. Elementary school boundaries influence the neighboring behavior of school children—the patterns of mutual visits within childhood peer groups. Except for immediate neighbors and relatives, a child's range of peer acquaintances tends to be limited to schoolmates. The geographical distribution of a child's playmates is thus partly influenced by the boundaries of school districts. Because the neighboring behavior of adults is often influenced by prior contacts made by children, school boundaries may become a factor in defining neighborhoods. The importance of children to the process of neighborhood integration has been stressed by Whyte in the course of his observations in Park Forest,[14] and in the researches of Roper who found that the bulk of neighboring behavior in middle class settings was due directly or indirectly to the visiting patterns of young children.[15]

Not only does the school through its district lines help determine adult interaction, but the school as a social institution functions as a locus for much community interaction. The PTAs of South Shore are the strongest community organizations in the area with the possible exception of some churches and the commission. To the extent that friendship patterns and a "we feeling" arise from participation in such a voluntary organization, the school tends to set the boundaries of the community.[16] The stable attendance zone of Bradwell school thus served as an additional pull away from South Shore.

Parish Boundaries

Three Catholic churches are located within South Shore and their parish boundaries include most of the territory regarded as con-

14. William H. Whyte, Jr., *The Organization Man* (Garden City, Doubleday and Co., 1956), p. 378.

15. Marion Roper, "The City and the Primary Group" (unpublished Ph.D. dissertation, Department of Sociology, University of Chicago, 1934).

16. The significance of the location and boundaries of schools is particularly interesting in light of Chicago's neighborhood school system which presumes the neighborhood to exist prior to the school and not vice-versa.

stituting South Shore according to *Fact Book* and commission criteria. Parish boundaries, as depicted in Figure 3, indicate that for two of these churches (St. Bride's and Our Lady of Peace), parish territory extends beyond South Shore; only one parish (St. Philip Neri) is wholly contained within the community. It is noteworthy that the clergy of St. Philip's have been most active in South Shore community affairs and that St. Philip's is an important source of financial support and leadership for the South Shore Commission.

When interviewed about their community, Catholic respondents occasionally mentioned their parishes. All Catholics were well aware of the existence of these parishes and could give approximations of parish boundaries. The responses of Catholics to a non-Catholic interviewer probably led to an understatement of the degree to which parishes function as sources of community identification. Catholics

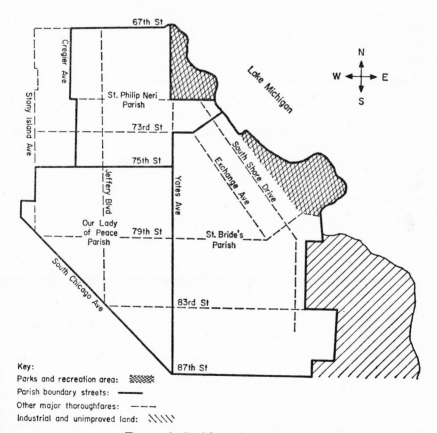

Key:
Parks and recreation area: ▨▨▨
Parish boundary streets: ━━━
Other major thoroughfares: ─ ─ ─
Industrial and unimproved land: \\\\\

FIGURE 3: Parishes of South Shore

indicated that when interacting with their coreligionists, they often identified themselves and other Catholics in terms of their parishes and seldom in terms of such community areas as "South Shore" or neighborhoods like "The Highlands."

Wards and Precincts

The city of Chicago's seventh ward encompasses approximately 75 percent of South Shore's territory (using the commission's definition) but the ward also takes in land as far south as 87th Street. The jagged boundaries of the ward are depicted in Figure 4. Neither the ward as a whole nor any of its ninety-three precincts was ever referred to by respondents as communities or neighborhoods, but it should be noted that there were no known party workers or other political figures among those interviewed.

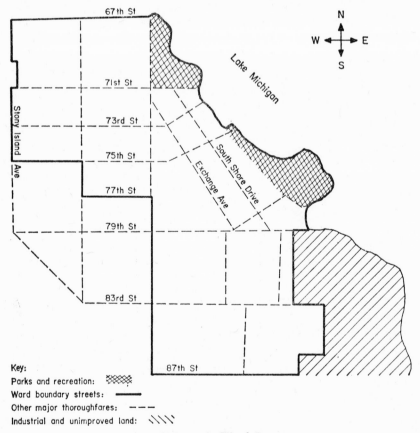

FIGURE 4: Ward 7

SOUTHEASTERN SOUTH SHORE: A NEIGHBORHOOD
WITHOUT BOUNDARIES

That the southern boundary of Ward 7 is well outside of
South Shore (at 87th Street) may be an additional symptom of the
ambiguity of South Shore's southern boundary and of the indefinite
status of Chel-Win, Bradwell. The southern boundary (83rd Street)
possessess none of the features we discussed that help determine
boundaries in other parts of South Shore. The southern boundary
line is not a clear edge—it is not a wide boulevard and its small
clusters of commercial development do not differentiate it from
similarly developed parallel streets nearby such as 81st, and 85th.
Similarly, there is little difference in physical structure, social class,
and racial or ethnic stock in the areas north and south of 83rd
Street—although there was a *gradual* decline in social status and
decreasing proportion of residents who were Jews with increasing
proximity to the center of the steel mill area at about 87th Street
and the lake. Local ward, parish, and (until recently) school boundaries all treated 83rd Street as an internal community street.

The clarity of boundaries on South Shore's northern, eastern,
and western borders can be attributed to the presence of features
which are absent in the ambiguous southern border. Perhaps this
lack of any clear-cut boundaries in the area inhibited residents from
developing an identification with either South Shore or, for that
matter, with the next Community Area to the south (South Chicago,
or as described by some indigenous residents, The Bush). The only
clear source of boundaries was thus the attendance zone of the
Bradwell elementary school—and because this attendance zone included only whites, an additional reason was present for a lack of
identification with South Shore and its problem.

The independent stance thus assumed by Bradwell residents may
have exerted a paradoxical effect on the commission's goal. There
may have resulted an enhanced confidence in Bradwell's future
white status which may have inhibited white mobility out of the
area, thus aiding the racial balance of South Shore as a whole. On
the other hand, Bradwell's opposition to commission activities may
have had an opposite effect by obstructing programs designed to
keep whites living in adjoining areas. Regardless of the net effect
which the Bradwell problem had upon South Shore's racial composi-

tion, it is noteworthy that the behavior of Bradwell's residents seemed to be consistent with, and perhaps can be explained in part by, the boundary characteristics of the area in which they lived. The larger point is that the processes by which people determine boundaries to differentiate their geographical world are also processes which have consequences for community racial change and the programs created to deal with the change.

4
The South Shore Commission

THE powers and resources of the South Shore Commission were derived from the organization's voluntary constituents; its ability to survive, grow and act was contingent upon convincing many persons, within and without the area, that it was indeed the legitimate source of authority in decisions affecting the future of South Shore. Blacks and whites, school boards and police captains, building commissioners and real estate dealers, all eventually became commission supporters who cleared their plans and aimed their talk at the leaders of the South Shore Commission. In this chapter, I will discuss the nature of this organization, the roles played by its leaders, and the ideologies they brought to their work.

EARLY HISTORY

The commission was an outgrowth of the South Shore Ministerial Association, an organization of local clergymen who met monthly to discuss church-related problems and to exchange ideas and community news. In 1954 a priest, a minister, and a rabbi helped to establish a more broad-based and comprehensive organization—the South Shore Commission.

The Ministerial Association was (and remains) a source of pride to local churchmen and rabbis who consider their early ecumenical spirit as evidence of South Shore's rather unique progressivism and brotherly spirit. Clergymen urged their parishioners and congregants to join with members of the other faiths to participate in the life of the commission. They caused their governing boards to make contributions from institutional budgets and they themselves served on commission committees and as officers.

It is unclear from interviews with present-day leaders as to when and how control of the commission shifted from the hands of the clergy to those of lay persons. The early impetus for the organization's development was supplied by the clergy—a pattern apparently quite common in the development of community organizations in urban areas.[1] Clergymen I interviewed spoke of the transfer of leadership in South Shore as a deliberate strategy of the church leaders; lay founders of the commission remember the transfer as a result of the clergy's lack of organizational skills. Said one important lay founder: "The clergy were floundering around with the thing . . . finally we came in and set things up on a going basis for action. Then the commission could really get going." Whatever interpretation we accept, the clergymen provided an important, and perhaps crucial, early stimulus which legitimized the commission and its goals in the eyes of most residents

ORGANIZATION AND STAFF

The first temporary head of the commission was the reform rabbi who was active in the organization's founding. After his six month term ended, members elected a local banker as the first president under a formal constitution. From then on, lay persons held the top commission office. The commission's constitution specifies as governing body a seventy-five-member board of directors whose collective will is to be reflected in the decisions of an eighteen-member executive committee drawn from the board's ranks. The executive committee is led by six officers: a president, three vice-presidents, a treasurer and a secretary. All officers and board members are elected to one year terms with re-election possible an unspecified number of times. This is the formal structure of the commission.

Election of officers and board members automatically follows from recommendations of leadership slates selected by a nominating committee of the board. Commission leadership is, in effect, a self-

1. Examples of church leadership in stimulating community organization in racially changing areas are reported in Fisher *et al.*; Philip A. Johnson, *Call Me Neighbor, Call Me Friend* (New York: Doubleday, 1965).

perpetuating group although new leaders were often sought out and made a part of the governing body. As with many voluntary associations, the board of directors was too large and unwieldy for rapid decision making, and much policy was determined by the executive committee and approved post hoc by the board. On several occasions during the study period the executive committee proved itself capable of swift action—the kind of response to an "emergency" impossible for a seventy-five-member board which meets once a month.

GROWTH AND DEVELOPMENT

Actual decision making came into the hands of the executive committee because the commission grew into an organization with complex, large scale operations. The commission's greatest surge in membership and budget size came after 1964, following the election of an energetic new president who was to serve three terms, and the appointment of a new executive director. This team, during the next three years, expanded the number of family memberships, broadened the commission's base of financial support, and escalated the scope and intensity of its activity. A smaller and smaller role in commission affairs was played by bankers and clergymen who had been important in the early days; and a declining proportion of the commission's budget was derived from contributions made by the bank and religious institutions. The continuous growth of the commission in terms of membership base and budget size is reflected in the data in Table 8.

TABLE 8

BUDGET SIZE AND NUMBER OF FAMILY MEMBERSHIPS,
SOUTH SHORE COMMISSION

Year	Annual Commission Budget (in dollars)	Number of Family Memberships
1955	16,450.66	934
1958	29,347.40	1,496
1962	49,353.99	1,455
1964	51,545.06	2,126
1966	90,000.00	3,500

SOURCE: The South Shore Commission.

The 1966 commission budget represented an almost doubling in size over a two-year period. The funds were used to support programs for school improvement, youth recreation programs, building code enforcement, crime control, area redevelopment planning, various real estate activities, an art-league workshop, and the publishing of a monthly community newspaper (*The South Shore Scene*). The commission had approximately twelve active committees during the study period, each responsible for the administration of at least one on-going program. Committee chairmen were most often board members as well; committee members frequently were not. In addition, the commission sponsored block clubs and "area councils"—although block club organization did not receive very high priority, with the result that the clubs never exceeded twenty or twenty-five at any given time.[2]

With the proliferation of activities, the commission's full-time paid staff also grew. Its executive director came to be assisted by a director of law enforcement and block organization, a housing director, and a manager of tenant referral, and two full-time secretaries. In addition, various volunteers served as clerical aids in addition to those active in committee work.

SOURCES OF ORGANIZATIONAL CLEAVAGE

Although the commission was founded well in advance of racial change, the early organizers were aware that black in-migration was a genuine possibility in the not too distant future. The commission was seen by most of its founders as an instrument for generating an appropriate response to the change.

There were two distinct views on what would be the most appropriate response, and the two opposing conceptions of the commission's role came to constitute the most fundamental cleavage within the organization and the community. The two groups may be characterized as the exclusionists and the integrationists. Each group had its own style of action, a particular social base within the community, and a general political ideology that went beyond

2. Block clubs rise and fall in South Shore with frequency and without notice; it is difficult to determine how many are functioning at any given time. At times the commission stated that 110 out of a possible 325 blocks were organized, but in a September 1965 interview, the block club director indicated that only twelve clubs were meeting on any sort of regular basis.

the issue of race but which was used in community debate to justify positions taken.

Most of the commission's early leaders had conceived of the organization as a kind of protective society, which, by encouraging proper property maintenance, land use planning, and tenant screening, would preserve the community as an exclusively white and generally middle-class area. The early founders, in other words, were primarily exclusionists. Their ranks included officials of the only bank in South Shore, a few country club leaders, and several local residents of city-wide eminence and rather substantial wealth. The organizational style preferred by these persons was secluded decision-making ("executive session"), minimum attention to such issues as representation or the broadening of support and participation, or using grassroot energies as a strategy for goal attainment.

Early in the commission's history, members drawn from this group attempted to prevent black in-migration by the formation of a syndicate which purchased several buildings in the Parkside area in order to preclude their being opened for black occupancy. This action was taken shortly before large-scale black in-migration into the Parkside area began, and proved to be as futile a strategy in South Shore as in other communities in which it has been attempted.[3]

The political views of the exclusionists were generally on the "right"; almost all were opposed to open-occupancy legislation (even after South Shore itself had gained large numbers of black residents). Some were against government medical aid for the aged and, when hearing of incidents of crime or violence in the community, related such events to what they considered the declining "moral fibre" of the country and the "breakdown of law and order." Despite (or because of) the general political conservatism of these persons, the exclusionists, like practically all commission leaders, were enthusiastic supporters of Chicago Mayor Richard Daley and the Cook County Democratic Machine.

The integrationists, although also supportive of the Daley organization, differed markedly from their exclusionist colleagues. They tended to be persons sympathetic toward grassroots "self-help" activity—both because they felt it ideologically appealing and be-

3. See, for example, Albert J. Mayer, "Russel Woods: Change without Conflict—A Case Study of Neighborhood Racial Transition in Detroit," in Nathan Glazer and Davis McEntire (eds.), *Studies in Housing and Minority Groups* (Berkeley: University of California Press, 1960), pp. 298–320.

cause it was seen as an important strategic asset for achieving goals. The ranks of the integrationists tended to be filled with professionals (as opposed to businessmen), Jews rather than Catholics and Protestants, and the "young" (early 40s). Their politics tended to be liberal; their sympathies were generally with the "Negro cause"— at least in its more moderate manifestations. They were generally appalled both by what they regarded as extremists of the left (for example, Saul Alinsky[4] and "his" Woodlawn Organization) as well as by extremists of the right (for example, Goldwater, "Southern bigots," and others explicitly opposed to civil rights for blacks and basic welfare measures such as social security).

Prominent among residents holding this conception of the commission's role was a group active in the social action committee of a reform Jewish congregation led by a rabbi whose role as the commission's first president was mentioned earlier. Soon after the commission had begun operating, this important South Shore congregation (recently moved from Hyde Park in response to racial change in that area) built its imposing edifice on South Shore Drive in what the rabbi refers to today as "a decision to test our faith." "We knew that change was coming to our neighborhood, but we also felt that this was a place where we ought to sink our roots," the rabbi commented in an interview. Several members of the congregation played leading roles in commission activities throughout the organization's history.

Generally, the integrationist group sponsored the commission's plans and its members carried them out. Securing the support of the exclusionists was necessary, both for the benefits which could be derived through their direct aid (such as important contacts with members of the city's business and political elite) and also in order to maintain a consensus within the organization. They always tried to convince the exclusionists to go along with actions distasteful to them "for the benefit of the community." Such efforts were often successful, in part, thanks to the talents of the commission president, who always listened respectfully to all parties, but deftly maneuvered

4. Alinsky's Industrial Areas Foundation organized the Woodlawn community in the late 1950s; Alinsky himself was not active in Woodlawn during the study period. For an account of the founding of the Woodlawn Organization and its running battle with the University of Chicago, see Charles Silberman, *Crisis in Black and White* (New York: Random House, 1964). For a description of Alinsky's organizing strategy, see Saul D. Alinsky, *Reveille for Radicals* (Chicago: University of Chicago Press, 1946).

discussions away from broader moral and political questions—always focusing attention on immediate and specific problems in order to avoid the antagonisms which otherwise could have easily developed.

This exclusionist-integrationist classification is based upon a rough construction of attitude and action syndromes derived from remarks made by current leaders, historical records of statements and positions taken by early participants, and on observations made during the study period of positions taken by commission leaders. Some persons, of course, were conservative on one issue and liberal on another. There were not two mutually exclusive groups; instead there was a continuum of positions represented in the commission with many persons genuinely in the middle and thus impossible to categorize. I also recognize that this conservative-liberal dimension is without any clear operational definition or demonstrable social-psychological root. I am merely adopting the lay political social-psychology widely prevalent among South Shore residents at the time.

In this limited sense, it can be said that there were two distinct groups operating within the commission, having two different ideal types of persons within each. Commission leaders themselves perceived the difference and used this classification in reconstructing the organization's history and in describing recent organizational events. The exclusionists were most often called "the conservatives"; the integrationists were called "liberals," and occasionally "progressives" or "activists." As might be expected, many persons who were placed in one camp or the other by their colleagues referred to themselves as moderates—individuals who considered themselves to have positions between the two extremes and who were thus, in their view, more pragmatic, open, and responsive to change than their more "ideological" colleagues.

SOURCES OF CONSENSUS

Although there was an important ideological split between commission participants, there was also sufficient basis for agreement to enable the organization to operate smoothly, to enjoy constant growth, and to have decisions made with a minimum of rancor. One reason for the ensuing consensus lies perhaps in the rather homogeneous origins of the commission leadership. Although

attempts were always made to draw board members from all geographical regions of South Shore, there was always a class bias
within the leadership. Low income and blue collar persons were
never represented, even though 27 percent of the 1960 Community
Area population was engaged in blue collar work. Similarly, blacks
came to be represented on the commission board and executive
committee only after 1963 and they remained under-represented in
commission councils throughout the study period. In 1967, only six
of seventy-five board members were black, despite the fact that approximately a third of the community's residents were black at that
time. The occupational backgrounds of South Shore's seventy-five
board members are set forth in Table 9.

TABLE 9
OCCUPATIONS OF MEMBERS OF THE BOARD OF DIRECTORS,
SOUTH SHORE COMMISSION, 1966–1967

Occupation Type	Number of Directors
Managers, Proprietors	22
Professionals, Higher Status (e.g., doctor, dentist, lawyer, newspaper editor)	15
Professionals, Lower Status (e.g., schoolteacher, social worker)	11
Clergymen	10
Public Officials	3
Miscellaneous White Collar	2
Housewives	10
Other	2

SOURCE: Author's interviews, various issues of *South Shore Scene.*

Various reasons can be suggested for this under-representation of
the poor, the blue collar, and the black. First, as has often been
noted elsewhere, such persons may not be joiners[5]—and they may

5. For evidence which indicates that there is a positive relationship between
status and participation in voluntary associations, see Mirra Komarovsky, "The
Voluntary Associations of Urban Dwellers," in Logan Wilson and William Kolb
(eds.), *Sociological Analysis* (New York: Harcourt, Brace, 1949), pp. 378–392.
That blacks may, however, be as prone as whites to take part in such organizations
is argued in Anthony Orum, "A Reappraisal of the Social and Political Participation of Negroes," *American Journal of Sociology,* LXXII, No. 1 (July, 1966), 32–
46.

be especially reluctant to participate in a group where style and tone are set by articulate middle-class professionals long skilled in organizational activity. It is also true, at least for blacks, that due to the recency of their arrival in the community, the broad network of contacts and neighborhood commitments which come with long-term residency were lacking—thus inhibiting contact with commission leaders and activities and perhaps decreasing the desire to participate in community affairs.

But there are other possible reasons for explaining the particular make-up of the commission leadership. The commission tended to choose its board members on the basis of the benefits which could be derived by associating an individual with the organization. The wealthy, the well-connected, and the expert were sought out—if only to lend the commission letterhead prestige. Over the years, and particularly after the 1963 election of the new integrationist commission president, there was a tendency to drop dead weight from the board, regardless of the individual's position or status. But the qualities sought in a board member remained largely the same. Despite the general ascendancy of integrationists within the organization, the commission was still most concerned with power, expertise (and to an increasing degree, energy and commitment to the organization), but not with representation. In terms of power and expertise, local blacks could not compete for positions of leadership and for the informal approval of commission members.

GOALS AND THE STATEMENT OF GOALS

The near homogeneity of class and race among commission leaders was perhaps the basis for a common allegiance to the single goal which from the beginning had served to unify them. Simply put, the aim was to keep South Shore a community in which middle-class white occupancy would always be tenable. In earlier commission days, some hoped that only whites would live in the area; others envisioned an "integrated" community with a minority of middle-class blacks in residence. Differences in preferred strategies emerged from these different conceptions of the community's future and the larger ideological positions on which such conceptions were said to be based. But commission leaders always shared the desire to keep South Shore a community in which many whites, *including themselves,* would always live. In a sense, therefore, commission leaders came to be more divided in terms of strategy and style than on questions of immediate community goals.

The early split between exclusionists and integrationists continued to be a part of commission life and almost every board meeting I observed during the study period showed some manifestation of it. After 1960, the terms themselves increasingly lost any meaning as black migration into the community continued unabated, making some sort of integration an inevitable outcome of any conceivable commission strategy. Yet there was still the same line-up on most issues; those who had earlier been exclusionists were now opposed to commission support for a statewide open occupancy law, while the integrationists were in favor. The exclusionists opposed encouraging black membership in the commission; the integrationists saw such membership as crucial to reaching organizational ends.

Primarily because of opposition from the exclusionists, racial integration had nowhere formally been stated as a commission aim. In interviews during the summer 1965, commission staff members and leaders maintained the fiction that organizational goals were without racial content, consisting only of community improvement and keeping South Shore "a good place to live." Until 1966, public statements by community leaders, as well as the extensive amount of literature produced by the commission, referred neither to race nor to integration.

The Function of Euphemisms

Although commission leaders felt obliged to use euphemisms in place of statements on the actual goal of the organization,[6] the phrases "good community" and "a good place to live" were well understood by local whites—and perhaps by many black residents as well. Most of the commission's resources and most of the discussions taking place within the organization were, in one way or another, devoted to the issue of South Shore's racial composition. Similarly, discussions within commission meetings, which attempted to appraise the effectiveness or worthiness of a specific program, almost always turned on the question of how it was affecting the area's racial composition. When commission leaders openly asked

6. For a discussion of the role of euphemisms in a changing community, see Eleanor P. Wolf, "The Baxter Area, 1960–1962: A New Trend in Neighborhood Change?" *Phylon*, XXVI (Winter, 1965), 348–361.

whether or not "we are going to make it," "making it" always had the same meaning—preventing "inundation" (another term frequently used).

The language of commission leaders occasionally led to confusions at board meetings—especially for those few members (primarily blacks) who, perhaps because they had only recently come upon the scene, were not as familiar with the terminology being used. Two incidents illustrate the kinds of interactions which occurred. At one board meeting, leaders had a long discussion of what one should tell people who "spread stories" that South Shore "is not going to remain a good community." Much advice was given— generally reiterations that "we will succeed, you have to make them understand and not be swayed by rumor mongers." Under the misconception that his remarks were relevant to the discussion, a black board member spoke of his own confidence in the community's ability to "succeed"—citing instances of good property maintenance and the organization of block clubs in his predominantly black neighborhood. The ensuing dialogue between speakers was one of great confusion because the black member was addressing himself to issues only tangentially related to race—issues which he considered important in themselves to any good community—whereas the whites present were concerned primarily with keeping whites in South Shore. The black man's point was received as a non-point; his listeners could not respond to an irrelevant remark. He thus received no feedback and his repeated interjections got him nowhere.

A similar incident occurred during a discussion of urban renewal in the all black Parkside neighborhood. Whites present were anxious that something "be done about Parkside" precisely because of its all-black status; blacks wanted action in Parkside because of the *kinds* of blacks who were moving into the area and what they regarded as a deficit of community facilities. A black commission member explained during board proceedings: "We've drawn welfare types and we don't want it; we need middle-class Negroes, not the kind we already have so many of." But for whites, renewal was seen primarily as a means of lowering the proportion of blacks in the community. Said a white commission leader: "This [urban renewal clearance] will mean the *rebirth* of Parkside." To blacks present, of course, Parkside had never died; one wonders what meaning such a statement could have had for them. Such divergent conceptions of community need, and the action priorities to which they could have led, never became clearly articulated in commission meetings; instead, such latent differences were always drowned in a chorus of ambiguous agreement that what was needed was indeed a "good community." The effect of this system of euphemisms was to blunt dissension among persons who might otherwise have disagreed and to provide both whites and blacks with a comfortable vocabulary with which they could talk "together" about different things.

External Forces Influencing Goal Statement

This need to avoid direct reference to racial goals stemmed from some additional considerations. First, it was not just a few commission leaders who were opposed to the goal of integration; many community residents (especially those living in the southeast portion) had similar views and regarded such a goal as tantamount to encouraging black occupancy. In addition, there was the fear that by labeling South Shore an integrated community, potential residents in other areas of the city would bypass South Shore as a place to live and an exodus of whites already in residence would be accelerated.

Despite this reticence, most commission leaders felt that they were suffering the negative consequences of an integration policy without being able to have the advantage of making a direct appeal to those whites who might *prefer* to live in a biracial area. They also felt that whites in South Shore as well as in the rest of the city *knew* that South Shore was changing, but were not aware that strenuous efforts were being made to modify the pace and form of that change. Thus what appeared to some leaders to be an exodus of whites fleeing change may have in reality been whites who moved only because they could see no sign of any attempt to influence the change process.[7]

This lack of commitment to integration led to accusations by some that the commission was an anti-Negro exclusionist group; fears developed that the Woodlawn Organization (a "militant" Alinsky group active in the community just to the north) would begin organizing in Parkside on this issue. Word reached commission

7. Commission leaders were themselves divided on the question of whether or not whites were deserting South Shore but even those who thought "people" were staying did not seem to have full confidence in that judgment. Others considered it "wishful thinking."

leaders that Woodlawn Organization officers had publicly stated that South Shore was their "target"; the existence of a rival organization competing for black membership within the commission's territory (especially an organization believed to be as radical as this one) was regarded as a menace to the community.

From the opposite end of the community (both ideologically and geographically) came organized resistance to the commission from the Chel-Win Association. This organization was formed on the basis of two principles: "Socialism" was taking over America, including its local communities, and the South Shore Commission was abetting a Negro takeover of South Shore.

An officer of Chel-Win (the only organization official who would consent to an interview) saw the South Shore Commission in this way in the spring of 1965: "The commission has been trying to bring Negroes into the area. They've been trying to create a run-down all-Negro neighborhood. There's a group in the commission, I don't know exactly what the name of it is, I think it's something like "Open House." [8] This group meets with people in the city and various leaders to bring Negroes into the area. His views on integration were expressed in this way:

It's [South Shore] the only area left in Chicago that's a decent place to live and I mean that. That's a fact. There's no such thing as an integrated neighborhood. There never has been such a thing since the beginning of history. . . . Mayor Daley knows that; we have no complaint with Mayor Daley. He's just taking orders from Washington and from the man up there. That means Johnson.

The Chel-Win Association limited its activities to the neighborhood from which it derived its name: Cheltenham and Windsor Park. Its membership figures were private; its activities generally limited to monthly meetings at which such topics as Communists in the civil rights movement or victory in Vietnam were discussed.[9] It had an overlapping leadership with the Bradwell School PTA and several Chel-Win officers also occupied high PTA positions. Unlike

8. This evidently is a reference to the Open House Committee of the South Shore Commission, which, in its attempt to attract *whites* to the area, holds annual tours through some of South Shore's more elegant homes.

9. For a report of these meetings, see: "Calls Student Riots Caused by Commies," *Southeast Economist* (Chicago), August 8, 1965, and "Chel-Win Will Hear Marines," *ibid.*, April 10, 1966.

the commission, Chel-Win's leadership was lower middle class (the officer quoted above owned a small laundry) and the organization had no Jewish leaders.

The Chel-Win Association was thought by most persons in the community to be of rather small importance, and was believed to operate on a small budget with a membership of perhaps 100 persons. Several clergymen who had churches within the Chel-Win area had never heard of the organization. But its existence was a threat to the commission and raised the possibility that if the commission went too far, Chel-Win would be able to mobilize a powerful opposition. Some commission leaders were in sympathy with it; the Chicago school superintendent was said to be on close terms with Chel-Win leaders and did appear in several posed photographs with notoriously "conservative" Bradwell PTA officers who were also active in Chel-Win.

Resolution: A Commitment to Integration

For such reasons as these, the commission was reluctant to "push" integration; it was, for example, prevented from formally supporting state open occupancy legislation even though most commission leaders considered that such legislation, by "opening up" the suburbs, would relieve pressure on South Shore. The Commission avoided the issue under the pretext that as a non-profit organization it could not play a political role without endangering its tax-exempt status. The same status did not prevent the commission from generating support for civic bond issues and for state legislation such as a gun-control law.

In the end, an explicit commitment to integration was made necessary by the reality that so large a proportion of South Shore's population had become black and that this fact could be lost upon few. Although the wrath of persons who supported such organizations as the Chel-Win Association would be risked, even many persons in the commission who had earlier opposed either integration or an organizational commitment to it came to believe that it was strategic to make integration an explicit commission goal. The first announcement of this change came in a policy statement published in January of 1966. It said: "The Board of Directors of the Commission feels that it is important from time to time to restate [sic] the position of the commission, in order that new residents may be informed of our position." The statement then stressed the organization's commitment to non-discrimination in housing and (in language derived from earlier proclamations by the Hyde Park-Kenwood Community Conference) proclaimed the community's desire to maintain a "stable, integrated community of high standards." [10] By spring of 1967, this sentiment was articulated in an officially approved statement of the commission's vision for South Shore: "A truly integrated urban community, not merely a transition from all white to all Negro; a community attracting both whites and nonwhites in such proportions that a racial balance is maintained; a working together to achieve good living for all its residents; this is South Shore's dream." [11]

MOTIVATIONS OF LEADERS: WHY PEOPLE CARED

Despite its rather visionary connotations, the integration goal statement had the same origin as earlier commission goal formulations: the consensus among South Shore whites that their community was to remain as much as possible like it had always been. South Shore had been one of Chicago's "good" communities, the height of "social perfection," in one local booster's view.[12] Its present-day leaders wanted to preserve their community so that they themselves could remain in the neighborhood in which they had lived their adult lives, built their friendships, and enjoyed the satisfactions of a community long associated with a certain degree of worldly success.[13] For the area to have become predominantly black would have meant that South Shore would have been "lost." A prominent South Shore matron, a member of the Chicago School Board, expressed the same sentiment when she exclaimed at a mass community meeting: "I plan to stay in South Shore; I ask each of you to stay in South Shore. . . . Because if we can't succeed in

10. See *ibid.*, January 30, 1966.
11. South Shore Commission, *South Shore Community Plan* (Chicago: South Shore Commission, 1967), p. 26.
12. John C. Spray (ed.), *Chicago's Great South Shore* (Chicago: South Shore Publishing Co., 1930), p. 33.
13. The crucial importance of status connotations of a given residential area in influencing out-migration is discussed in Mayer, "Russel Woods," as well as in Nelson Foote, *Housing Choices and Housing Constraints* (New York: McGraw-Hill, 1960).

having integration in South Shore, you can *forget* Chicago." Without whites in residence, a geographical area (whether a community or an entire city) was seen to cease having a relevant existence.

Many commission leaders worked extremely hard to guarantee the continued existence of their community. The three-term president of the organization (spoken of earlier) spent as much time on commission activities as on his own business. It was not uncommon for leaders to spend twenty to thirty hours a week on commission activities and during emergency periods the total was even higher. For commission officers, every night of the week was spent in organizational activity, although for some, other organizations such as charity and professional groups also took up part of their leisure time.

This effort was expended, in most cases, to aid a community for which there was strong affection, and *not* to protect vested financial interests. The individuals who worked hardest for the commission during the study period were precisely those whose business and professional lives were oriented to the city as a whole or to other community areas. When asked to explain, these persons could not say why they worked so hard for South Shore. In the words of one otherwise highly articulate community leader: "I'll be damned if I know why I do it. I just like South Shore; I have an attachment to the area."

The most active of commission leaders were men who, like the one just quoted, had lived in the area for many years, had children who had grown up in the community, and who felt a "responsibility" to prevent South Shore from "going to pot." [14] These people were by nature joiners; all had long histories of participation in community, professional, and charitable organizations.

This generalized tendency toward organizational participation was consistent with another striking fact about commission leaders (including integrationists): They did *not* conceive of themselves as

14. Other students have observed the salience of voluntary organization and heightened community significance to urban residents as a result of impending or actual racial change. See, for example, Davis McEntire, *Residence and Race* (Berkeley: University of California Press, 1960). Natalie Rogoff, "Racial Attitudes in a White Community Bordering on the Negro District," unpublished Master's dissertation, Department of Sociology, University of Chicago, 1947; Mikva, "The Neighborhood Improvement Association: A Counter-Force to the Expansion of Chicago's Negro Population" (unpublished Master's dissertation, Department of Sociology, University of Chicago, 1951).

pioneers. It was true that they knew that a community similar to their own had never before achieved racial integration and that their own success would be a first. The "stable integration" of Hyde Park was taken to be a result of the extraordinary wealth and power of the University of Chicago which, it was said (again and again), "tears down a building as soon as a Negro moves in." Unlike at least some organizers in Hyde Park,[15] commission leaders were not motivated by a desire to create new forms of social interaction or a new kind of neighborhood. Rather, integration was accepted (or seized upon) as a necessary strategy for the preservation of South Shore. For the most active commission leaders (the integrationists), the fact that they could be working for integration rather than exclusion in the course of preserving their community was a source of great personal satisfaction. These were persons who read rather widely and were cognizant of the "crises in the city"; they could speak of creating a "total dynamic environment for living" [16] and of the "need" to maintain middle-class white residency within the Chicago city limits.[17] By working for their own community, they could make a personal contribution to what the press, the politicians, and the academicians had labeled a worthwhile goal. Among persons with a general propensity to be active in community affairs, there was a fusion of affection for South Shore with a personal ideology which called for involvement in activities relevant to major social problems. The result was a commitment to an organization devoted to racial integration and community preservation.

Just as the opinion leaders helped to provide a general context supportive of organizations like the commission, they also provided direct support and encouragement as well. Politicians of both major parties, of a wide variety of city, state, and county agencies, were never anything but laudatory about the commission and its goals. At public meetings, at private dinners and at press conferences, the commission and its leaders were praised for their community spirit, organizational energy, wisdom and the worthiness of their aims. Local and national news media (including radio and television)

15. This impression of the motivations of early Hyde Park organizers is derived from conversations held with participants as well as from Abrahamson, *A Neighborhood Finds Itself* . . .

16. *South Shore Community Plan*, p. 11.

17. This objective was also the key goal of Mayor Richard Daley as announced by an aide after his 1967 election victory. See: "Daley Pledges 'Golden Age' for City," *Chicago Daily News*, April 5, 1967, p. 12.

similarly praised the commission; there was not a single critical notice appearing in any medium during the entire two-year study period. The *Christian Science Monitor* interviewed commission leaders and then published a laudatory article headlined "Self-Help Pays Off in South Chicago." [18] Another national publication, *City*, published a similar piece, filled with optimistic prognostications and praise for the commission's commitment to self-help and integration.[19] Although the content of these notices was often misleading and uncritically accepting of commission public relations statements, it served to legitimize commission activities not only to the public at large, but in a dramatic way to organizational participants as well. These stories in the media were received with pride and self-congratulation; they were regarded as a sign of organizational success and also of the worthiness of participation in the South Shore Commission.

Several specific examples of this rather uncritical but morale-boosting reporting should be cited because it is the response which such organizations typically receive from the media. The *Christian Science Monitor* reported there to be fifty active block clubs in South Shore. Yet an inspection of the *South Shore Scene* for ten consecutive issues in 1966–1967 reveals references under "Block-Club Corner" to only eighteen different block clubs. When it is realized that one of the functions of the *Scene* was to publicize the existence of such clubs, the small number of groups listed must be taken as indicative of a very weak block-club system. Only twelve block clubs met on a regular basis. In discussing a different topic, the *Monitor* reported in the same article that only 2 percent of the area's homes are for sale annually, whereas (as reported in Chapter Eight) it was actually found that 2 percent of the area's homes had "for sale" signs in front of them at *one given time* during the study period. Still another example: *City* reported, "Pressure from South Shore has kept average class size in elementary grades to thirty-three pupils, and the plan states a goal of thirty." In fact, thirty-three pupils was the city-wide average and reflected a policy of the Chicago School Board to keep class sizes equal in all parts of the city, which they generally were.

Nevertheless, the media's approving distortions provided an additional source of evidence for a proposition which commission leaders

18. *Christian Science Monitor,* July 21, 1967.
19. *City,* I, No. 3 (September, 1967), 30–32.

came to take as self-evident: the residents of a community have the right to determine the community's future, including (and especially) the kinds of people who will live within its boundaries. A well-known real estate analyst and Chicago civic leader (Downs) has argued that city communities must be provided with such autonomy (which *is* characteristic of politically independent suburbs) if the "cultural homogeneity" necessary to attract middle-class whites to city areas is to be made possible.[20] Only through such autonomy, Downs argues, created perhaps through community control of zoning and building standards, can cultural levels be controlled. Similar points have been argued by minority group activists under the concept of "community control," albeit with rather different social goals in mind and with a more negative response from the press, politicians, and academia. Autonomy for South Shore, as for any city sub-unit, could not realistically be gained through formal legislation;[21] the appropriate vehicle was thus community action through the South Shore Commission. With integration as a goal and community autonomy as a strategy, the South Shore commission was placed on a morally and intellectually sound foundation—one which brought pride to its leaders and one upon which appeals for city-wide support for organizational efforts could be confidently based.

20. Anthony Downs, "Metropolitan Growth and Future Political Problems," *Land Economics,* XXXVII, No. 4 (November, 1961), 311–320.
21. Recent (unsuccessful) attempts in Berkeley, California, to subdivide that city into separate autonomous police jurisdictions had a similar end and suggest a possible method for creating such autonomy through government reorganization.

5
Competing for Whites:
Techniques
of Community
Preservation

M IDDLE-CLASS whites in the Chicago area have a wide choice of where to live; whatever area attracts them does so because it is perceived to provide maximum advantages for the money paid. Most South Shore whites could choose between relocating within the community (the array of dwellings within South Shore was wide), or moving to a suburb, the fashionable Chicago Near North Side or to nearby Hyde Park—a neighborhood where racial stability and an intellectual environment were widely perceived to be guaranteed by the presence of the University of Chicago.

Although many South Shore residents had probably developed sentimental attachments to their community and may have been part of a social network of friends and acquaintances which could not be easily replaced, they, like their counterparts living in other Chicago areas, were generally aware of alternative areas of residence that provided many, if not all, of the advantages of living in South Shore. South Shore whites, it can be assumed on the basis of the high median incomes of the area, were in a position to take advantage of such alternatives. Unlike in certain working class communities of black or immigrant populations, in South Shore neither ignorance of available alternatives nor a lack of means could be expected to lead a majority of residents to remain in the community.

Consistent with this view of reality, South Shore's leaders saw the role of the commission, in the phrase of the organization's logotype, to make their community "*the* place to live." That way South Shore could keep middle-class whites already present and, as present ones died off, attract new replacements from other areas.

Two strategies were used to reach this goal. The commission attempted to create neighborhood conditions it thought important to attract whites and to make these neighborhood assets generally known to prospective white residents. Secondly, an effort was made to directly facilitate white move-ins by recruiting white, middle-class residents through a tenant referral service and other means. These two general strategies for neighborhood preservation will be discussed in this and the following chapter.

IMPROVING COMMUNITY CONDITIONS: THE
SOCIAL ENVIRONMENT

Various commission programs were aimed at creating a social environment (as opposed to a physical one) which would be attractive to middle-class whites. This was thought to be an environment characterized by safety, quiet, and the kind of people whose status and life style make them "good neighbors" and whose children make good pupils and schoolmates. The commission brought to bear upon this goal a diverse array of instruments and strategies, the most important of which will be presently described in terms of the neighborhood problem which each was designed to solve.

Crime: Making South Shore Safe for Integration.

Perhaps no community problem disturbed South Shore's white residents more than the increase in crime which was thought to have accompanied racial change in the areas of the community which had become heavily black. In light of the available evidence, it seems that such perceptions were anchored in reality.

Available police records of crime by city block made possible a comparison of frequency of crime reports in South Shore for two comparable six-month periods—one in 1964 and one in 1966.[1] During this two-year period there was a dramatic increase in the proportion of Chicago's total number of serious crimes ("Part I" Crime—homicide, rape, major burglaries, thefts, and assaults) in that part of South Shore north of 76th Street and a slight increase in

1. Comparison with earlier periods was not possible; before 1964 crime data was recorded only by precinct and South Shore is divided by precinct boundary lines. I computed crime data from print-outs in police department storage files.

the relative frequency of reports of such incidents in the area south of 76th Street.[2] During the two-year period under study, the great majority of South Shore's blacks were living north of 76th Street; in 1966, for example, the three elementary schools north of 76th Street had a mean black enrollment of 86 percent; the four elementary schools south of 76th Street had a mean Negro enrollment of 15 percent. Aside from the notorious limitations of official statistics, the data substantiate the hypothesis that an increased incidence of serious crime had accompanied black occupancy in South Shore.

The same pattern held for less serious crimes ("Part II" Crime— disorderly conduct, vandalism, etc.) and other miscellaneous police activity. There was a sharp increase in police reports of such incidents in the area north of 76th Street; in the area south of 76th Street the police reports of such incidents increased at about the same rate as in the city as a whole. However, many calls to the police within this category[3] have nothing to do with crime, consisting of such police activity as special guard details or helping a pregnant mother or an injured person to the hospital. The bulk of cases in this category are of the sort which are not clearly criminal.

Table 10 contains the official data upon which the general conclusion rests that white South Shore residents were accurate in their perception that crime increased in that area of the community in which a significant proportion of the population was black. Part I and II crime increased in this area not only in absolute levels, but also in relation to crime in predominantly white South Shore and to city-wide changes in crime totals over the same period.

In response to this rise in area crime, the Chicago Police Department (which allocates personnel on the basis of the crime load of

2. 76th Street was used as the cut-off; it simplified computation because that was how police print-out data appeared. The street is also a serviceable boundary for separating white from black South Shore. It was the only cut-off point "tried."

3. The category here actually represents a combination of two police department categories—Part II Crime and Other. These two police categories were combined for present purposes because the line between them is a thin one which has led to gross variations in crime rates within each over time. Thus, for example, according to police records, the aggregate total of Chicago Part II crime *declined* by approximately 300 percent from 1964 to 1966 whereas the number of incidents classified as "other" increased at a similar rate during the same period. Obviously, the changes reflected variations in classification methods—although police officials interviewed could recall no change in classification policy over the years.

TABLE 10

CHANGES IN THE NUMBER OF REPORTED CRIMES
IN SOUTH SHORE, BY DISTRICT, 1964 AND 1966

Year	South Shore District 3 (North of 76th St.)		South Shore District 4 (South of 76th St.)		City-Wide	
	Part I Crime	Other "Crime"	Part I Crime	Other "Crime"	Part I Crime	Other "Crime"
1964	4,936	8,329	3,925	5,190	450,024	660,542
1966	7,024	13,740	4,380	7,375	478,460	940,541
Change[a]	+2,088	+5,411	+455	+2,185	+28,436	+279,999
Percent change	+42	+65	+12	+42	+6	+42

[a] Increases in crime indicated by these figures are due, in part, to the fact that the 1966 figures correspond to a longer time period than the 1964 figures. The period for 1964 for which crime totals were available was April 30 to October 14; for 1966 the analogous period was April 28 to November 9. The table should be used only to make comparisons between areas and for contrasting a specific area with the city as a whole.
SOURCE: "Weighted Workload by Location, Semi-Annual Work Load Reports," Department of Police, City of Chicago. Computed from raw block data by the author.

a given area) raised the number of beats[4] in South Shore from four and one-quarter to six between 1962 and 1966. (In the Hyde Park area to the north where crime was falling during the same period, the number of beats decreased by a similar amount during the same period.[5]) The commission hailed these beat changes as increased police protection and used them to sell South Shore. But actually, the beat increase was a reflection of the rising need for police protection, as indicated by police records.

A more reliable indicator of crime rates in the area was the increase in emergency room service provided by Jackson Park Hospital, located at Stony Island Avenue and 75th Street. This hospital, situated at the north-south "center" of South Shore, experienced a three-fold increase in the number of emergency room patients treated during the period 1960 to 1966.[6] Most of this in-

4. These are "winter beats" rather than "summer beats" (beat structures are changed each season) which reflect heavier demands for police services due to the area's extensive beach and park facilities.
5. Information provided by Southeast Chicago Commission.
6. A second hospital was also within the commission's South Shore boundaries but, unlike Jackson Park Hospital, did not primarily serve the South Shore area. This hospital, perhaps because it was located on South Shore's southeastern edge in an all-white area, had stable rates of emergency room service and no increase in treatment of violence victims.

crease, according to the hospital's medical director, was the result
of a tendency of black residents, as compared to white, to make
more extensive use of hospitals for routine medical needs. But it
was also the case that the number of patients treated for gunshot
and stab wounds had "skyrocketed." In the words of the medical
director: "I would estimate that we are now getting roughly ten
times the number of gunshot and stabbing cases that was true five
years ago. Most of these are from within South Shore. Now we're
getting them from Jeffery Boulevard, which was unheard of. And
then there are the beatings . . . we get many, many beatings." [7]

South Shore residents were well aware of the area's increase in
crime; they witnessed and heard from their neighbors about many
incidents of purse-snatching and burglary. They also read about the
many criminal acts occurring in the community on the pages of the
twice-weekly community newspaper, *The Southeast Economist*. The
paper maintained a policy of helping South Shore and the commission as much as possible. For example, despite the rise in
crime rates in the area, *The Southeast Economist* printed between
July 1965 to April 1967 a total of eleven articles indicating that
crimes had gone *down* in the area during various short-term periods
and only six that crime had risen. This was possible by playing up
news that a certain *kind* of crime (for example, auto thefts) had
declined and ignoring other kinds of crime rates which had gone
up. Similarly, the newspaper simply refrained from reporting crime
data for those periods when the news was particularly bad.

On the average, one of every four editions of the *Southeast
Economist* contained news of some crime which had occurred within
South Shore's boundaries. During the two years for which I inspected
copies of the newspaper, there appeared ten stories on South Shore
murders, five on robberies with serious assaults, eleven on major
robberies without assaults, one on a non-fatal stabbing, two on
suspected kidnappings, one on a thwarted bombing attempt (of a
Catholic church), one on a case of arson, two on drug raids, one
on rape, and one on a hit-and-run driving case. In addition, thirteen
articles appeared which discussed black gang activities in the com-

7. The Jackson Park Hospital medical director made a study of his own in
1964. He found that over a three month period in that year there were thirty-
eight shootings with black victims and seven shootings with white victims. But in
both racial groups, the same number (seven) received fatal wounds, suggesting
that shooting may be more prevalent among South Shore's blacks because it involves expressive behavior rather than serious intent to kill.

munity. The paper did not report all South Shore crime, but perhaps it reported enough to confirm local residents in their conviction that crime in the area was rising and that "you can't trust statistics" which might indicate the contrary.

These rather concrete manifestations of crime were accompanied in South Shore by an intense fear among many residents of venturing into the streets—especially at night. Clergymen at various religious institutions indicated that night-time activities were either curtailed or completely dropped because many parishioners, especially old people, refused to leave their homes after dark. Some community leaders, especially commission officers, often argued that residents greatly exaggerated the amount of crime that occurred in the community and felt that gossip and rumor often turned molehills into mountains. Yet the rising crime rates suggest that the fears may have been well founded.

An increase in crime in South Shore had repercussions which would not occur in a different community—such as one in which high crime rates had been experienced in the past or where residents were migrants from areas where violence was not uncommon. In South Shore an act of violence was *abnormal* [8] in the perspective of white residents who in fact had always lived in a community where such incidents seldom, if ever, occurred. Residents repeated over and over, "Such things just never happened before in South Shore." The fear which residents experienced was mixed with, and perhaps intensified by, a feeling of incredulity that such events were occurring in "their" South Shore.

There were often incidents which, although frightening to some white residents, certainly had nothing to do with crime, vandalism, or potential violence. One incident was described by an elderly white woman who told how the neighborhood's change had affected her own life:

"About two weeks ago I heard my buzzer. . . . I was all alone in the apartment. Then I heard a knock-knock. . . . I never do this, I don't know why I did it, it was after dark—I opened the door just a crack leaving the chain up. . . . Well, there—just standing there— was this big black colored man."

Q: What did he want?

8. For a discussion of criminal normality in a different context, see David Sudnow, "Normal Crimes: Sociological Features of the Penal Code in a Public Defender Office," *Social Problems*, XII (Winter 1965), 255–275.

A: Why, he asked me if there were any children living in my building. I told him "no"—and then thank goodness, he left me alone.

The "colored man" in question was probably registering children for a summer day camp which was being organized in the area at the time.

South Shore had become the "turf" of a Negro youth gang headquartered in nearby Woodlawn which called itself the "Mighty Blackstone Rangers." The Rangers were notorious throughout the South Side of Chicago; many criminal acts of all degrees of seriousness were attributed to them. In particular, the Rangers were generally considered to be systematically involved in extorting money from high school pupils, assaulting and robbing local residents, and engaging in various petty acts of vandalism. One frequent form which such vandalism took was the painting of South Shore walls and facades with the Ranger imprimatur (BSR) and various messages to opposition peer groups (for example, Disciples Ain't Shit). The northern wall of the overhead pedestrian bridge that crossed South Shore Drive linking the community to the lakeside parks at 67th Street, was boldly inscribed "Blackstone Rangers," thereby intimidating the thousands of South Shore residents who passed under this "gateway" to their community on their way home from a day's work in the Loop. Once a graffito was in place, usually applied with black spray paint, it tended to remain (the bridge remained marked for about a year)—serving as a constant reminder to residents of what seemed to be the uncontrollable lawlessness in their midst.

The commission devoted much energy to what was formally termed "law enforcement." In cooperation with the South Shore Chamber of Commerce, it instituted a radio patrol network whereby groups of residents cruised community streets on weekend nights (and in some areas, every night) watching for infractions of the law which could be radioed to the police for action. Businessmen contributed funds for equipment; residents provided organization and manpower. In one area during a particularly difficult period, some residents were working seven nights in a row in four to six hour shifts. Commission leaders and local police officials thought the patrols highly effective; they were widely credited with the prevention of looting of South Shore stores after a tornado and after the Chicago blizzard of 1967, which was accompanied by looting and vandalism in some other city areas.

When arrests were made in South Shore, either as a result of the patrols or by police acting on their own, the commission followed the case, and often appeared in court "making the court aware of the community's interest in the outcome." [9] Between June 1966 and June 1967, commission officials, by their own estimate, appeared in court over sixty times for criminal cases. The commission generally attempted, often with the help of volunteer resident lawyers, to make sure that charges were pressed, that witnesses were found to testify against the accused, and that maximum sentences were pronounced. The commission was particularly anxious that "something be done about" the Rangers and pressed local police officials to "get the ring-leaders" and to never lose an opportunity to incarcerate suspected youthful troublemakers. The police, when pressed for action (as at community meetings) always assured residents that everything possible was being done to "make life miserable for the punks," but that various "legalisms" and the actions of some "bleeding hearts" prevented them from removing the Rangers from the community. The pressure on the police to get the Rangers was intense, and was generated most strongly by the integrationist liberals who saw vandalism and crime as destructive to their ambitious plans for the social and physical rejuvenation of the community.

In one important incident, the community was shocked by what was termed a riot in the high school lunch room, believed to have been begun by a group of gang members who (it was reported), at a predetermined time, chanted in unison "Blackstone, Blackstone, Blackstone" to a crowded audience of lunching students. A melee then ensued in which, it was alleged, Rangers overturned food trays, broke windows, threw dishes, and assaulted other pupils— resulting finally in minor injuries to approximately six students. Immediately after the fracas, police, school officials, and commission leaders were on the scene, initiating procedures for apprehending and prosecuting the culprits and for assuring the community that such events would never occur again. After a long series of court proceedings in which commission leaders played a prominent role, some of the alleged perpetrators were removed from the South Shore community, despite the fact that even after strenuous pleadings, no students would come forth to testify as witnesses. Three black

9. From an undated letter mailed to commission members in 1967 and signed by the commission executive director.

youths were incarcerated, another was sent by his family to live with
a brother who served in the military in Germany, and the eleven
other alleged leaders were permanently expelled from South Shore
High School.

Youth Guidance

The youths who committed acts not serious enough to result in
incarceration but were still deemed undesirable by community
standards (for example, petty theft and truancy) were eligible to
participate in the commission's "Youth Guidance Program." Under
the direction of a South Shore volunteer psychiatrist, white residents
invited black youngsters on family outings and assisted the youths
with school work and job needs. In the main, the adult was to "help
his [the youth's] self-esteem grow so that he can be a good citizen
and a productive member of society." [10] A total of seventy-five
youths had participated in the program, and according to the commission, they were all "staying out of trouble" as a result of their
experience.

Although commission funds were generally not used for these
purposes, the organization also encouraged other area institutions
(e.g., YMCA, Young Men's Jewish Center, churches) to expand
street worker and teen-age programs such as a youth job center
(Operation Encouragement), free or low-cost day camps and
special schools (with 2,944 children attending in summer, 1966),
and teen-age recreation centers. South Shore leaders claimed that
their community had a greater number of summer youth programs
than any comparably sized area of Chicago. The commission itself,
in cooperation with the Illinois Institute of Technology work-study
program, employed six college students to supplement various youth
program staffs. It also deployed seven Neighborhood Youth Corps
workers to various locations in the community.

Schools

Conditions in the local schools were taken by many residents to
be an important determinant of South Shore's future, though for
most white households, the state of the public schools was irrelevant.
Because so many of the community's whites were middle-aged or

10. From a letter to the editor requesting volunteers. See *Hyde Park Herald*
(Chicago), November 30, 1966.

older, only 23 percent of the area's households had children under eighteen years of age at the time of the 1960 Census. In part because of the large number of Catholic residents, only 15 percent of the area's households had children who attended *public* schools or had children under school age but likely to attend public schools in the future.[11] It can be deduced from 1960 census data that no more than 32 percent of South Shore's *population* was in any direct way concerned with (or likely to be involved in) public schools. This was the percentage of the area's population which included public school pupils, pre-school age children whose parents were likely to choose public education for them, and the parents of such pupils and children.[12]

For these South Shore residents (and those whose children had attended South Shore schools in their youth), a declining "quality" of the schools—institutions which were regarded as once representing superior public education—was perceived to be a major com-

11. An estimate of the proportion of South Shore white married couples *likely* to send pre-school age children to public schools was taken to equal the 1960 proportion of area pupils attending public schools (computed on the basis of published census data, Table P-1, *U.S. Censuses of Population and Housing: 1960*, Final Report PCH (1)-26, Chicago, with data for four tracts bisected by South Shore boundaries computed by halving totals referring to such tracts). The proportion was multiplied by the number of married couples with children under eighteen in South Shore (Table P-1, *ibid.*) to yield an estimate of the number of white households either sending or likely to send children to public schools. This figure, taken as a proportion of all area households (number of housing units, Table H-1, *ibid.*) yielded the 15 percent estimate contained in the text.

If it is true, as was widely believed in South Shore, that persons with children have been disproportionately likely to have left the area and that Catholics (as opposed to Jews) have been more likely to remain, then the estimated percentage of white households directly concerned with public schools would have constantly declined *below the 15 percent figure* in the transition from 1960 to the present.

12. The number of pre-school children (four years of age or younger) in South Shore in 1960 was computed from published census data (Table P-2, *ibid.*) with bisected tracts treated as described in footnote 11. The number of such children whose parents anticipated public school educations for them was computed by multiplying the computed number by the proportion of school age children attending public schools in 1960. This product was then added to the number of South Shore parents (number of couples with children under eighteen times 2) plus the number of pupils in public schools, to yield the total number of South Shore whites directly concerned with public education in 1960. The total, expressed as a proportion of the 1960 population, yields the estimated percentage of the area's *white population* which was directly concerned with public schools. As explained in note 11, as transition progressed this percentage probably became smaller.

munity problem. The state of the high school caused most concern in the community—probably because of its symbolic function as *the* high school for South Shore and because the age and size of its student body focused additional attention upon it. It was the kind of middle-class school which traditionally had sent most of its graduates to college, but which never won the outstanding reputation reserved for a city's very best schools.

School officials in South Shore insisted that racial change had not resulted in any watering down of the academic curriculum at the high school—despite the fact that 45 percent of the 1966 freshman class were reading below grade level.[13] Instead, the educators interpreted parents' concern about the *quality* of schools to be in reality a concern over the *clientele* of the schools. Similarly, parents of students who expressed desires to leave the community because of the quality of teaching or curriculum were thought by school officials to be "rationalizing" in order to cover up their real desires to move to a higher status community or one where life would be more fun. This interpretation of both parents' and students' attitudes is consistent with a position taken by Wolf, who argues: "although initial explanation of the phrase 'a good school' may be made in terms of 'good teachers, pleasant buildings, good facilities' . . . they [parents] have considerable respect for the power of peer culture, group contagion, and social climate." [14] The association of negative attributes with black pupils may cause many white parents to resist sending their children to schools with blacks. Some South Shore parents also voiced concern that their children's chances for admission to a good college would be prejudiced by their coming from a non-prestigious secondary school.

The commission strenuously attempted to bolster the "quality" of public education in South Shore. It made sure that academic curricula were as full-ranging in both elementary and secondary schools as they had always been. A special program for gifted children was established at one of the six public elementary schools (Bryn Mawr) under a two-year grant (renewed in 1966) from the state of Illinois.

Most important, the commission worked diligently to provide white residents in the area with neighborhood schools which con-

13. Source of this datum is the principal of the South Shore High School.
14. See Eleanor P. Wolf, "The Baxter Area, 1960–1962: A New Trend in Neighborhood Change?" *Phylon,* XXVI (Winter, 1965), 348–361.

tained a large proportion of white children. The first elementary school to become virtually all black (97 percent) was Parkside in 1964. Working with PTA organizations at Bryn Mawr, O'Keeffe, Mann, and South Shore high schools (all very active groups), the commission and its schools committee made many attempts to prevent such an occurrence from taking place in any additional South Shore schools.

At the beginning of the study period, it was the O'Keeffe school which was closest to moving from integrated to an all-black status; in the fall of 1964, 67 percent of its children were black. In addition to inducing whites with children to move into the O'Keeffe area, efforts were made to alter school racial compositions through direct action from the Chicago School Board. In order to do something about the increasing "resegregation" of O'Keeffe and the prevention of a similar situation at the already integrating Bryn Mawr school, various plans were laid for a policy of managed integration of local schools. The first plan to receive serious consideration was known as the Bryn Mawr Petal Plan—a scheme of permissive transfers which aimed to achieve racial balance in the area by selecting Bryn Mawr students from other school attendance zones on the basis of their race. That is, children at all South Shore elementary schools would be eligible to transfer to Bryn Mawr (a school located in the geographical center of South Shore), but permission to transfer would be based upon how such a transfer would affect the racial balance both of the sending school and of Bryn Mawr.

Opposition to the Bryn Mawr plan came from the PTA of the all-white Bradwell school, which adamantly opposed any compromise of the "neighborhood school" principle. After months of consideration, the Chicago School Board was advised by the attorney serving in the superintendent's office that because discrimination on the basis of race was implicit in the plan, it was illegal. Citing this advice, the school board dropped the Bryn Mawr plan from further consideration.

Partially as a result of the fact that a similar racial quota plan was successfully instituted in the Chicago suburb of Evanston after the Chicago School Board had made its decision, Bryn Mawr parents were emboldened to force action through the courts. A suit was filed in circuit court by Bryn Mawr parents (two white couples and two black couples) on behalf of their four children. The suit, filed on November 18, 1965, charged that the Board of Education, by not acting to guarantee integration in South Shore was in disobey-ance of the Illinois Armstrong Act which directs school boards to take into consideration the prevention of segregation in revising school district boundaries. The parents proposed a quota for Byrn Mawr of 50 percent black and 50 percent white. In December 1966, their suit was dismissed on the grounds that the effect of a racial quota would be to bar some students from attending a school "solely because of color," thus violating their constitutional rights.[15]

Although no other scheme for integrating community elementary schools reached so advanced a stage as the Bryn Mawr plan dur-ing the study period, other proposals were in the talking stage. One idea was to have each South Shore elementary school serve only two grade levels. All South Shore children entering the first grade would change school buildings every two years as they moved through the local elementary school system. Excluded from the plan would have been the all-black Parkside and almost all-black O'Keeffe schools, which if included, would have brought so many black children into each of the school buildings that at least some would have had black majorities. Commission officials were wary of publicizing such a plan lest the Bradwell PTA's inevitable opposi-tion preclude its acceptance by the school board. Bradwell PTA officials were already complaining vociferously that commission school proposals always had the effect of endangering the neighbor-hood school principle and that "we are being manipulated for the interest of others." [16] Perhaps because of this opposition, enthusiasm for this consolidated elementary school plan appeared to be waning (even among commission leaders) at the close of the study period.

The South Shore School-Community Plan

Despite its difficulties in gaining approval for managed integration, the commission was able to make some major gains for South Shore in its dealings with the school board. These gains were widely be-lieved to be a result of the fact that two local residents (both South Shore boosters) served on the eleven-member board and also a result of the cordial relationship which existed between the com-mission president and Benjamin Willis, the superintendent of

15. *Chicago Daily News,* December 8, 1966.
16. *Southeast Economist* (Chicago), June 18, 1967.

Chicago schools during most of the commission's history. Speaking of the commitments which the School Board made to South Shore and of his many personal meetings with the school superintendent (a man who had been under bitter attack by civil rights and other community groups during this period), the commission president remarked: "I'm really the only community president he can deal with. We get along very well."

The payoffs to South Shore were several. First, the School Board created in the spring of 1965, a new and relatively autonomous school district covering exactly the same territory as that specified by the commission to constitute South Shore. The redrawing of boundaries had the effect of bringing slightly larger numbers of white students into the area served by South Shore High School. Concurrent with a redrawing of boundaries, the Chicago Superintendent of Schools, in enunciating the "South Shore School-Community Plan," stated that neighborhood integration was (in part) the responsibility of the public schools and that in setting attendance boundaries and in making curriculum decisions, the goal of preserving integrated communities should be considered. In the superintendent's words to the Board of Education: "The South Shore School Community Plan . . . is a demonstration program which has as its primary purpose assisting a community which is undergoing racial change to stabilize as an integrated community, retaining both white and Negro families, and to prevent a 'de facto' resegregation by race." [17] This plan, the content of which came as a direct response to commission demands, represented the first time the Chicago schools assumed the position that the school could or should be a vehicle for influencing community racial composition. It is significant that the same superintendent remained unresponsive to demands by civil rights advocates that the same principal be applied to the integration of neighborhoods in which blacks did *not* live.

Under the South Shore School-Community Plan, South Shore was to be given priority over other school districts so that whites would find the area's educational facilities so attractive that they would remain in the community. The schools were to engage in

17. Benjamin C. Willis, "Statement to the Board of Education: School-Community Plan," Office of the Superintendent of Schools, City of Chicago, April 12, 1965.

full-scale cooperative arrangements with "the community." The South Shore Commission was explicitly recognized as the representative community institution and thus the second party to the school-community partnership. Much in the way of specific improvements were promised to South Shore under this spring 1965 plan; much (although not all) was in fact delivered.

Of key importance to the community was that construction was authorized for a second physical plant for South Shore High School. The new structure, well under construction at the end of the study period, was said to be the most expensive secondary education building ever built in Chicago.[18] Features of the new building included carpeted classrooms, air conditioning, a theatre in the round, ice-skating rink, and a library four times as large as any previously existing in Chicago schools. Significantly, funds were allocated for South Shore's school, and construction was under way, well before relief was promised to four other southeast schools—all significantly more overcrowded than was South Shore. Funding the new $5 million addition on a priority basis was sharply criticized by Chicago civil rights leaders as an "example of lack of concern for quality education for all." [19]

A further irritation to civil rights leaders was the fact that original plans called for funding the new school from a 30 million dollar grant from the federal government designed for improvement of educational facilities in Chicago poverty areas. Because South Shore was not a poverty area, funding the new school from such a source was seen as part of a Chicago "conspiracy against Negroes." [20] Perhaps because of this opposition, together with fears that federal officials would oppose the expenditure, the school board instead funded the new building out of general revenues.

Although community leaders were pleased that South Shore was to gain a superior physical plant for its high school, there was still

18. *Southeast Economist* (Chicago), September 19, 1965.

19. *Ibid.*, September 3, 1965. The quote is from Al Raby, convener of the Coordinating Council of Community Organizations (CCCO), an "umbrella" group representing over thirty organizations involved in Chicago civil rights activities. The more overcrowded high schools were Harlan, Hirsch, Bowen, and Hyde Park. Raby's complaint was also directed at the fact that Chicago's public schools were more highly segregated than those of any major non-southern U.S. city. See: U.S. Commission on Civil Rights, *Racial Isolation in Public Schools,* I (Washington, D.C.: U.S. Government Printing Office, 1967), 4, 5, 48, 49.

20. *Southeast Economist* (Chicago), September 3, 1965.

apprehension that the increasing size of the area's black population would mean that a majority of children in the new school would be black when it opened its doors in the winter of 1968. With construction of the new building under way, the commission proposed that the structure be declared an academic high school with students in general curricula (non-college oriented) to attend the old building across the street or a vocational high school out of the area. Thus even if a majority of high school students in the area were to be black (as was virtually guaranteed to be the case on the basis of projections from existing elementary school enrollments), a majority of students in the new building would be white. The chairman of the commission schools committee remarked: "If this [new] school could be used for all of the academically superior, college bound students in the southeast area, it would help maintain a racial balance." [21] At the close of the study period, school officials had not yet announced curriculum plans for the new building.

Although it represented the largest investment of public funds in the area, the new high school was not the only significant budgetary commitment of the School Board to South Shore. A former Hebrew school building in the area was purchased by the School Board to serve as a district educational saturation center (the first in Chicago), housing district administrative offices and a program for high school computer science training. Other innovations under the plan which were instituted included the creation of an evening junior college at the high school, the establishment of a local citizens' advisory council, special reading clinics and remedial classes for below grade-level students.

The provision of the plan calling for school-community cooperation was carried out. The district superintendent and the high school principal (both new to the community and to their jobs) became enthusiastic commission boosters and appeared often at community functions. Many school playgrounds and other school facilities were regularly made available for community use. This cooperative school-community stance enabled the commission to spring into immediate action after the school "riot" (described earlier) occurred. Said a past commission president, one who was in the school when the incident occurred: "Our community was organized and ready to act when needed. Our police and school authorities and our com-

21. *Ibid.,* December 4, 1966.

munity and youth service organization knew one another, were able to meet together within seven hours of the disturbance, and had machinery in motion to meet with the public almost immediately." [22]

The response of the community was, in fact, rapid. The police informed the commission immediately after the disturbance ended; a meeting of commission leaders, school officials, police, and local clergy was held the same day, and the decision was made to increase police surveillance within and around the school and to create an "adult presence" in the school by using parent volunteers within the building. All of these actions (and others) were taken, and South Shore, in spring, 1967, had about forty parent volunteers who had worked in the high school (more, it was said, than in any other Chicago school building).

Social Class

Commission leaders were always concerned that blacks entering South Shore be equal or superior in their occupational and educational status to the whites whom they replaced. If such could be guaranteed, it was reasoned, the impact of black immigration upon resident whites would be minimized.

Many community leaders were therefore disturbed by what they regarded as a lack of sensitivity by real estate dealers to class distinctions among blacks. White real estate dealers were castigated for not practicing good screening techniques which could be designed to guarantee that South Shore got the "good Negro." For their part, the real estate dealers thought it genuinely difficult to find such Negroes. As one such businessman remarked: "Everybody wants a Ralph Bunche—and there aren't many of those in either race." Black real estate dealers agreed that South Shore was *not* the prestige Negro area in Chicago; that distinction was felt to belong to Hyde Park and to Chatham (an all-black neighborhood consisting predominantly of single family homes, also on the South Side). The "good Negroes" perhaps did not *want* to live in South Shore, preferring areas like Chatham where everyone "had a home of one's own" and where, consequently, control of property maintenance was in the hands of residents.

In any event, evidence suggests that at least a small number of

22. *Ibid.,* February 19, 1967.

South Shore's blacks were poor. Cook County welfare data indicate that whereas there were only thirty-three Aid to Dependent Children cases in South Shore in June, 1960, the number had risen to 244 six years later.[23] Excluding blindness and old age assistance (which are not as closely related to class as are other case load types), the case load total for all other forms of public assistance rose in South Shore from 50 in 1960 to 147 in 1966—despite the fact that city-wide case loads for such programs actually dropped during the same period. The absolute number of what were termed by South Shore whites as "welfare types" was thus not great compared to many other urban communities. But like the increased amount of crime occurring in the area, it was abnormal in South Shore and thus received a great deal of notice. The phrase "ADC building" had gained common currency in South Shore—a building so described connoted that the area surrounding such a structure had reached the lowest possible ebb.

The commission took two specific approaches to influence the kinds of blacks rented to in South Shore and the level of services provided them. First, the commission attempted to convert the local real estate industry to what was referred to as "constructive attitudes toward neighborhood change." Many meetings were held between commission officials and various real estate men in the area. The three largest firms, responding to a commission request, sponsored two mass "education" meetings in which approximately 900 real estate salesmen, rental agents, and janitors were exhorted by the president of one of the sponsoring companies to maintain properties well and to "undertake an effort of positive promotion for South Shore to attract good quality tenants and owners." Janitors were told by another important real estate man that they were the "eyes and ears" of the community and that they should be the first to report overcrowding, other signs of illegal occupancy or neglect, and poor housekeeping.

A second commission approach was the creation, in June of 1967, of a central screening service. Under this program, real estate firms were to submit the names of questionable apartment applicants to the commission. A fee of $4.00 was collected from the applicant or

23. Welfare data furnished by officials of the Cook County Department of Public Aid.

absorbed by the management firm. Of this amount, seventy-five cents was used by the real estate firm to carry out a credit check; the balance was turned over to the commission which dispatched a staff member to the home of the applicant for an unannounced inspection of the level of housekeeping and the conditions under which the family was living. Information so gathered was then turned over to the real estate firm, which was thus placed in a better position to appropriately handle the application. In addition, an alphabetical list was begun of all "undesirable" applicants—to be consulted in case the same persons should make a second attempt to move into South Shore.

At the close of the study period, the program was still in its infancy; during the pilot program only eighteen home visits had been made, but of these sixteen were described by the commission as clear rejections. The three real estate firms involved, according to a commission official, were shocked by the reports of overcrowding and communal living discovered, and were happy to have the information. On the basis of these pilot results, it was decided by the commission and the participating firms to make the screening service a permanent commission program available to all local real estate dealers.

Even before the visitation program began, however, the commission made a practice of bringing to the attention of local real estate firms the existence in their buildings of persons with criminal records or "in trouble with the police," and, generally pressed for eviction. Also, through its close cooperation with local school authorities, the commission was able to learn of additional undesirable renting situations in South Shore. School officials learned from children the numbers of persons living in their households and other occupancy conditions of their family. The information was turned over to the commission, according to one of the organization's leaders, in cases where occupancy standards or building code laws were being broken. Again, pressure for eviction was placed upon the real estate firm involved. In a statement characteristic of many made by both school and commission officials, a commission officer remarked: "Because of our excellent rapport with the schools we're able to find out about these goings on and get rid of them. We're just not going to put up with these kinds of people in South Shore." This example of school-community cooperation was not part of a regular, systematic program, but did occur when school officials uncovered conditions regarded as particularly undesirable for the welfare of the community.[24]

All of these activities were based on the commission's explicit premise that, in the words of one commission leader, "we have the right to determine the kind of people who are going to live in our community." Said another, "We have a right to say to the real estate industry: 'We have certain standards which must be met.'"

IMPROVING COMMUNITY CONDITIONS:
THE PHYSICAL ENVIRONMENT

Housing

South Shore tried to maintain a physical environment conducive to middle-class white residency. A city building code enforcement program had always been a part of the commission's strategy; a member of the staff devoted most of his time to inspecting South Shore properties for code violations, bringing pressure upon building owners to correct deficiencies and carrying complaints to the attention of the Chicago Building Department, and when necessary, into the courts.

In July 1966, the commission was successful in having the city's first "housing service center" established in South Shore to carry out door-to-door building inspections, to assist local residents in procuring low interest federal loans and grants to upgrade their properties, and (in the words of the center's coordinator) "to prevent or eliminate overcrowded situations and to rectify conversion by illegal structural changes." [25] According to the head of the Chicago Building Department, South Shore was chosen for this first service center because of the "excellent type of community leadership" in the area.[26]

Even after the establishment of the center in South Shore, the commission continued its own surveillance. During the period from June 1966 to June 1967 the commission received 1,015 citizen

---

24. The view that undesirables should be removed from South Shore was shared by many residents, black and white. One black resident, writing in a letter to the editor of the *South Shore Scene* stated: "How can citizens help? Contact landlords and real estate firms regarding the youthful leaders of crime and violence. If they live in South Shore, let's get rid of them." See *ibid.*, November 1966.
25. *Southeast Economist* (Chicago), July 24, 1966.
26. *Ibid.*

complaints involving local street, alley, and building conditions. The nature of these complaints and their disposition were as follows:

130 were investigated by the commission and found to be unfounded;
411 involved street and alley complaints which were referred to local aldermen whose function it was in Chicago to handle such problems;
265 resulted in compliance after meetings with owners (in some instances more than one meeting was required);
209 were referred to the Neighborhood Center;
125 complied after being ordered to do so by the city building department;
 81 complied after being ordered to do so through court action;
  3 resulted in buildings being demolished under court order.

Commission staff members estimated that they were in court on housing cases on the average of twice weekly—an effort which resulted in the levying of eighteen fines amounting to a total of $2,843 —an amount actually paid on properties on which repairs were also made.

Concurrent with commission housing surveillance and the efforts of the Housing Center was a program by the Chicago Dwellings Association (CDA)—an agency of the city government which purchased and rehabilitated housing for use by middle-income residents. CDA had chronic funding problems and difficulties in locating structures which could be rehabilitated at a cost below that of new construction.[27] CDA actions within South Shore were consequently modest in scale (involving the rehabilitation of two apartment buildings), but this was CDA's major city-wide activity during the period.

Given the commission's efforts and the priority treatment the area received from city officials, a commission leader's predication that "in three years there won't be a single code violation in all of South Shore" seemed quite reasonable.[28] Yet increasing physical deterioration could be observed in the area—especially in the all-black apartment districts. The level of attention to landscaping, building exteriors, and trash removal had noticeably declined.[29]

27. For an account of an unsuccessful attempt by a non-profit organization to rehabilitate housing on a break-even financial basis, see: *New York Times,* March 9, 1967, pp. 1, 38.

28. *Southeast Economist* (Chicago), February 19, 1967.

29. In Chicago, trash removal from apartment buildings is the responsibility of the building owner and not of the city.

Although to resident blacks such conditions may have seemed superior to other black neighborhoods, South Shore whites often called Parkside "a slum." [30] For the more subtle forms of building maintenance, the commission seemed unable to function as effectively as when dealing with illegal practices.

Thirty-one interviews[31] with South Shore area real estate dealers revealed a conviction among almost all white building managers that after a property "goes Negro" the most profitable course to follow is either to lower the level of maintenance expenditures or at least to modify maintenance practices in such manner that "beautification" suffers. One officer of a large and highly respected South Shore real estate firm indicated that it was standard practice to decrease building services when blacks moved into a structure because "you've had some lean years; now's your chance to make a buck." Other area real estate men cited increased costs due to vandalism, overuse of facilities by large numbers of children and the "unurbanized" life style of blacks as eating up maintenance funds normally spent in keeping buildings attractive. Officers of other firms cited the fact that many white janitors were bigoted and would not expend energy to maintain a black-occupied building at a quality level. Regardless of the reasons, it seemed clear that the appearance of the community was gradually on the decline, which most observers attributed in part to black migration into the community.

A Plea for Amenities: The South Shore Community Plan

The commission had always been interested in bringing to South Shore new parks, modern shopping centers, and glamorous boulevards that would attract and retain whites. It was active in stimulating the landscaping of a parkway on Stony Island Avenue and in the creation of a small urban renewal project (quietly getting under way in the early summer of 1967) which cleared approximately four front blocks of housing in the Parkside area. The commission had also been instrumental in having the O'Keeffe area (and eventually all of South Shore) designated as an "unassisted urban

30. Rossi and Dentler found that in Hyde Park (before urban renewal) whites considered the community to be badly deteriorated, while blacks were generally pleased with its physical condition. See: Rossi and Dentler, *The Politics of Urban Renewal: The Chicago Findings* (New York: The Free Press), 1961.

31. The nature of these interviews and the techniques used are discussed in Chapter Two.

renewal conservation area," thus making residents and potential developers eligible for low interest construction and rehabilitation loans.[32] The commission encouraged homeowners and businessmen to "spruce up" their properties and the local Chamber of Commerce to establish parking facilities and other improvements.

Late in the study period, the commission embarked upon a more ambitious approach to the renewal of the community's environment. An analysis of South Shore's problems and the commission's proposals for their solution was released in the form of *The South Shore Community Plan: A Comprehensive Plan for Present and Future by the Residents of South Shore.*[33] A series of commission subcommittees, all working under the direction of an energetic young South Shore architect, devoted almost two years of spare time to produce it. In its near-final form (as released in the spring of 1967), the plan contained over 100 pages, including architectural renderings and illustrative maps and graphs.

Although the *South Shore Community Plan* was called a "human plan" by its authors because it contained provisions for educational curriculum development and recommendations for "managing integration," most of the excitement generated by the document involved its bold proposals for new construction and physical rehabilitation. Profusely illustrated with characterizations of what the "new" South Shore would look like, the plan came as an answer to those who had been looking for large-scale physical intervention "like in Hyde Park." The most spectacular proposal of the plan was the construction of Project 71—a major regional shopping center and high-rise apartment complex covering the despised Illinois Central Railroad tracks on 71st Street as a replacement for the existing obsolete and overbuilt retail shopping district.

The plan also called for clearance of deteriorated buildings, construction of new housing including clusters of high-rise apartments, new parks, new traffic patterns, and the conversion of a seldom-used railroad stub into an attractive pedestrian mall traversing al-

32. Little ever came of this designation. Only seven loan applications had been filed at the end of the study period, even though parts of the community had been eligible for years previous. A developer attempted to build a 221d3 housing project near the lake shore; the zoning variation he needed was successfully blocked by the commission, which considered such moderate income housing inappropriate to such a prime lakeside area.
33. *South Shore Community Plan.*

most the entire community. As expressed in the pages of *The South Shore Plan,* the community was to be recreated in the image of the professional planner's ideal: "If you were to hop a helicopter and fly over the South Shore of the future . . . like an exciting montage, you would see a variety of housing forms skillfully woven together by broad bands of green malls. You would see the old fashioned grid patterns softened by circles of foliage . . . clusters of high rises scattered through the landscape and pedestrian ribbons tying the community to the shore." [34]

Despite the fact that community and metropolitan newspapers gave the South Shore Community Plan and Project 71 prominent coverage on the day of formal announcement,[35] the Chicago real estate journal, *Realty and Building,* relegated the news to a fifth of page 7—enough space for a picture of the proposed Project 71 and five column inches of description. The picture caption referred to the plan as one "suggested" by the South Shore Commission; any project of comparable size and scope would have merited the term "proposed" or "planned" (which are the words ordinarily used) and almost certainly would have received prominent front page coverage if the editors considered it likely that the development would ever be built.

Indeed there were many reasons to justify a restrained response to the news of South Shore's future redevelopment. First was the matter of *time;* large scale renewal projects need many years of planning, deliberating, acquiring, condemning and building. Even in Hyde Park, renewal took a generation. South Shore, although recommended by the city for "demonstration cities" funds along with five other Chicago communities, was in danger of losing its designation as the size of the federal program and Chicago's share of it was increasingly cut. South Shore had the additional problem of not being a community likely to attract prospective developers—being relatively distant from the city center and not adjacent to any major institution.[36] It could be argued that to rehabilitate South Shore—

34. *Ibid.,* pp. 1f.
35. A description of the plan and a large photograph containing Project 71 and the commission president dominated page 3 of the *Chicago Sun-Times,* the editor of which was a commission board member. A total of fifty-nine column inches was devoted to the story. See *Chicago Sun-Times,* April 14, 1967. Similarly, the *Southeast Economist* devoted seventy column inches to the same news.
36. The difficulties of making redevelopment pay in such a grey area where site

a community with almost no substandard housing; to create parks in an area already surrounded on two sides by regional parks and recreational facilities; and to build new stores to replace old ones torn down because they were obsolete—to do such things as these could well be regarded as an unwise use of public resources in light of more pressing demands elsewhere. Despite these impediments, by the early summer of 1967 the commission had begun a round of visits with financiers, developers, and federal and local officials to translate the *South Shore Community Plan* into a reality.

CREATING A POSITIVE IMAGE FOR SOUTH SHORE

South Shore's many programs and plans to enhance the conditions of community life would have had little effect unless they helped to create a positive image of the community among Chicago whites. An important instrument for communicating the most positive possible image to the whites already in residence was the *South Shore Scene,* a commission-published and edited monthly mailed free to 25,000 area families and businessmen. Community leaders could project in *The Scene,* and in press releases for other media, those aspects of South Shore which conformed to the most idyllic suburban life style and those few cultural institutions (e.g., a commission-sponsored art league and gallery) which represented "high culture." [37] Almost all materials contained a dramatization of the community's lakefront location amidst beaches and parks and its large number of fine homes.

Open House Day

In order to make the most of these assets, the commission sponsored an annual "Open House Day" patterned after the annual

---

acquisition costs are relatively high and housing demand (among upper-income persons) relatively low are discussed in the following works: Charles Abrams, *The City Is the Frontier* (New York: Macmillan, 1966); Bernard Frieden, *The Future of Old Neighborhoods: Rebuilding for a Changing Population* (Cambridge: M.I.T. Press, 1964).

37. The headlines of a series of feature articles on new white residents appearing in the *South Shore Scene* during 1966 may illustrate the content of the "dynamic urban-interesting life" campaign of the period: "Dull Lives? Not for Residents Here" (*ibid.,* May 1966); "South Shore Charms Meet Urban Needs" (*ibid.,* March 1966); "Music Plays Vital Role in Lives of Residents" (*ibid.,* September 1966).

Open House Days which had been held for years in Hyde Park. Organized by a commission committee consisting primarily of upper-middle-class housewives, Open House consisted of guided tours through some of South Shore's more impressive residences. Over 100 community residents were said to have planned and executed Open House activities which in 1967 also included an art display and jazz concert.

Each year more people turned out for Open House Day; in the spring, 1967, over 1,500 persons were said to have taken the tour —the great majority of them whites. Open House Day enabled South Shore to put its best foot forward—to show that much luster remained in what was once one of Chicago's prime neighborhoods. People were still living graciously in South Shore, people who obviously could afford to move had they cared to. One year, Open House included a tour through the home of a wealthy black family, demonstrating that integration brought "the good Negro" to South Shore.

It is impossible to know how many "visitors" were already residents of South Shore, or how many were in the market for housing or were influenced to move into the community. But Chicago newspapers generally gave Open House Day full page coverage in the society sections, complete with photographs of elegant South Shore interiors. The positive publicity was the kind of payoff which could increase the demand for housing in South Shore, thus justifying in itself the effort expended on the program.

The coverage given Open House Day, like the response of the media to Project 71 and various commission programs and demands, were made possible by the general city-wide consensus that the commission's goals were worthy, and by the specific relationship which commission officials enjoyed with the mass media. Editors of two Chicago metropolitan dailies were on the commission board; numerous local television and radio executives (including a prominent news director) were South Shore residents and active members of the commission. These advantages, coupled with the energetic attempts of other community residents, provided a prodigious public relations program.

SOUTH SHORE AND CITY POLITICS

In a city often characterized as the last bastion of machine politics, South Shore leaders paid little attention to politics at the community level—they seldom sought gains for the community by working through aldermen or precinct captains. The commission generally succeeded in maintaining cordial relations with the two local aldermen (both Daley machine functionaries) who served South Shore. In certain routine matters such as garbage collection and street repairs, complaints received by the commission were referred to aldermen for correction. At various commission ceremonial functions, such as the annual full-membership meeting, aldermen were introduced and given a round of applause as "visiting dignitaries," but they were not invited to speak. Like precinct captains and other political workers, they were treated courteously on the few occasions in which they came into contact with the commission, but they were never considered very important to the goals of the organization. Their reelection was rather half-heartedly supported by commission leaders; the commission never formally backed candidates for election but there was an obvious consensus of support for the Democratic Party and for Mayor Daley.

Many commission leaders worked for Mayor Daley's reelection in the campaign of 1967 and for passage of his bond issue proposals. They were convinced that with the possible exception of school authorities, virtually all power in the city of Chicago rested in Daley's hands. Commission leaders considered the needs of their community to require nonroutine measures; the kind of actions asked of the city government were not part of any existing policy and thus were beyond the power of aldermen and minor officials. The commission leaders' strategy was to gain the Mayor's support, to communicate that support to the heads of various city departments, and then establish direct links between city officials and themselves. Commission leaders held at least four closed meetings with the Mayor during the study period and various committee chairmen and commission officers met at least as frequently with city department and agency heads—several of whom were themselves South Shore residents and commission board members.

Thus, the commission's approach was to deal with the top, to encourage personal contacts between commission leaders and agency heads—whether in the building department, the Board of Education, or nonpolitical groups such as local newspapers and civic organizations. The commission's approach was tenable for several reasons. First, its leaders were at home in the offices of important people (many leaders being important people themselves). Second, many commission leaders, through business or professional activities, were already on good terms with the officials. Finally, South Shore's appeal was based on an ideological position which they shared: Something should be done to "save" a community like South Shore from becoming all black.

Most of South Shore's programs depended upon the cooperation of outside groups (primarily city agencies); without their assistance it is doubtful that the commission could have created and sustained its range of programs and the devotion and energy of its leaders. In order to improve local schools, reduce crime, find jobs for teenagers, or renew the physical environment, outside resources were required. In light of the natural style and connections of its leaders, and the realities of politics in Chicago, the commission's strategy for gaining the priority goods and services to make their community attractive to middle-class whites was appropriate.

THE IMPROVEMENT PARADOX

Given the validity of the dual market racial change model outlined in Chapter Two, there are certain reasons to suspect that most of the commission programs were not likely to succeed. One key practical "problem" with the improvement strategy is that programs which make a community more desirable to whites tend to make it more desirable to blacks as well. In South Shore, as in most changing areas, there was a tendency to mistake a frequent co-occurrence of black residency and physical deterioration for a causal relationship in which deterioration *brings about* black occupancy. But because upwardly mobile middle-class blacks are the initial "integrators" of white areas,[38] bolstering the quality of the environment would tend to create greater demand by these persons. As other researches have shown, black in-migration is *not* most likely to follow paths of deterioration and decay, but rather occurs in white areas which are substantial enough to be desired by the black middle class, although obsolete enough to be spurned by a

38. See Taeuber and Taeuber, *Negroes in Cities* (Chicago: Aldine, 1965), pp. 163, 164. The Taeubers conclude: "Negroes in Invasion tracts are of higher educational and occupational status, are more likely homeowners, and less likely to be crowded than Negroes in Negro areas."

white middle class with superior options.[39] South Shore whites were convinced that the beauty and good physical condition of their community was its greatest asset. In fact, once a middle-class community becomes defined as one which is open for Negro occupancy, its beauty may be (from the standpoint of whites) one of its greatest liabilities.

To the extent that commission programs made South Shore more attractive to both races equally, intervention would have no effect on racial change. To the degree that such extra amenities were *particularly* appealing to whites, transition would be delayed; to the extent that the particular appeal was to blacks, transition would be accelerated.

Most commission programs were developed and continued as part of a general scheme of community improvement, without precise analysis of a program's probable differential impact on the Negro and white markets. This was perhaps inevitable. The kind of data such analyses required were unavailable and would have required a massive research program in themselves. But even with such analyses, there may have been no easy answers. The heart of the problem in South Shore was that no institution or other asset could be used to generate a *particular demand among whites as opposed to blacks*. As already indicated, the creation of amenities in South Shore, short of making the area so desirable that it served a population paying rents completely beyond the reach of almost all Chicago blacks (and most whites already there), would make South Shore more valuable to members of *both* races. This is the problem inherent in efforts such as "Project 71" or other partial redevelopment schemes. Similarly, any development of new housing serving persons of moderate income and rented on a color-blind basis would also fail to stimulate white, as opposed to black, demand. And this would probably be the result of any scheme to improve local schools, street safety, parks or recreation facilities. More direct integration programs, such as the Bryn Mawr School Petal Plan, would also increase black demand, assuming that the attraction of integration is as strong (or stronger) to blacks as to whites. Only South Shore's image-building public relations efforts, aimed at white media, were at least on target, though Chicago blacks also read at least some of

39. See, for example, Annette Fishbein, *The Expansion of Negro Residential Areas in Chicago.* Unpublished master's dissertation, Department of Sociology, University of Chicago, 1962.

the media which carried the South Shore message, and might take the advertised claims more seriously.

There were ambitious programs under discussion which, if carried out, would have bolstered the local white and not the local Negro market. One such possibility was the creation in South Shore, either on cleared land or on lakeside property purchased from the declining South Shore Country Club, of a research park which would attract potential tenants through its proximity to the University of Chicago and which would fill South Shore apartments with white scientists, executives, and technicians. Another possibility was to bring a new, major Catholic university to either location. This would also have bolstered the white market as faculty, students, and researchers sought convenient housing. It is probably not a coincidence that the Archbishop of Chicago, about to embark upon a major archdiocese building program, was the invited keynote speaker at the June 1967 Annual Full-membership Meeting of the commission.[40] At the close of the study period, both the research park and the new university were still in the "talking" stage and no commitments had been made by any parties necessary to the realization of either venture.

Another ambitious approach to integration which was discussed in South Shore, and which held significant potential for influencing racial patterns, involved the applying of racial quotas to South Shore buildings. It was true that the commission had issued an edict to local real estate officials specifying that their transactions were to be half with Negroes and half with whites, but such pronouncements were not taken seriously by many local real estate dealers. Only if firms cooperating with the commission gained control of vast blocks of area housing could such a program come to pass.

There was a continuing attempt to transfer a large number of buildings in a certain strategic neighborhood to the ownership or management of one of Chicago's prestige real estate firms, a firm which had a reputation for making good on its policy of managing some of its structures under a racial quota system (approximately 20 percent Negro) and with high maintenance standards. The commission worked "hand in glove" (the words of a commission leader) with this firm, alerting it to the availability, or likely availability, of particularly "poorly managed" structures which, after pressure upon

40. The Archbishop, however, was forced to withdraw his earlier acceptance of the invitation for he was to be in Rome receiving his Cardinal's hat on the day of the commission meeting.

owners by the commission, were likely to sell for "reasonable" prices. The aim was to produce single ownership of all apartment housing in one well-bounded area so that complete environmental control could become possible.

On the assumption that enough properties would become available for purchase, the firm in question was said by commission officials to have made a commitment of three million dollars for property acquisition—an investment estimated to be capable of purchasing 30 million dollars' worth of South Shore property.[41] I was unable to discover first-hand how much of this property had been acquired at the close of the study period and how much of it could ever be expected to be purchased. The question whether enough properties were to be purchased to influence significantly the area's racial composition remains moot. But such action is one interesting method of bypassing the vicissitudes of the dual market through cooperation between a community organization and a real estate firm of "good reputation" and the willingness to invest large amounts of capital in an unprecedented venture.

The commission understood the possibilities of such a scheme because of a growing awareness that the processes of real estate buying and management were the key to the area's future. Programs of community improvement, while still regarded as important, lost their centrality in commission leaders' thinking. Intervention in local real estate dealings became increasingly pervasive during the study period. The most important mechanisms for such intervention are the subject of the next chapter.

41. Because the area in question had earlier been designated as an unassisted urban renewal area, construction and rehabilitation loans were available at below market rates.

6
Tenant Referral Service:
Exploiting
the White
Market

T HE limited white market for South Shore housing was exploited through the commission's Tenant Referral Service (TRS), which ensured that available area housing was brought to the attention of as many white prospects as possible. The Tenant Referral Service was located in the commission office—two adjacent storefronts centrally located near the major shopping district on 71st Street. Persons interested in renting a South Shore apartment visited the commission's office, where they could specify the size of apartment desired, the top rent they could pay, their family's composition, and provide personal references. They were then presented with a choice of approximately six available apartment units which seemed appropriate to their means and needs. These listings were drawn from the current TRS file of vacant apartments, which was constantly replenished by calls from landlords. The commission did not contact landlords directly; it received notices of vacancies from real estate firms. If the prospective tenant had no automobile, community volunteers were available for chauffeur service.

PROGRAM GROWTH

There was a steady increase in the number of persons who made use of the Tenant Referral Service. After a modest beginning in 1958, the program accelerated rapidly during the year 1963, when according to commission officials 900 families were "served" by TRS. In 1964 the volume of persons who applied for TRS services doubled, rose again in 1965 to 2,521, and reached a total

113

TABLE 11

NUMBER, RACE, AND GEOGRAPHICAL ORIGIN OF FAMILIES
SERVED BY TENANT REFERRAL SERVICE, 1963–1966

| | | Race | | Origins | | | | |
Year	Families Served	White	Negro	South Shore	Hyde Park	Out of Town	Other Chicago Areas	University of Chicago
1963	900	810	90	540	NA	NA	360	NA
1964	1,800	1,440	360	880	NA	NA	920	NA
1965	2,521	1,560	951	865	187	520	462	487
1966	3,190	1,435	1,755	1,085	342	487	749	527

SOURCE: Records of the South Shore Commission.
NA: Not available.

of 3,190 families in 1966. The progress of Tenant Referral Service is summarized in Table 11.

SEARCHING OUT THE WHITES

The most striking trend in TRS's history was that an increasing proportion of those served were black. In response to this trend, TRS tried strenuously to increase the proportion of white clients. It tried to guarantee a stream of white applicants at least large enough to absorb vacancies in white or mixed buildings.

The annual tours of the Open House Committee were one source of new leads, and so were contacts with major corporations and institutions in the Chicago area in need of executive housing. A commission leader estimated that more than 100 personal visits were made to such officials; an additional 500 mailings were made to other organizations in the metropolitan area. Special emphasis was placed on contacting universities and research organizations—institutions thought likely to attract large numbers of persons who would not regard racial integration as a neighborhood liability. In addition, the commission advertised the existence of TRS in the *Hyde Park Herald* and the University of Chicago's student newspaper. Needless to say, only those institutions likely to yield white prospects were approached.

Personal contacts made by commission members also gained new applicants for TRS. Readers of the *South Shore Scene* were encouraged to spread the word of South Shore and the TRS to their business associates, clients, and out-of-town friends. A member of the commission's board of directors was manager of the local real estate operations of the University of Chicago; through his efforts, many university students and faculty members were referred to the TRS office. According to commission records, 527 families were referred to TRS by the university in 1966; in addition 342 more Hyde Park families visited TRS during that year. The commission also profited from the fact that some of its members were officials at other large Chicago institutions and corporations, such as Illinois Institute of Technology, Illinois Central Railroad, American Airlines, and various area banks and manufacturing enterprises.

GAINING LISTINGS

Quite obviously, the value of TRS to prospective tenants was dependent upon the size, quality, and variety of apartments on the commission lists. With the increasing number of rentors who applied for housing through the commission, TRS gained a reputation among area brokers for being effective. After almost four years of operation, virtually all large real estate agents in the South Shore area had used TRS, and so had many of the smaller management firms and local owners.[1] The commission listed, at any given time, between 75 and 250 apartments for rent. (This extreme variability primarily reflects seasonal variation. For one agent I interviewed, TRS had completely replaced public advertising as his routine source of new tenants.)

Some real estate dealers reported more sparing use of the TRS. For example, one medium-sized operator indicated that he generally turned to the commission only when he had experienced difficulty in finding a desirable tenant through the listings in his own office. Thus, only a small portion of his vacancies ever reached the TRS list, although this may have been, in terms of the commission's goals, a crucial portion. Difficulty in finding desirable tenants generally meant difficulty in finding *white* tenants; it thus may have been that by serving landlords who were struggling to maintain a certain unit for white occupancy, the commission may have had a

1. South Shore respondents were probed on these matters as part of the general survey described in Chapter Two.

greater effect on racial patterns than was reflected in the size of its listings.

STRATEGIC PLACEMENTS

The commission did not refer applicants randomly to the buildings and neighborhoods of South Shore. In the words of one commission official, referrals were made with the goal of "keeping whites moving into integrated buildings. That's where we put our primary efforts. Whites must see other whites moving into the building after Negroes have once moved in. Otherwise they will empty out. We definitely focus on integrated buildings and integrated areas."

When a black applied for an apartment at TRS, it would not have been useful to refer him to a racially mixed building if there was a good chance that a white tenant could be found. Indeed, continued integration of the same building would eventually have led to complete resegregation and the defeat of the key purpose of TRS. Also, the commission was generally inhibited from referring blacks to buildings which were *all white*. To do so would have integrated parts of the community whose residents were opposed to such integration and whose landlords often listed their apartments with the understanding that no blacks would be referred.

The South Shore Organization for Human Rights, a small, locally based civil rights group, often alleged that the commission maintained two separate lists of available units—one for prospective black tenants and another for whites. Two tests of the commission's policies came to my attention during the study period; both resulted in the same findings. A leader of the Organization for Human Rights summarized her findings:

I sent Gloria (a white woman) in to the apartment referral desk, and she asked for five rooms . . . (with various specifications), and then I went in two hours later and asked for the same thing and I had all the addresses Gloria had . . . and I was told by the lady at the desk that she had absolutely nothing on Jeffery for the amount I wanted to pay. She had one for the white girl for $120, and she had one for me for $165. I ended up receiving three referrals, and Gloria had gotten six. I had one at $135, and two at $165; Gloria had two at $120, one at $125, two at $130 and one at $135. . . . When Gloria then called these places, she was asked by several of them "Are you white, because I wouldn't rent this to Negroes."

The second test was carried out several months later, and resulted in similar findings, with Negro rentals generally higher than white, but with one apartment appearing on both lists (and at the same rental level).

Allegations that such practices existed were explicitly denied by commission staff members in their public statements. Yet in light of the goals of the organization and the policies of many landlords who provided listings, there would seem to be little doubt that race was indeed a determinant of who was referred where. The strategy was a reflection of the commission's program of managed integration, based upon the following board-approved statement: "A policy of managed integration is essential in order to achieve a stable, integrated residential community. This means that all real estate transactions within the community should be approximately 50 percent Negro and 50 percent white. It involves *setting up artificial restraints* until such a time as the community can achieve racial stability by normal population turnover [emphasis added]." [2] Although some commission members thought the phrase managed integration either too Machiavellian or were concerned that it implied policies inconsistent with existing anti-discrimination legislation, most commission leaders became convinced that managed integration was the only kind of integration possible. As one staff member stated:

I don't believe in some magic number as a tipping point. You use as your tipping point the time when whites won't move in anymore. You do it building by building. You don't have to use a magic number like 20 percent like in Prairie Shores (an integrated urban renewal project also on the south side of Chicago) or 25 percent like Jim Downs[3] says. But you do have to *manage* integration in some way and of course you can do it easiest where all the property is in the hands of one company.

A tenant referral service, including differential treatment of whites and blacks, facilitates a form of managed integration ordinarily not feasible in areas where control of rental housing is

2. See *South Shore Scene* (Chicago), December 1966.
3. James Downs is chairman of the Board of the Real Estate Research Corporation, Chicago.

spread among many hands. At the same time, an organization involved in such activities exposes itself to the condemnation of civil rights groups and possibly finds itself in opposition to city and state fair housing legislation and executive orders.

The Chicago Fair Housing Ordinance declares that it is the policy of the city to "assure full and equal opportunity to all residents of the city to obtain fair and adequate housing . . . without discrimination against them because of their race, color, religion, national origin, or ancestry." More specifically the Ordinance specifies:

no owner, lessee, sublessee, assignee, managing agent or other person, firm or corporation . . . *or any agent of any of these,* should refuse to sell, rent, lease, or otherwise deny to or withhold from any person or group of persons such housing accommodations because of the race, color, religion, national origin or ancestry in the terms, conditions, or privileges of the sale, rental or lease of any housing accommodation or in the furnishing of facilities or services in the connection therewith [emphasis added].[4]

As an agent of owners and other agents, the commission was occasionally accused of discriminating on the basis of race and thus of disobeying the fair housing law. However, the practices of TRS were never ruled upon by a Chicago public body or tested for legality in the Illinois courts.

The Chicago Commission on Human Relations, whose duty it was under the law to initiate proceedings against any party suspected of disobeying the fair housing law, was well aware of the commission's activity.[5] It chose, in the words of one South Shore Commission officer, to "look the other way" because a genuine attempt was being made to achieve integration—although the Commission on Human Relations did strive for "conciliation" in cases where blacks alleged discrimination by individual South Shore landlords.[6] Without such cooperation (or at least tacit approval) from the

4. The Chicago Fair Housing Ordinance is reprinted in Chicago Real Estate Board, *1966 Yearbook of the Chicago Real Estate Board* (Chicago Real Estate Board, 1966), p. 254.

5. This impression is based on several discussions held with the director of the Chicago Commission on Human Relations.

6. This irked one commission officer, who when addressing a commission meeting, said: "This is where they can make their brownie points—in South Shore, which is already an integrated community.

Commission on Human Relations, the community's largest program would have been placed in jeopardy.[7]

A difficulty of the opposite sort arose from the fact that TRS did serve blacks. To some residents of South Shore (such as the members of the Chel-Win Association), it appeared quite improper for the commission to help blacks locate in the area when the influx of blacks into South Shore was precisely the situation to be combated. For example, the commission assisted (however reluctantly) 1,755 black families to locate South Shore apartments in 1966. Given the commission's many Negro members and some white members who were pro-Negro, TRS had no choice but to serve both races.

It should be noted, however, that by serving blacks as well as whites certain advantages accrued to the commission besides the wherewithal to placate black and pro-Negro members. Because TRS never sought out potential black tenants, it may be that those Negroes who applied for TRS services would have attempted to move into South Shore anyway; by having blacks apply through TRS, some could have been discouraged from moving into the area and others could have been placed in locations where their presence would be least damaging to the commission's racial goals. TRS could screen out tenants who were considered lower class or otherwise undesirable for the community. These persons could be told there were no vacancies or encouraged to locate elsewhere. Similarly, the commission could attempt to guarantee that the first blacks to integrate a particular building would be of the type who would not frighten neighboring whites into leaving the area.

Despite these strategic advantages, commission leaders felt obliged to minimize in their public pronouncements and in statements to members the extent to which blacks were being served. Although TRS was a frequent subject at public meetings in the community, the question of racial composition of those served was never raised by commission leaders. When the commission boasted of the new families it was attracting to South Shore through TRS, audiences were left to equate new families with new *white* families. In my conversations with area residents on such occasions, they invariably

7. For a case study of the methods and effectiveness of a human relations commission see Leon Mayhew, "Law and Equal Opportunity" (unpublished Ph.D. dissertation, Department of Social Relations, Harvard University, 1963).

interchanged phrases like "500 new *white* families" for the speaker's announced "500 new families that have come to the TRS in the last two months." The speaker (always a commission officer or staff member) never, in citing such data, used the phrase "white families," but left it to his audience to infer that he would surely not be boasting about the commission's ability to attract black families.

A more blatant act of understating the degree to which blacks were served by TRS occurred at a commission meeting at which I was present. This was one of the few occasions when someone asked what proportion of those served by TRS was Negro. The reply: "about 20 percent." This figure was not at all consistent with data in commission records which indicated that the most recent figure was 55 percent; the 20 percent figure was two years old. Such distortions probably had two purposes: to keep morale high and to keep fuel away from the fire of those who opposed any assistance of black in-migration.

EFFECTIVENESS OF TENANT REFERRAL SERVICE

Because the commission did not contact landlords after referrals were made, there was no way of knowing whether the prospective tenant actually located in the area. The commission attempted to determine the proportion of TRS clients who took up residence in South Shore by contacting 750 of the 2,521 families served during 1965. Of these, 75 were found to have rented elsewhere; the remainder were confirmed to be South Shore residents.

Of the 675 families contacted who located in South Shore: 200 were black and 475 were white; 275 had located in the precariously integrated O'Keeffe neighborhood (190 of whom were white); 200 came from outside the city (all but 13 of whom were white); and 90 came from the Hyde Park area on the north (all of whom rented in the O'Keeffe neighborhood). Unfortunately, it cannot be known from such data how many whites locating in South Shore would have moved into the community anyway, regardless of the existence of the commission or TRS. But some degree of commission effectiveness would seem to be reflected in the fact that so many persons had located in the O'Keeffe area (where emphasis was deliberately being placed) and that so high a proportion were out-of-towners (representing a pay-off of contacts with Chicago universities, hospitals, and large corporations).

Confidence in these findings, however, is limited by the fact that only the city phone directory was used to trace clients, thus eliminating from the sample those who ended up in the suburbs. The white proportion of those found in South Shore was likely inflated, given that blacks are less apt to have phones, and thus less likely to end up in the sample. The cited survey reports undoubtedly overstate the degree of the commission's success, consistent with the organization's known tendency to inflate figures which point to its own effectiveness.

UNINTENDED CONSEQUENCES

Although the major goal of TRS was bringing whites into the area, it had other, unanticipated consequences which served the commission's strategy. Regardless of the racial composition of clients, the sheer volume of referrals made the commission a significant force in the local real estate market. As one commission officer stated: "We control the white market. We don't control the Negro market—at least not yet, but we've got a foot in the door there too."

Some idea of the commission's impact on local real estate may be gained by juxtaposing the TRS figures with the size of the rental market in South Shore. A rough estimate of the number of persons changing residence in the area during a single year can be derived from 1960 census data which indicate that "during the course of a single year between 19 and 22 percent of the country's inhabitants move from one house or apartment to another." [8] Given 25,675 tenant-occupied dwelling units in South Shore,[9] about 20 percent of them, or 5,135, changed occupants in 1966. Many, if not most such units, changed hands without ever being placed on the market;

8. See Donald Bogue, *The Population of the United States* (New York: The Free Press, 1959), p. 375. Mobility in apartment areas is higher than in the nation as a whole and so mobility estimates derived from the national norm may be misleading. According to the Institute of Real Estate Management, 28 percent of apartment units fall vacant each year (*New York Times,* November 10, 1963). Other factors, however, such as the high economic and educational status of South Shore residents, as well as the community's old age structure would tend to have the opposite effect, perhaps compensating for the underestimate of mobility (see Bogue, pp. 377–387).

9. This figure was deduced from census data in a manner described in Chapter Seven.

they were, for example, transferred from one friend to another with landlord assent but without ever having to be put before the public. The fact that 3,190 families were referred to specific apartments during that year would indicate that the commission was an important factor in the local market.

An officer of one of the largest real estate firms in the area could agree: "The tenant referral service, I think, is certainly effective. But the commission has become a part of the real estate market now and it's playing a role that really should be played by the real estate industry. It makes them effective, but I don't know if I approve from the realtor's point of view." Said another real estate dealer, the president of a company noted for its reluctance to keep buildings all-white or to attempt to keep whites in an integrated building: "The commission is strong. They'll cut you off from tenant referral. We rent to anybody, anywhere. But you've got to watch yourself. You have to keep up the place or they'll blacklist you and then owners would boycott you. When you're going to open up to the colored, you've got to think about the commission."

Statements such as these attest to the fact that TRS provided the commission with some degree of power over local real estate dealers —power which could be used to generate cooperation with various commission programs aimed at keeping whites in the area and guaranteeing that certain standards of physical maintenance and tenant screening would be continued regardless of the racial composition of a building. The commission also used its power and facilities to encourage landlords to stop writing off buildings as "gone Negro" after the first black move-in.

The commission had instruments for generating cooperation from landlords. A firm could be blacklisted in the community; requests for zoning variations or building permits could be blocked. Through commission pressure on appropriate civic bodies, an offending firm could be excluded from participation in development or management of newly constructed urban renewal structures such as the hoped for Project 71. Finally, a firm could be harassed on a day-to-day basis for building code violations in structures which it owned or managed. Besides providing the commission with still another lever of influence over real estate firms, TRS placed the commission directly in the real estate market, thus providing its leaders and staff with the kind of sophisticated, intimate knowledge of local building and market conditions which made the commission generally more effective in dealing with landlords no matter what the issue.

DISCOURAGING BLACKS

The goal of encouraging white residency in South Shore implies the concomitant goal of discouraging black occupancy. In South Shore there were no signs that violence had ever been used to prevent blacks from remaining in the area, as had occurred in other Chicago neighborhoods during earlier periods. South Shore people generally regarded one another as not the "type" to engage in such activities.

Combatting "Panic-Peddling"

The commission was particularly anxious that "panic-peddling" not occur in the local single-family home market. A panic-peddler was defined as an unethical real estate dealer who, in his desire for profits, encouraged a white exodus and rapid property turnover in the community. The effect of panic peddling was seen to be the rapid opening up of new areas of South Shore for black occupancy, which would jeopardize the commission's goal of a "balanced" community racial composition. The panic peddler was said to be encouraged by the possibility of gaining large numbers of fee commissions or by the potential for gaining exorbitant profits by buying cheaply from frightened whites and reselling at a premium to housing-starved blacks. A South Shore clergyman complained bitterly of the unscrupulous real estate activities practiced in the neighborhood of some of his parishioners. He stated in an interview: "They [panic peddlers] send hooligans out in the middle of the night—making a racket and throwing booze bottles all over the place. Then the next morning, after you've been up all night without any sleep, there's a black face asking you if you'd like to sell."

Commission leaders closer to the local real estate scene agreed with South Shore real estate dealers who when interviewed considered South Shore generally free of both speculation and extreme scare techniques. Indeed, except for reports such as the one just quoted, I found no evidence of such activities in the course of the study.[10] But commission leaders did think there was a problem

10. The "evidence" in question includes interview data discussed in Chapter Two and property transfer data described in Chapter Eight.

caused by real estate dealers who, sensing that change was imminent, sent mass mailings or made phone calls to home owners
offering their services. For commission officials this constituted
harassment or panic peddling but to the real estate dealers such
"promotions" were a legitimate means of creating new business;
for unestablished firms and black-owned companies, these strategies
were seen as the *only* way in which business could be done in an
established white neighborhood.

Such activity, legal or not, had the effect of making more efficient
the functioning of that portion of the real estate market which the
commission would like to have seen operate as inefficiently as
possible: the transfer of white properties into black hands. Commission strategies were all aimed at making more efficient those
persons, institutions and processes which had the opposite effect.
This was the cause of the friction between the commission and those
whose business it was to bring blacks and housing together.

Various techniques were available to the commission in its efforts
to discourage *any semblance* of panic peddling in South Shore. In
addressing a meeting of local real estate dealers, called by the commission, the executive director announced: "Some firms, the great
majority located outside of South Shore, focus on a block after the
first Negro family has moved in, attempting to use the family as a
reason for present owners selling their homes. We believe this is
the worst type of exploitation and will fight these practices with
every means at our disposal." [11] One of the means at the commission's disposal was to exact a verbal assurance from an offending
firm that its objectionable practices would be ended. From June
1966 to June 1967 the commission received twenty-five complaints
alleging some form of panic peddling; all resulted in appropriate
assurances from the offending firm.

Another commission alternative was to press court action
(through the Chicago Commission on Human Relations) against
any firm which explicitly alluded to race in its attempt to gain a
housing listing. Because such business behavior was in violation of
the Chicago Fair Housing Ordinance, a firm found guilty of mentioning race could lose its real estate license, be fined, or both. It
is noteworthy that the only real estate company ever to face court
action (for any offense) under the Chicago Fair Housing Ordinance

11. *Southeast Economist* (Chicago), November 14, 1966.

was a black-owned firm, which was accused of panic peddling in a case initiated by the South Shore Commission.

Still another strategy of the commission was to encourage South Shore residents to use only reliable firms in their real estate dealings. At one point, according to a commission official, a list of recommended firms was drawn up. It consisted of companies which were owned by whites, had been doing business in the community for many years, and had cooperated with the commission. Black real estate men construed this as an attempt to freeze them out of the community—an area which they considered a likely target for increasing the limited market which racial segregation permitted them to enjoy in Chicago. Perhaps because of the vociferous objections raised by those dealers not listed, the commission's recommended list was never widely circulated.

A Fair Housing Center

Probably the boldest technique for discouraging additional black occupancy was the commission's support for the creation in South Shore of Chicago's first Fair Housing Center. The purpose of the Fair Housing Center, which was established in the spring of 1967, was to make blacks aware of housing opportunities in the all-white communities throughout the metropolitan area.

The center was operated by the Chicago Conference on Religion and Race and the Leadership Council for Metropolitan Open Communities; the latter organization had been formed in response to the grievances expressed in a dramatic series of civil rights marches (led by Martin Luther King) into Chicago white neighborhoods in the summer of 1966. Both groups were Chicago "blue ribbon" committees (made up of the city's business and religious elite), formed with the stated intention of satisfying civil rights demands by opening up the entire metropolitan area to black occupancy.

The aims of these two groups and those of the South Shore Commission were in harmony. In the process of integrating communities where no blacks lived, South Shore (a community in which too many blacks lived) could be helped to preserve its integration. The commission and the center were thus in positions appropriate for mutual cooperation; unwanted blacks arriving at TRS in search of housing could be shunted to the referral service at the Fair Housing Center, where they could be helped to locate outside of South Shore. Blacks applying at the commission's TRS were, after being provided with South Shore listings, referred to the Fair Housing Center for additional housing leads. The Fair Housing Center, having no listings in the South Shore area, provided information and when necessary, chauffeur and escort service, to facilitate moving into distant all-white communities. Cooperation between the organizations was facilitated by locating the Fair Housing Center four doors north of commission offices, and in the same building. This study ended just as the center was beginning its work: no data can be presented on the volume of its activity or its success in placing blacks outside of South Shore.

THE NET EFFECT

By having its own tenant referral service in operation on so large a scale, the commission may have had some influence over local real estate patterns. Particularly in the O'Keeffe area, whites and blacks were renting in some of the same buildings and on some of the same blocks—perhaps for a longer period of time than is common in changing areas.[12] Because university people were generally unfamiliar with the Chicago area and often short on household-hunting time and motivation, the availability of TRS may have been instrumental in their choice of South Shore as a temporary home. For other new white residents, TRS may similarly have been important in the process which led them to locate in South Shore. All conclusions are tentative; all are based on guesswork.

Despite its high volume of activity and the fact that it may have successfully created small pockets of biraciality, it is possible that TRS (by bringing together prospects and vacancies in a central place) served primarily to make market mechanisms operate more *efficiently* than they otherwise would have, without significantly altering the overall pattern of racial transition in the community. It is even possible that by boosting the efficiency with which new tenants find vacancies, and thus the processes which cause transition, South Shore's racial change was *accelerated*. Units which remain vacant do remain non-black.

12. The fact that both blacks and whites were simultaneously renting and buying in changing South Shore neighborhoods is not, in itself, evidence that South Shore was responding to commission intervention. The same phenomenon has been observed in other changing communities. See Chapter One; also Chester Rapkin and William Grigsby, *The Demand for Housing in Racially Mixed Areas* (Berkeley: University of California Press, 1960).

Whether the effect of TRS, combined with other commission programs, was great enough to distinguish racial change in South Shore from the classic pattern of succession thus remains very much in question; an attempt to provide a more definite answer is made in the following chapters.

Part III

Outcome: Measures of Integration Success

7
Distribution and Speed
of Racial Replacement

IF THE commission's activities had a significant effect upon South Shore housing markets, success would show in certain crucial indices of the speed and distribution of racial change. Specifically, if South Shore departed from the classic succession pattern, black migration should have been at a rate lower than is ordinarily found in a transition area. Further, those blacks who did enter should have been locating throughout the community in a relatively diffuse pattern. Success in achieving the first goal (one for which there was virtually unanimous commission support) would mean that South Shore showed signs of maintaining itself as a *biracial* community with people of both races within its boundaries; success in achieving dispersion (a goal for which there was less widespread enthusiasm) would indicate that some form of *racial integration* was being achieved as well.

A key indicator of the extent to which the goals were reached is the speed and pattern of "racial replacements" in the community. Racial replacements are instances in which a South Shore white household vacates a dwelling unit which is then filled by a black household. Because South Shore is a mature area with few housing units constructed since 1960,[1] net black household migration into the community can be assumed to reflect numbers of racial replacements for a given area over a given period of time.

1. For information on new construction in South Shore prior to 1960, see Evelyn M. Kitagawa and Karl Taeuber (eds.), *Local Community Factbook, Chicago Metropolitan Area, 1960* (Chicago Community Inventory, University of Chicago, 1963). New construction in various areas of Chicago subsequent to 1960 are reported in summary form in each year-end issue of *Realty and Building* (Chicago: Realty and Building, Inc.), Vols. CL–CLVI.

Two bodies of evidence are relevant to the question of the degree to which intervention in South Shore yielded significant results. A comparison of rates of racial replacement (as derived from hospital birth records) in South Shore with those of other changing areas in Chicago can provide evidence of the degree to which organizational intervention can alter the *speed* of racial change. Changes in the racial composition of local elementary schools can be used to show the speed as well as the distribution of racial replacement (at least for families with children).

SCHOOL RACIAL COMPOSITION

Because Chicago school attendance zones are the immediate residential areas surrounding the schools, the racial composition of the schools can be taken as a symptom of the population composition of school attendance areas. The measure is only a crude index of racial composition; as indicated in Chapter Five, only 32 percent of South Shore's population was concerned with local schools. Even so, patterns of racial distribution among school-age populations are an important clue to more general patterns of racial distribution.

Official racial head-counts have been made each autumn by classroom teachers in Chicago schools since 1963. Data are thus available which specify the racial composition of each South Shore public school at four points in time: autumn of 1963, 1964, 1965, and 1966. These data are reproduced in Table 12.

A neighborhood experiencing racial integration should yield signs that black migrants are populating all area schools at least to some degree. There should be some support for the notion that the traditional pattern of movement of blacks from one neighborhood sub-area, complete transition of that area, concomitant with migration into the next adjoining sub-area, is not occurring. Or, if there is not integration but some minimal form of biraciality that is being preserved, there should be evidence of a neighborhood sub-area (and the school which serves it) withstanding the change—or at least changing at a relatively slow rate.

The South Shore school data contain little which would suggest that either integration or biraciality was being achieved. In 1966 the schools in South Shore that served significant numbers of both races appear to be schools on the racial border in the process of transition; the community's predominantly white schools seem to be white because they happen to remain geographically remote

TABLE 12

RACIAL COMPOSITION OF SOUTH SHORE SCHOOLS

School Name and Location	Proportion of Student Body Black				Distance of School from Black P.O.I.[a] in Blocks
	1963	1964	1965	1966	
Parkside	90.3	96.6	97.8	99.1	3
O'Keeffe	39.8	67.3	85.4	93.9	6.5
Bryn Mawr	16.3	37.2	55.2	66.1	10
Mann	7.0	26.6	43.0	55.1	17
Bradwell	0.1	.2	.7	3.7	22
Sullivan	0.0	0	0	2.3	30
South Shore High[b]	1.5	7.0	24.8	41.8	

SOURCES: 1963 data: *Chicago Sun-Times*, October 24, 1963. 1964, 1965 data: *The Southeast Economist* (Chicago), October 17, 1965. 1966 data: *The Southeast Economist* (Chicago), October 23, 1966.

[a] Black P.O.I. refers to the original geographical point of black in-migration into South Shore.

[b] High school boundary zone was modified between 1964 and 1965 with the inclusion of Parkside and O'Keeffe and the exclusion of a larger all-black elementary school as "feeder" schools in the fall of 1965. The net effect of this change on the high school's racial composition was negligible. Distance of black P.O.I. is not applicable.

from the line of succession. The racial composition of South Shore schools are a function of distance from the original point of black in-migration (P.O.I.) taken to be the corner of Stony Island Avenue and 67th Street. The location of South Shore's schools and the original point of in-migration are portrayed in Figure 5.

Column 6 of Table 12 indicates how many blocks each school is distant from the point of in-migration. Because north-south blocks are generally twice the length of east-west blocks, one north-south block is taken to equal two east-west blocks. City blocks are used as units of measurement because they appear to be the most meaningful units of distance for city residents. A neighborhood experiencing the classic transition pattern should exhibit an inverse relationship between the proportion of black students in a school and the distance of that school from the P.O.I. The closer the correlation coefficient of the relationship between the two variables is to minus unity, the greater is the degree to which a given area is experiencing the classic pattern. Figure 6 portrays the inverse relationship between distance from the P.O.I. and the proportion of an elementary school's student body which is black for each point in time for which racial head-count data are available. The correlation coefficients are increasingly high and significant for each year: 1963, −.81; 1964, −.93; 1965, −.96; and 1966, −.96. These findings,

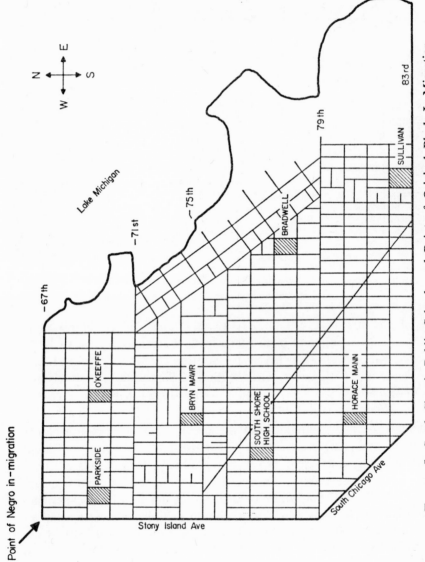

FIGURE 5: South Shore's Public Schools and Point of Original Black In-Migration

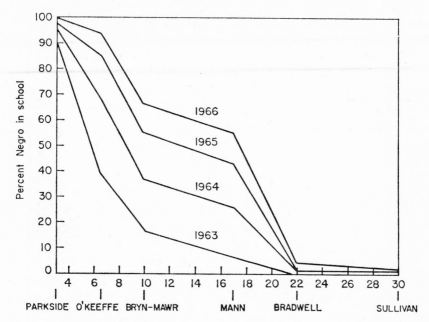

Number of blocks distant from point of original Negro in-migration

FIGURE 6: Elementary School Racial Composition as a Function of Distance from Point of Black In-Migration

considered together with the fact that the high school which is "fed" by these schools changed from 7 percent black in 1964 to 41.8 percent black in 1966, indicate that South Shore was in fact experiencing the classic succession pattern.

RATES OF RACIAL REPLACEMENT

It is impossible to know exactly how many blacks live in South Shore at any point in time between census intervals. However, estimates of the population size and racial composition of all of Chicago's Community Areas have been made for two points in time since the 1960 census: April 1965 and April 1966. These estimates, prepared by the Hospital Planning Council for Metropolitan Chicago, are derived from hospital birth records of mothers' residence.[2] They make possible a comparison of the speed of racial

2. See Hospital Planning Council for Metropolitan Chicago, "Chicago Regional Hospital Study" (Chicago: Chicago Association of Commerce and Industry, December, 1966). (Multilithed.) I am indebted to Pierre de Vise for interpretation of these data.

change among all communities, including South Shore, which were contiguous to black residential areas in 1960 and which experienced an increase in black population over the ensuing six years. Community Areas were selected for comparison which met the additional criteria of being less than 90 percent black in 1960 and more than 10 percent black in 1966. Some areas which have experienced minor increases in black population were excluded from consideration; communities where the population was 90 percent black in 1960 were considered to have already experienced transition; those which in six years had not experienced at least a 10 percent black occupancy were taken to not yet constitute changing areas.

Thirteen Community Areas (CA's)[3] met the criteria established. South Shore can be compared with twelve other Community Areas to determine whether or not there are any signs that it was experiencing transition at a rate slower than what would be expected of a changing community in the 1960s. Many of these other communities were regarded by South Shore residents as areas which in their words were "going overnight." South Shore leaders frequently cited the work of the commission as the reason for what was perceived to be the slow and orderly pace of racial change in South Shore compared to the "panic" which grips less sophisticated and organizationally undeveloped communities. Additional explanations made reference to the community's unique natural amenities, the existence in South Shore of educated people whom real estate dealers can't frighten, and the presence in the area of the type of person who maintains his property well.

The basic assumption underlying these views does not seem justified when the rate of racial change in South Shore is compared with that of other community areas going through a similar experience during the same period. For each such area, Table 13 presents data relevant to the rate of racial replacement: the percent change in black population between 1960 and 1966, and the total number of black migrants to the area during the period 1960–66. The location of these Community Areas in the context of Chicago's changing "racial line" is portrayed in Figure 7.

3. The community areas correspond to regions originally demarcated by the Chicago Community Inventory as constituting relatively homogeneous, cohesive communities. See Kitagawa and Taeuber, *Community Area Factbook*.

TABLE 13

RACIAL CHARACTERISTICS OF THIRTEEN CHANGING CHICAGO COMMUNITY AREAS, 1960–1966

Community Area	Total Pop. 1960	Total Pop. 1966	Black Pop. 1960	Black Pop. 1966	Percent Black 1960	Percent Black 1966	Percent Black Change	Net Black Gain	Adjusted Percent Replacement Rate[a]
South Shore[a]	73,086	72,434	7,579	31,581	10.4	43.6	33.2	24,002	42.6
West Garfield Park	45,611	42,848	7,459	29,107	16.4	68.7	52.3	21,648	38.7
Auburn-Gresham	59,484	57,369	138	19,890	0.3	34.7	34.4	19,752	35.78
South Shore[a] (Commission Boundaries)	73,476	...	152	18,559	0.2	25.3	25.1	18,407	32.6
East Garfield Park	66,871	68,904	41,462	54,820	62.0	87.5	25.5	13,358	28.05
Englewood	97,595	91,197	67,488	75,620	69.2	82.6	13.4	8,132	21.57
W. Englewood	58,516	56,257	6,933	17,665	11.9	31.4	19.5	10,732	19.31
Washington Heights	29,793	31,074	3,776	11,560	12.7	37.2	24.5	7,784	13.48
Greater Grand Crossing	63,169	61,102	54,482	59,208	86.2	96.9	10.7	4,726	11.35
Chatham	41,962	45,224	26,872	39,797	74.0	88.0	14.0	12,925	11.06
Near North Side	75,509	78,302	24,940	29,818	33.0	37.6	4.6	4,878	6.30
Avalon Park	12,710	12,348	50	3,161	0.3	25.6	25.3	3,111	5.56
Armour Sq.	15,783	12,678	6,687	8,016	42.3	63.2	20.9	1,329	4.60
Roseland	58,750	59,055	13,358	14,730	22.8	24.9	2.1	1,372	2.16

SOURCES: 1960 data from *Local Community Fact Book*; 1966 estimates from "Chicago Regional Hospital Study" of the Hospital Planning Council for Metropolitan Chicago (Chicago Association of Commerce and Industry, December 1966, multilithed).
[a] The meaning of column 10, on the extreme right, and the distinction between the two South Shore entries are explained in the text.

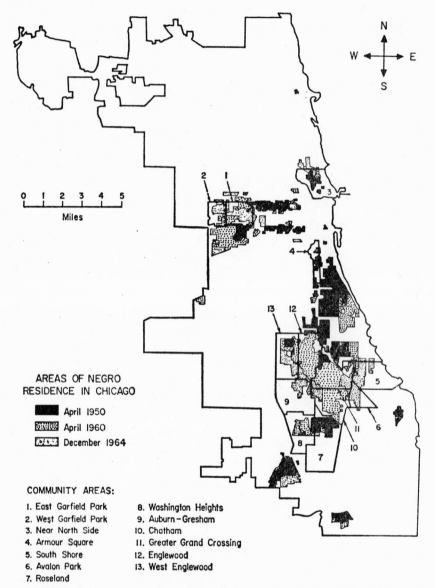

N
W ← → E
S

0 1 2 3 4 5
Miles

AREAS OF NEGRO
RESIDENCE IN CHICAGO

■ April 1950
▨ April 1960
▨ December 1964

COMMUNITY AREAS:

1. East Garfield Park
2. West Garfield Park
3. Near North Side
4. Armour Square
5. South Shore
6. Avalon Park
7. Roseland

8. Washington Heights
9. Auburn–Gresham
10. Chatham
11. Greater Grand Crossing
12. Englewood
13. West Englewood

FIGURE 7: Areas of Black Residence in Chicago, 1950, 1960, 1964, with Special Reference to Communities Changing between 1960 and 1966

Interpreting Table 13

Several explanations will facilitate interpretation of Table 13.[4] First, South Shore is treated twice: once on the basis of *Fact Book,* Community Area boundaries and once on the basis of boundaries specified by the South Shore Commission and used elsewhere in this study. I include rates based on Community Area boundaries because the Hospital Planning Council Study reports its findings (and collects its raw data) in terms of these demarcations. I deduced from the reported data an adjusted rate for South Shore based on the commission's boundaries.

The operation was complicated by the fact that there is no way of knowing how many of the 1960–1966 estimated black migrants into the Community Area of South Shore located in the area west of Stony Island (thus filling in those partially black tracts) and how many migrated across Stony Island into South Shore (as defined by the commission). To handle the ambiguity, the assumption was made that during 1960–1966, the *entire* population of the tracts west of Stony Island became black, an assumption approximately consistent with Urban League estimates and elementary school racial data for the area. The number of whites living in the west-of-Stony Island tracts in 1960 can thus be considered equal to the net number of blacks who migrated into those tracts between 1960 and 1966.[5] It follows that by deducting this number from the total number of 1960–1966 black South Shore migrants, we arrive at

4. Comparisons of columns 2 and 3 in Table 13 reveal the somewhat surprising fact that almost all changing areas declined in total population during the six-year period. Several hypotheses may be suggested to account for this. First is the fact that the white populations of these areas were generally old; thus the on-going process of "emptying nests" within white households may account for the declines. Another possibility is that white families with children were more likely to leave the community as a result of change than families without children. In any event, the comparison suggests that even in communities such as Greater Grand Crossing, which were in the final stages of transition, the phenomenon described by the Duncans as Negro overcrowding or piling up may no longer be occurring in Chicago transition areas. See Otis Dudley Duncan and Beverly Duncan, *The Negro Population of Chicago* (University of Chicago Press, 1957), pp. 142–156.

5. The use of 1960 whites as a proxy for 1966 Negroes rests on the assumption that the total population of South Shore's tracts remained relatively stable over the period—an assumption consistent with available population estimates and the fact that these are neighborhoods with little new construction since 1960.

the number of black migrants who took up residence in tracts *east* of Stony Island, that is, in South Shore as defined by the commission. To the extent that our assumption of complete transition between 1960 and 1966 for the west-of-Stony Island tracts is incorrect (and it is *not* completely correct), our estimate of black migration *understates* the extent of black in-migration into South Shore (commission boundaries).

The Results

Regardless of which definition of South Shore is used, the community appears to be one of the fastest changing areas—or at least not extraordinarily slow in its racial replacement rate. In terms of change in percentage of the area population which is black, 1960–1966, the Community Area of South Shore was a clear second only to West Garfield Park—a low-income West Side neighborhood adjacent to the scene of Chicago's 1966 summer riots. Community Area South Shore changed at a pace just under that of Auburn-Gresham, a community at the southwest edge of the 1960 racial line. When using the more conservative measure based upon commission boundary specifications, South Shore emerges in a near tie for third place, along with three other communities—all changing at approximately the same rate.

A More Refined Comparison

It may be inappropriate to compare South Shore with communities which had racial compositions in 1960 in the range of 70 or 80 percent black. Such neighborhoods could not possibly have increased much in black percentages after 1960, there being such a small proportion of whites left to be replaced. By comparing South Shore only with areas which were less than 50 percent black in 1960, the greatest differences between neighborhoods disappear. The low income area of West Garfield Park still appears as the fastest changing area (52.2 percent), the Community Area of South Shore (33.2 percent) is in a near-tie with Auburn-Gresham (34.4 percent) for second place, followed by a clustering of change rates in the range of 20 to 25 percent among five of the remaining areas: Avalon Park, 25.3 percent; South Shore (commission boundaries), 25.1 percent; Washington Heights, 24.5 percent; Armour Square, 20.9 percent; and West Englewood, 19.5 percent.

Following this cluster are two community areas where special conditions prevail. The community area of the Near North Side experienced little growth in the size of its black population—a reflection of the fact that this is the area of Chicago's famous "gold coast and the slum." [6] The white portion consists of homes and apartments for Chicago's wealthiest families; the black slum dwellers who share the "community" are not symptomatic of a succession process capable of replacing the whites of the Gold Coast. The other Community Area with only a small change in its racial composition between 1960 and 1966 was Roseland, an area which is really two quite different neighborhoods with a broad industrial belt separating the two sub-areas. The northern portion has been predominantly black since 1950; the southern portion has tended to remain white. The inclusion of this area among those experiencing racial change can thus be viewed as an artifact of inappropriate Community Area boundary demarcations. Near North Side and Roseland are not comparable with the other areas which appear to be more genuine instances of racially changing communities.

Disregarding these two areas, it would seem that among the most similar changing areas, South Shore is not an extraordinary case. Depending upon how the area is defined and the assumptions of population movement made, it can be viewed as either typical of the group in its speed of racial replacement or close to being the very fastest changing area of Chicago. In any event, the evidence suggests that the organizational efforts and various amenity benefits found in the area do not differentiate it in terms of racial replacement rate from other changing communities.

An Alternative Index of Replacement Speed

There is a second way to express the rate of racial change other than by citing percentage differences in racial composition—and by this method South Shore turns out to be changing even faster relative to other areas. A problem with using changes in percentage black over a given period is that no account is taken of the fact that the *size* of community areas differ, leading to a misleadingly

6. See Harvey Zorbaugh, *The Gold Coast and the Slum* (University of Chicago Press, 1929).

low rate of racial change for larger communities such as South Shore. The assumption is made, consistent with previous South Shore data cited as well as with the bulk of the literature on the subject, that racial change occurs ordinarily by what a South Shore rabbi termed the "ink blot" principle, with blacks expanding from one block to the next adjoining block with only limited "skipping" about.[7] Thus, if one Community Area has 100,000 residents and a second one has 50,000 residents, and 10,000 blacks replace whites in the same size border of each, the smaller Community Area will have changed 20 percent whereas the larger area will have changed only 10 percent—which gives a very misleading impression of the relative "success" of the two areas in discouraging black in-migration. If both Community Areas have attempted to discourage any additional black in-migration (and this *is* likely the goal of all Chicago border communities[8]), can it be argued correctly that one community area was twice as successful as the other?

A case can thus be made that a larger community can enjoy a slower change rate based upon percentage differences—only because the vastness of its population permits a larger white data base made possible by the existence of white areas as yet untouched by the racial change process. Such considerations augur for the use of absolute numbers of net black migrants between time periods or a size-standardized rate as alternative measures of the speed of racial change. Absolute figures and the percentage change standardized for area size[9] are set forth as columns 9 and 10 in Table 13. South Shore, by these measures, emerges as the most rapidly changing of Chicago's changing areas when Community Area boundaries are used (24,002 replacements, 42.6 percent change). Using data based upon the commission's boundaries, South Shore remains as one of the fastest changing communities (18,407 replacements, 32.6 percent change), but lags behind West Garfield Park (21,648

7. Richard Morrill, "The Negro Ghetto: Problems and Alternatives," *Geographical Review*, LV (1965), 339–361.

8. See Zorita Mikva, "The Neighborhood Improvement Association" (unpublished Master's thesis, Department of Sociology, University of Chicago, 1951).

9. Standardized percent change rates were computed by multiplying the ratio of total Community Area population to mean Community Area total population times percent change rate as revealed in column 8, Table 13.

replacements, 38.7 percent change) and Auburn-Gresham (19,752 replacement, 35.8 percent change). Among the seven communities deemed in the previous section to be most similarly situated vis-à-vis racial change, South Shore again emerges (regardless of how the area is defined) as one of the more rapidly changing transition areas.

Replacement Rate, 1965–1966

The effects of organizational efforts such as those of the South Shore Commission may perhaps only become manifest after a period of incubation, as residents come to sense the commission's presence and gain hope, as realtors modify their practices in light of commission activities. For this reason it may be that during the most recent year for which data are available, 1965–1966, the speed of racial change in South Shore may have been appreciably less than that of other changing areas which although similarly situated geographically, were organizationally less adept.

Evidence on this question is provided through inspection of Table 14. Data are again based on April estimates derived from hospital birth data. Using this one year period as a basis for comparing changing areas, South Shore comes closest to showing signs of a slower rate of racial change than other changing communities. Among the twelve changing areas, South Shore was the fifth most rapidly changing during the 1965–1966 one-year period.[10] Among the areas which had a racial composition of under 50 percent black in *1965,* South Shore was the fourth most rapidly changing. These eight areas, the net number of black migrants (1965–1966) within each, and change rates expressed in terms of number of racial replacements as a percentage of total community population, are listed in Table 14.

The two slowest changing communities have already been discussed; special conditions exist in both Roseland and the Near North Side which disqualify them from comparison with other racially changing communities. With this done, South Shore emerges—in terms of *percent replacement rate*—with the fourth fastest change

10. The impression that South Shore's rate of change may have declined slightly during the year 1965–1966 is supported by the school data cited in Figure 6. It can be seen that rates of change in public schools were lower in 1965–1966 than in either of the two previous periods.

TABLE 14

RACIAL CHARACTERISTICS OF EIGHT CHANGING CHICAGO
COMMUNITY AREAS, APRIL 1965 TO APRIL 1966

Community Area	Net Black In-Migration 1965–1966	Annual Percent Replacement Rate
Auburn-Gresham	8,410	14.14
Avalon Park	2,438	5.85
Washington Heights	1,440	4.63
South Shore[a]	3,024	4.17
West Englewood	1,932	3.43
West Garfield Park	1,684	2.96
Roseland	728	1.24
Near North Side	346	0.40

SOURCE: All data deduced from population estimates of the Hospital Planning Council
for Metropolitan Chicago, "Chicago Regional Hospital Study."
[a] Differences between commission and *Fact Book* boundaries lose their significance
after 1965, since virtually all new racial replacements were within South Shore boundaries by either community definition.

rate of the six remaining communities. It should be noted that with
the exception of rapidly changing Auburn-Gresham, the four fastest
changing areas have very similar replacement rates; it is thus not
clear that South Shore's actual replacement rate is significantly
slower than any community's except Auburn-Gresham. Further, in
terms of absolute numbers of black migrants (a reasonable criterion,
already discussed), South Shore is in second place—again following
only Auburn-Gresham. Although South Shore's change rate may
have declined slightly compared to other areas in 1965–1966, it
still does not display symptoms of a community in which intervention is making any significant difference in the speed of racial change,
especially when that change is measured in terms of absolute numbers of migrants.

SUCCESSION IN PREVIOUS DECADES

    In their analysis of rates of racial succession in Chicago
during decades between 1920 and 1950, the Duncans conclude that
due to the more rapid growth of Chicago's black population during

the 1940–1950 decade, transition was most rapid in neighborhoods changing during that period.[11] This rapid growth continued through the 1950s and only after 1960 is it generally thought to have significantly decreased. Thus it is reasonable to suppose that the speed of neighborhood transition—because of more modest rates of black population increase and the consequent decline of pressure (differential market demands)—was less rapid in Chicago after 1960 than before.[12]

Data presented earlier indicated replacement rates during the six year period 1960–1966 of between 20 and 50 percent for the most comparable Chicago community areas. Comparisons derived from the census of neighborhood transition during the ten year period 1950–1960 yield change rates ranging as high as 80 percent for certain Community Areas.[13] Whether or not there were six year intervals *within* these decades with change rates significantly higher than our 1960–1966 figures cannot be deduced from census information. The data is indeed inconclusive, but it seems reasonable to conclude that the speed of change in South Shore (and in the other communities most comparable to it) results, at least in part, from what may be a more satiated black housing demand, and thus a more relaxed form of community change than was the case in the past.

Nevertheless, intervention in South Shore had not had the effect of differentiating either the speed or pattern of racial change in the area from that occurring in other communities changing simultaneously. Variations which did exist can perhaps be explained by still other differences among communities (see Table 15) although an analysis of such variations (including those not indexed by census material) would involve an extensive study in itself. The purpose of

11. Duncan and Duncan, *The Negro Population of Chicago,* pp. 99–101, 110, 120–121.

12. The Taeubers report a rise in the vacancy rate in Negro residential areas in 1960. The difficulty in using such information as evidence for decreased "pressure" within Negro areas is that many such vacancies doubtless represent units in structures which have been vacated for urban renewal clearance, highway construction, or legal condemnation owing to code violation. All such forms of vacancy occur disproportionately in Negro areas and all occurred with greater frequency in 1960 than in earlier census years. See Taeuber and Taeuber, *Negroes in Cities,* p. 164.

13. Kitagawa and Taeuber, *Community Area Factbook.*

TABLE 15

A COMPARISON OF HOUSING AND SOCIOECONOMIC CHARACTERISTICS AMONG SIX RACIALLY CHANGING CHICAGO COMMUNITY AREAS

Population Characteristic	Auburn-Gresham	Avalon Park	Washington Heights	South Shore (CA)	West Englewood	West Garfield Park
Percent foreign stock	44.7	38.9	34.6	42.2	38.1	31.0
Percent under 18 years old	26.1	31.2	31.1	21.4	31.7	34.9
Percent 65 years and older	14.1	11.3	10.7	15.7	10.8	8.1
Median school years completed	10.7	12.2	11.7	12.2	9.5	9.0
Percent of all workers in manufacturing industries	24.8	25.4	25.7	21.0	31.0	39.4
Percent of male workers in white collar occupations	41.9	55.5	46.1	62.6	30.4	26.3
Percent male labor force unemployed	2.4	2.6	2.6	3.5	5.2	4.8
Median family income	$8,014	$8,697	$8,523	$7,888	$6,695	$6,122
Percent housing units owner-occupied	53.1	74.1	74.5	21.1	50.0	20.5
Percent housing units built 1950 or later	8.5	20.6	24.8	6.2	3.2	0.5
Percent housing units in substandard condition	2.1	0.4	0.8	2.0	4.2	9.1
Median value, owner units (in 1-unit structures)	$17,900	$18,500	$17,600	$19,500	$17,600	$14,550
Percent of persons 5 and older living in different house in 1955 than 1960	42.2	45.5	43.6	54.6	45.5	66.8

this chapter has been a more modest search for the evidence of South Shore's uniqueness. We have found, as a result, that although the classic notion of succession may have to be modified to take into consideration a somewhat slower rate of change, two independent sources of data examined indicate that the transition of South Shore does not constitute an exception to the general contemporary pattern.

8
Property Turnover:
Measuring
White
Flight

I⊤ IS commonly assumed that residential racial succession is accompanied by instability. First, there is instability in the obvious sense that racial composition is changing. Second, there is instability in the less trivial sense that the amount of household turnover in the area is particularly high—presumably due to a tendency for whites to flee a changing neighborhood.[1] The latter sort of instability is the focus of this chapter. For operational simplicity, it is defined as the extent to which the proportion of residential properties placed and sold on the housing market is appropriate to the age, housing type, location, and other nonracial characteristics of a particular area. An increase in such property turnover is often regarded as a cause of neighborhood change and as a key inhibiting factor to the development of residential racial integration in American cities. Thus, a commonly favored intervention policy in changing areas has involved an attempt to convince local whites to remain and to create the amenities which will help keep them in residence.[2]

CONSEQUENCES OF STABILITY

In addition to its relevance to intervention policy, there are other reasons to investigate whether racial change can occur

1. Davis McEntire, *Residence and Race* (Berkeley: University of California Press, 1960), pp. 77–87.
2. See Abrahamson, *A Neighborhood Finds Itself* (New York: Harper and Row, 1959); William Biddle and Loureide Biddle, *The Community Development Process* (New York: Holt, Rinehart and Winston, 1965); John Fish et al., *The Edge of the Ghetto: A Study of Church Involvement in Community Organization* (Chicago: University of Chicago Divinity School, 1966).

within a context of relatively orderly mobility patterns. In a setting characterized by flight, the slowly developed institutions and voluntary associations which bind people to one another and to the larger communities stand in danger of collapse as large numbers of persons suddenly depart and equally large numbers arrive. Rapid mobility does not permit local institutions to assimilate newcomers; it inhibits in-migrants from finding their way to the institutions which represent interests and views appropriate to their own. Rapid exodus by one group causes institutions to collapse because of rapidly declining financial and moral support. Rapid influx then overwhelms the few institutions which remain—thus inhibiting them from fulfilling the mediating functions often considered the crucial roles of urban organizations. The result may be a state of social disorganization which, according to the precepts of classic sociological theory, implies all the negative characteristics ascribable to anomic urban man.[3]

The problem of stability is especially crucial when the in-migrating and out-migrating groups are of different races, for the process of integrating newcomers into existing structures is made all the more difficult by racial antagonisms.[4] The success of attempts, like those actually made by certain South Shore clergymen and community leaders, to integrate newcomers into the life of on-going community institutions seems to be contingent upon—as a minimum requisite —a degree of neighborhood stability normal to a community of South Shore's size and type. When commission leaders spoke of the need for stability in South Shore, they usually had in mind both a freezing of the existing racial balance and keeping housing turnover at as low a level as possible. Achievement of the latter goal was

3. For materials relevant to this argument, see W. I. Thomas and F. Znaniecki, *The Polish Peasant in Europe and America* (Chicago: University of Chicago Press, 1922); Helena Znaniecki Lopata, "The Function of Voluntary Associations in an Ethnic Community: 'Palonia,'" in Ernest Burgess and Donald Bogue (eds.), *Contributions to Urban Sociology* (Chicago: University of Chicago Press, 1964), pp. 203–224; Maurice Stein, *The Eclipse of Community* (Princeton: Princeton University Press, 1960); William Kornhauser, *The Politics of Mass Society* (New York: The Free Press, 1959).

4. Studies which describe attempts to integrate Negro newcomers into existing white structures are: Biddle and Biddle, *The Community Development Process*; Abrahamson, *A Neighborhood Finds Itself*. For evidence that those who participate in community organizational life are most likely to reject Negroes, see Joseph D. Lohman and Dietrich Reitzes, "Deliberately Organized Groups and Racial Behavior," *American Sociological Review*, XIX (June 1954), 342–344.

often considered a requisite for the achievement of the former, but a low level of property turnover and population movement was also valued as a worthy end in itself.

With these considerations in mind, I attempted to determine the degree to which South Shore could be considered a stable community. In the last chapter, I concluded that South Shore was not stable in terms of racial composition. In this chapter, I examine the question of stability in terms of property turnover.

GENERAL STRATEGY

No completely satisfactory measure of neighborhood stability could be applied to South Shore, although I applied several approximate measures. The perfect measure would compare the number of persons who left the area to the number which would be expected to leave had racial change not begun to occur. Unfortunately, there is no way of knowing post hoc how many households would have moved under different circumstances than those which existed. Second, it was not possible, given the limited financial resources and time pressures of this study, to learn definitely how many South Shore residents left the area during the study period. The primary difficulty in even estimating the number of such persons rests in the fact that the majority of South Shore's housing stock consists of apartments which are vacated and occupied without being publicly recorded.

In addition to its relative invisibility, apartment mobility is also difficult to interpret—especially in a racially changing setting. In an earlier discussion (see Chapter Two) I indicated that whether a South Shore resident opts to remain or leave because of racial change may be a matter having less to do with his own attitudes toward blacks and his neighborhood than with the attitude of his landlord. Building managers make decisions about rent increases, maintenance standards, and the like that may cause a tenant to move who would otherwise have remained in the biracial setting. In a sense, a white tenant's departure may have been a result of racial change, but only because of the landlord's intervening behavior. Data on apartment mobility, although relevant to several issues raised, would be a faulty indicator of white residents' disposition to remain in terms of their own attitudes toward the in-migrating group. Instability among apartment dwellers does not necessarily imply that the instability would have occurred had the residents been homeowners instead of tenants.

Because it would be unfeasible as well as unprofitable, I did not attempt a direct measure of apartment mobility. Instead, I focused on owner-occupied homes, the legal transfer of which is recorded in various records and whose owners' desire to move is often made immediately apparent by the "for sale" sign in front of his property. Unlike tenants, homeowners are in control of their immediate environment; if they move as a result of black in-migration, their decision can be more easily ascribed to their own attitudes. Although findings relevant to stability among homeowners are not directly applicable to questions of stability within rental markets, the evidence derived from the homeowning market may provide clues as to the actual mobility among tenants—at least among those apartment dwellers who do not face landlord policies which encourage white departures. We may thus gain an approximation of the extent to which the area as a whole is stable, or at least the extent to which such an area *would be* stable if its housing stock were largely owner-occupied or user-controlled.

A Matched Comparison

No community is completely stable; one of every five Americans changes residence each year.[5] The precise question is thus not "Is South Shore stable?—but is it stable compared to other communities which are similar in every way except that they are not experiencing racial change. The method used was to compare South Shore with the non-racially changing community most similar to it.

The community selected for comparison was Rogers Park, one of Chicago's seventy-five Community Areas, and one which (except for racial composition) was strikingly similar to South Shore. Both areas are on the lake shore and almost equidistant from the Loop; South Shore begins sixty-seven blocks south of the city center, Rogers Park sixty-four blocks north. The far north location of Rogers Park, however, places it at a distance from the edge of the city's expanding black residential area; it is one of the least "threatened" of all communities. Compared to other parts of Chicago, there have been few "pressures" to integrate the area (although a few black families are said to be in residence); real estate men who

5. See Donald Bogue, *The Population of the United States*, p. 375.

were interviewed in the community reported almost a total absence of racial confrontation in their offices and all who were probed on the subject regarded the area as stable and "firm." Except for conditions of age and scattered decay also shared by other older areas like South Shore, a recent descriptive analysis of Rogers Park by a Chicago newspaper was accurate in its headlined description: "Rogers Park: A Community with Few Problems." [6]

The resemblance between the two areas, apart from the racial variable, was indeed strong: in income, education, and ethnicity of population; in condition, age, and type of housing stock; and in its physical appearance to the casual visitor. Table 16 presents a comparison of the two community areas along seventeen variables possibly relevant to residential mobility rates.[7]

Source of Data

Because of certain difficulties arising from the manner in which records are maintained by the Office of the Cook County Recorder of Deeds, I used an alternative source of property transfer data: the listings of property transactions in *Realty and Building* (hereafter *R & B*), the trade journal of the Chicago real estate industry.[8]

Because the editors of *R & B* reprint only some portions of the Recorders' records and ignore others like complicated land assemblages or property line revisions, I devised a primitive test for possible bias in the reprinted records. I made a geographical breakdown of total transfers for the listing in *R & B* and compared it with a similar breakdown included in the annual report of the Cook County Recorder of Deeds. Because it is the only breakdown made in the annual report, the comparison consisted of numbers of transfers within the city as opposed to the number within Cook County suburbs. The geographical divisions used in *R & B* permitted me to make a similar comparison of city versus suburbs. The

6. *Chicago Daily News*, April 6, 1967, p. 48. As part of the same series of articles describing various Chicago communities, the installment on South Shore was headlined: "South Shore: Can It Keep the Racial Balance?" (*Chicago Daily News*, March 23, 1967, p. 64).

7. Comparison is based on the Community Area of South Shore because data is conveniently available for these boundaries. The comparison of property transfers was based on South Shore boundaries adopted in Chapter Two (commission boundaries). The 1960 profile of South Shore would be similar regardless of which boundary set is used.

8. *Realty and Building* (Chicago), Vol. 156.

TABLE 16

A COMPARISON OF SOUTH SHORE AND ROGERS PARK COMMUNITY AREAS*

Variable	Rogers Park	South Shore
Population Characteristics		
Percent foreign stock	48.4	42.2
Percent under 18 years of age	21.0	21.4
Percent over 65 years of age	14.2	15.7
Years of median schooling	12.2	12.2
Percent with four years of college or more	12.8	13.3
Percent of "breadwinner" males in white collar occupations	74.0	62.6
Median family income	$7,465	$7,888
Percent of persons 5 years and older living in different house in 1955	61.1	54.6
Population per household	2.41	2.52
Housing Characteristics		
Percent owner-occupied	11.3	21.1
Percent sub-standard	2.6	2.0
Median value of units	$20,300.00	$19,500.00
Median rent	$110.00	$112.00
Median number of rooms per unit	3.9	4.2
Percent built 1950 or later	6.3	6.2
Year when building activity declined after housing stock "matured"	1930	1935
Location of community	Directly on Lake Michigan, 6400 to 7600 North.	Directly on Lake Michigan, 6700 to 8300 South.

SOURCE: All data is from Evelyn Kitagawa and Karl Taeuber, eds., *Local Community Fact Book: Chicago Metropolitan Area, 1960* (Chicago Community Inventory, University of Chicago, 1963).
* Use of commission boundaries for comparative purposes would further decrease the discrepancy between the two communities in terms of income and have negligible effects on other measures.

proportions derived from the two different information sources were nearly identical (0.40 vs. 0.42), giving some evidence that the data source is probably unbiased. This is, of course, an imperfect test but the best that available data permit. The numbers of transfers for any given area are understated in *R & B* records (and thus in the tables which follow) but are presumed to be equally understated among all areas.[9]

Procedures Followed

All property transfers reprinted in *R & B* for the period July–December 1966 were totaled for Rogers Park and South Shore.[10]

9. This rather glib assertion glosses over certain misgivings derived from several conversations with employees both at *R & B* and the Recorder of Deeds office. Those in the "data-making" process do not record and process with the uses in mind to which we have put "their" data. Materials, such as sheets recording a transfer, are handled in a most cavalier manner (especially at county offices). Nevertheless, I have not been able to demonstrate that this sloppiness had an effect on the data reported here. For further details on procedural matters, see Harvey Molotch, "Community Action to Control Racial Change" (unpublished Ph.D. dissertation, University of Chicago, 1968), esp. pp. 243–245.

10. For both South Shore and Rogers Park, properties are listed along with those of several contiguous communities under rubrics which cover larger regions than the two communities under study. I had to ascertain whether or not each entry corresponded to a location within the boundaries of either community. Because approximately half of all entries appear in *R & B* records with street addresses, it was possible in the case of these properties to determine whether or not they were in South Shore or Rogers Park by referring to road maps. For other listed properties, however, only the legal description of locations appeared in the entry—consisting of citation of subdivision names, block and lot numbers, generally beginning with the first relevant act of subdivision to occur after the Chicago fire.

It was thus necessary to translate these legal descriptions into street addresses —a process accomplished by matching the legal descriptions with street addresses as they appear on master maps held at the City of Chicago Bureau of Maps and Plats. The procedure I followed was to begin with the section of a given range and township specified on each property transfer record, to examine the descriptions in the margins of all maps covering that section (usually six in number), and to locate the property on the map by use of the code letter above each marginal description. For example, if a property's legal description was: "Lot 39 in Block 5 of Stinson's Subdivision of East Grand Crossing Subdivision of Section 25, Township 38, Range 14," the procedure would be as follows:

(1) Turn to atlas pages corresponding to Section 25, Township 38, Range 14 (as marked on top of maps as "25–38–14"); (2) read all marginal notations on these map pages until finding "Stinson's Subdivision of East Grand Crossing Subdivision"; (3) note the code letter affixed to the above description and locate this same code letter on the adjacent map; (4) locate "Block 5" in the area covered by the code letter; (5) locate "Lot 39" within Block 5; (6) read off the addresses which correspond to Lot 39; (7) determine whether or not the street address is within the relevant study area.

Additional steps had to be taken to learn what types of property were transferred (e.g., apartment buildings, single family homes, stores). The needed information was derived from Sanborn Maps which portray building outlines and describe structure type, by use, for every property in Chicago.

Property type (house, apartment building, or store) was determined by reference to Sanborn Maps for the relevant city area.

RESULTS: PROPERTY TRANSFER RATES

For each type of property existing in the two areas, the number transferred to new owners was divided by the total number of such properties located in the community to yield a series of property transfer rates for each locale. Regardless of property type, South Shore appears to be either as stable as Rogers Park or *more* stable than Rogers Park. The results are summarized in Table 17.

Interpreting Table 17

We can have two different comparisons of home transfers based on two different conceptions of what constitutes the appropriate base figure for total number of homes in each area. In the first instance, the total number of structures having one, two, three, or four units is used; in the second, the total number of owner-occupied dwelling units is used. These two different bases are used because neither is perfect. The problem is that census categories specifying structures having one, two, three, or four units include all such structures, regardless of whether one or more units within the structure is owner-occupied. Sanborn Maps, on the other hand, label with a "D" (the symbol used to indicate a private home) such one-, two-, three-, and four-dwelling unit structures which are *owner-occupied*. Other structures are labeled as small apartment buildings on Sanborn Maps. Because of this slight noncomparability of data, a case can be made that either owner-occupied or number of structures having one to four units is appropriate for our purposes. The number of cases within the ambiguity is small, however, because almost all such home structures are single-family dwellings. Moreover, the results are similar regardless of which source of base data is used.[11]

___

11. Several additional methodological explanations are needed: computation of base data was complicated by the fact that South Shore boundaries sometimes bisected census tracts. Thus the total number of owner-occupied dwellings was computed by use of census *block* data. Base totals for number of structures having one, two, three, or four units were derived by dividing the total number of two-family structures by 2, the number of three- and four-unit structures by 3.2 (an arbitrary figure based upon an estimate of the proportion of three- as

TABLE 17
PROPERTY TRANSFERS IN ROGERS PARK AND SOUTH SHORE

Property Type	South Shore			Rogers Park			
	Number of Cases (1)	Total Number of Such Properties in Area (Base) (2)	Transfer Rate Index (3) (1 ÷ 2)	Number of Cases (4)	Total Number of Such Properties in Area (Base) (5)	Transfer Rate Index (6) (4 ÷ 5)	χ^2[a] (7)
1- to 4-family structures	105	8,878	1.18%	43	3,083	1.39%	0.842[f]
1- to 4-family structures (using owner-occupied for base data)	105	8,320	1.26%	43	2,781	1.54%	1.153[g]
Condominium units	0	NA		5	NA		
Apartment buildings	20	NA		15	NA		
Apartment units (estimated)	282[b]	25,675[c]	1.09%	422[b]	20,393[c]	2.06%	7.851[f]
Retailing structures	7	NA		7	NA		
Retailing front lots (estimated)	13[d]	545[e]	2.38%	16[d]	496[e]	3.22%	0.67[g]
Miscellaneous and unclassified (vacant land, warehousing, etc.)	7	NA		5	NA		

[a] Results of significance tests are presented in spite of the fact that certain assumptions, such as independence, are not strictly met. They may serve nevertheless, as rough analytical guides. See David Gold, "Statistical Tests and Substantive Significance," *American Sociologist*, IV (February 1969), 42–46.

[b] Computed on the assumption of three apartments for each 25 ft. of width and 50 ft. of depth multiplied by number of floors in structure.

[c] Rentor-occupied units, U.S. census.

[d] Determined by visual inspection of Sanborn Maps with each 50 ft. of frontage taken to constitute one front lot.

[e] Refers to number of stores, U.S. census.

[f] Significant at .01 level.

[g] Not significant.

Variation by Structure Type

For apartment units, Rogers Park is significantly *less* stable than South Shore, with a higher transfer rate than in the racially changing community (p < .01). One of the classic explanations for instability in apartment areas experiencing racial change is that such instability is stimulated or at least intensified by operators who move into the local market and buy property which they "turn" and "milk dry" by forgoing maintenance.[12] As a result, it is said, whites are forced out. This view was held by many white residents of the South Shore area. A similar theme emerged often in interviews with real estate dealers who used the same theory, often expressed in different terms, to explain why neighborhoods "turn" where and when they do. The low rate of apartment building turnover in South Shore compared to Rogers Park indicates that such a process was not occurring. To the extent that such tactics are the source of mobility among tenants, this finding can be regarded as evidence of stability in the rental market. Perhaps tenants, like homeowners, were not fleeing South Shore.

The evidence suggests that such speculation did not occur in the home market either. The classic notion here is that certain real estate firms induce whites to sell their houses quickly and cheaply so that they can be resold by the real estate dealer to blacks at a premium price. During the six-month period under investigation, I found not a single instance where a home was sold and then resold in South Shore. Scheitinger,[13] in his study of the racial transition of Chicago's Oakland community in the 1940s, found many instances

---

opposed to four-family structures in the area), and adding the derived quotients to the total number of single-family structures. Data on number of units within structures are not published by census block; for those South Shore tracts bisected by boundary lines, totals were multiplied by the proportion of tract area located in South Shore, and resultant products were added to other tract totals. Total numbers of stores (treated as comparable to the number of fifty-foot storefronts) and numbers of apartments were derived from census tract data, with tracts overlapping community boundaries treated in a similar manner.

12. See Konrad Bercovici, *Around the World in New York* (New York: Appleton-Century Co., 1924); Paul Cressey, "Succession of Cultural Groups in the City of Chicago" (unpublished Ph.D. dissertation, Department of Sociology, University of Chicago, 1930).

13. Egbert F. Scheitinger, "Real Estate Transfers During Negro Invasion" (unpublished M.A. dissertation, Department of Sociology, University of Chicago, 1948).

of such double sales; and, somewhat more recently, Rapkin and Grigsby[14] found at least some speculation in changing Philadelphia areas. That none was uncovered in South Shore provides additional evidence of stability.

Variation Across Census Tracts

Although the overall rates of transfer are similar in Rogers Park and South Shore, there may be different patterns of turnover within the two communities which would imply that whites were, indeed, fleeing from at least *some parts* of South Shore. More precisley, it could be argued that in certain tracts (perhaps those recently opened to blacks), there was a high degree of turnover which was balanced by an extremely low rate of mobility in other tracts (for example, all-white areas) where residents freeze during a period of racial uncertainty.

The evidence, however, is not consistent with such an alternative explanation. Single-family house transfer rates in South Shore varied from a low of zero (in one small tract with few houses) to a high of 2.6; the analogous extreme figures for Rogers Park were 0.04 and 3.0. The standard deviation across tracts was slightly higher for Rogers Park (9.8) than for South Shore (7.9). Table 18 shows tract variations within the two communities.

Tract mobility rates are plotted on maps of the two communities in Figures 8 and 9. Inspection of these maps suggests that there is a tendency for South Shore's tracts of lowest mobility to be those closest to the lakeshore and most distant from predominantly black tracts. The fit is by no means perfect. Tract 636 (O'Keeffe) as well as Tract 638 were heavily black (and still changing) during the study period, although the transfer rates in these two tracts were extremely low. Because data are lacking on the precise racial composition of various tracts at the relevant point in time, it is impossible to relate mobility rates to racial composition in any exact manner. In general, however, the tracts with the highest transfer rates were also tracts in which racial change was occurring. But because of such exceptions as those noted, the converse statement cannot be made; it cannot be said that those tracts in which racial change was occurring had the highest transfer rates. Given the thinness of

14. Chester Rapkin and William Grigsby, *The Demand for Housing in Racially Mixed Areas* (Berkeley: University of California Press, 1960).

TABLE 18
VARIATIONS IN TRACT TRANSFER RATES
WITHIN SOUTH SHORE AND ROGERS PARK

South Shore			Rogers Park	
Tract	Transfer Rate[a]		Tract	Transfer Rate[a]
635	13.64		0001	3.89
636	1.47		0002	26.79
637	0		0003	20.73
638	0		0004	6.01
639	11.42		0005A	29.81
640	15.81		0005B	14.63
641	12.35		0006	7.58
642A	8.30		0007	7.78
642B	3.81		0008	5.95
643	25.90			
644	21.94			
662[b]	20.49			
663[b]	9.04			
664[b]	7.38			
665[b]	1.39			
Mean	10.20		Mean	13.68
Variance	63.68		Variance	96.12
Standard deviation	7.98		Standard deviation	9.80

[a] Number of property transfers per 1,000 homes in tract.
[b] Refers only to that portion of tract located within South Shore (commission boundaries). Base data derived from block census data.

available data, conclusions must be limited to the statement that if there was some relationship between turnover and racial change *within* South Shore, the extent of mobility, even in the most unstable tracts, was less than that which occurred in some tracts of communities like Rogers Park, where racial change was not occurring.

"FOR SALE" SIGN COUNTS

It might be argued that the stability characteristic of South Shore's home-owning population is an involuntary stability forced upon residents unable to find buyers (or at least "satisfactory" buyers) in a market depressed by racial change. To test this proposition, I compared South Shore with Rogers Park in terms of the

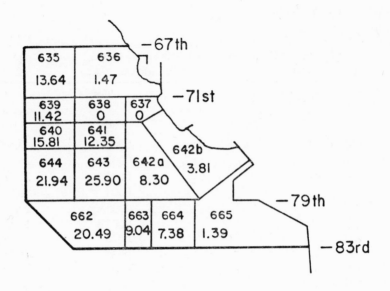

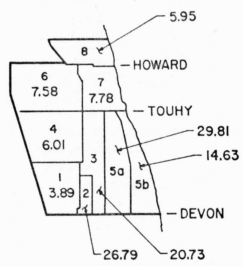

Key:

Community area boundary: ————

Tract boundary: ————

FIGURE 8: Tract Mobility Rates in South Shore

Key:

Community area boundary: ————

Tract boundary: ————

FIGURE 9: Tract Mobility Rates in Rogers Park

proportions of homeowners who *wanted* to sell their homes. In order to gain a measure of this mobility wish, every front block of both areas was inspected, and the total number of "for sale" signs in front of one-, two-, three-, and four-family homes was recorded and divided by the total number of such dwellings in each area to yield a Mobility Wish Index. The "for sale" sign counts were made twice for South Shore and once for Rogers Park. The comparison here is between counts for the two areas taken during the first week of December 1966. (Touring all the streets of South Shore required approximately four days, and Rogers Park required three.)

It is clear from the results shown in Table 19 that desired mobility is the same in Rogers Park and South Shore. Again, evidence indicates that South Shore is stable; there are no signs of flight by homeowners from the racially changing neighborhood.

A possible objection to the use of "for sale" signs as an index of a mobility wish is that there may be a difference in the degree to which home sellers use such signs in the two areas. For example, South Shore's white sellers may refrain from using such signs for fear of alienating their neighbors—or because they think the signs would endanger community morale, which they feel an obligation to protect. To be certain that such was not the case, a random sample of real estate firms in South Shore and all the real estate firms in Rogers Park (as listed in neighborhood telephone directories) were visited; officials were asked for lists of all homes they had for sale. Each home on the lists thus accumulated was visually inspected. The total number of signs in each area was computed and then divided by the number of homes listed for sale in each community. The results, as set forth in Table 20, indicate an equal propensity to sell with a "for sale" sign in the two areas.

TABLE 19

MOBILITY WISH INDEXES FOR SOUTH SHORE AND ROGERS PARK

	South Shore	Rogers Park
Number of signs	141	43
Number of housing units owner-occupied	8,320	2,613[a]
Mobility Wish Index	1.69%	1.64%

[a] There are 2,781 owner-occupied housing units in Rogers Park. Because one tract (a "peninsula" constituting the northeast tip of the area) was inadvertently not checked during the sign count, the number of owner-occupied units within that tract was subtracted from the total.

TABLE 20

PROPENSITY TO USE "FOR SALE" SIGNS TO SELL HOMES
IN SOUTH SHORE AND ROGERS PARK

	South Shore	Rogers Park
Number of dealers interviewed who had houses for sale	9	7
Number of houses on all lists	74	33
Number of signs	23	11
Number of signs as a percentage of total homes listed for sale	31%	33%

The Effects of "Racial Violence" Upon Stability

It is often observed by those commenting on racial change processes that, whereas a community can remain somewhat stable for a period of time, racial incidents are bound to occur, and that such incidents act as a catalyst for the white exodus. The high school lunchroom "riot" described in Chapter Five was the only such event which occurred in South Shore during the study period. It was an incident which was widely and prominently reported by the daily press, radio, and television, and was regarded as without precedent in South Shore.

Within the week of the riot, an emergency community meeting was held at the high school with an attendance (virtually all white) which flowed beyond the auditorium corridors and into classroom hallways. I was present at the meeting and circulated among the standing groups of worried parents, engaging them in conversation and picking up bits and pieces of conversations. Particularly at the meeting's close, after hearing pledges from local police and school authorities that their children would be protected from further harm, the consensus of the audience seemed to be that, in the words of more than one resident, "the whole thing [the security program] is a farce." From resident after resident, comments such as these were heard: "I'm going to put my house up for sale"; "I'm selling; there's nothing else that can be done"; "What else can I do but move?"; "I'm calling a broker."

In light of the expressed attitudes of so many South Shore residents, it is surprising to note that the high school incident seems to have had no immediate effect on the number of houses in the area placed on the housing market. A count of "for sale" signs was made on November 1–4, the days immediately following the high school incident. A second count (the one reported earlier for comparison with Rogers Park) was made between December 2 and December 6, approximately one month later. It is assumed that the first count describes the state of the housing market before the incident, for it would take several days for a homeowner to contact a broker, sign a contract, and have a sign placed on his property. The second count is assumed to reflect any changes wrought by the incident; a month would seem enough time to make the necessary arrangements to place one's home on the market. The November count revealed a total of 150 houses for sale; the count a month later indicated 141 houses were for sale. The slight drop is inconsistent with the notion that such incidents as described above must bring with them a swift and dramatic white exodus.

The second count of "for sale" signs suggests that South Shore's stability was probably similar to that of Rogers Park even at a time when flight would be most expected to occur. In addition to the high school incident, late 1966 was also the period in which South Shore had moved beyond many of the oft-cited "tipping points"— commonly stated as community racial compositions of 10 to 25 percent black.[15] The largest increase in black population of South Shore High School occurred during this period, with the data published widely in October 1966. Referring to one of the early press stories on the school's changing composition, one member of the commission board of directors had remarked: "When that was published another group of whites moved out. Everyone has a boiling point— the point where he says, 'This is enough. I'm getting out.' "

For some, 42 percent at the high school was it.[16] If there was to be a flight from South Shore, the moment would seem to have been at hand—at least in the light of remarks such as these and what are regarded as the standard "stages" of racial transition most often cited in the literature.[17] That available evidence generally suggests a lack of flight is thus significant.

15. Robert Weaver, "Integration in Public and Private Housing," *Annals of the American Academy of Political and Social Science,* CCCIV (March 1956), 86–97; Charles Abrams, *Forbidden Neighbors: A Study of Prejudice in Housing* (New York: Harper, 1955).

16. *Chicago Daily News,* March 23, 1967, p. 64.

17. See, for example, Ernest Burgess, "Residential Succession in American Cities," *Annals of the American Academy of Political and Social Science,* Vol. CXL (November 1928); Harold Gibbard, "Residential Succession: A Study in Human Ecology" (unpublished Ph.D. dissertation, Department of Sociology, University of Michigan, 1938)

SEEING, TALKING, MOVING

The question of South Shore's stability was a major topic
of conversation in the community and the frequent worried talk of
the assumed white exodus was quite inconsistent with the findings
reported here. When I informed several commission officers that
South Shore was indeed quite stable, they were somewhat in-
credulous—although anxious to incorporate the news into their
public relations materials.[18] Their skepticism was consistent with
my own earlier convictions (derived from a year's continuous observation in the community) that South Shore was, in fact, experiencing a flight of whites with rapid property turnover. The
gathering of counts of "for sale" signs and property transfers origi-
nated with a desire to document the *degree* of flight among homeowners; that there was to be no evidence of any flight was not con-
templated beforehand. The question thus arises: What was the
origin of the widespread impression of extraordinarily high property
turnover rates in South Shore?

Perhaps both the researcher and the researched were wrong because the idea of white people moving out is a spectre which haunts
South Shore. Each time a white resident sees a black on the street,
he or she is reminded that another white family has moved from the
area. In communities which are not changing racially, the departure
of certain residents and their replacement by others is invisible
to all except immediate neighbors and friends. In South Shore it is
evident to many more.

In addition, South Shore residents are aware that their community
is viewed as one with "problems" and that there are costs to be
paid by those who remain. While a resident may himself be willing
to pay the perceived costs, he doubts that other residents are similarly disposed. There is anxiety that whites will desert the area,
forcing *all* residents to bear the costs of relocation if the untenable
prospect of being the only white in a black neighborhood is to be
avoided. This anxiety heightens the attention given to any move-out,
and when combined with a folk knowledge of how racial change has

18. They did so, in a distorted way. As previously noted, the commission reported that only 2 percent of South Shore's homes sold each year. See p. 80,
Chapter Four.

occurred in other Chicago neighborhoods, it perhaps leads to an exaggerated appraisal of the number of whites who are leaving as a response to racial change.

Spokesmen for the commission, even in front of their own board of directors, did not call attention to the existence of white people who left the area (people who "threw in the towel"); to do so would have endangered community morale and exacerbated the problem. But many remarks made by commission leaders would suggest that they held a similarly distorted definition of the situation. Thus, in interviews, commission spokesmen dwelled on the issue of what types of South Shore people run from a changing area and under what conditions people are most likely to remain. Similarly, remarks would frequently allude to the need to convince residents that there was no reason for them to sell their South Shore homes. These are remarks made under the impression that a failure of confidence in the community's future had been responsible, to a significant extent, for high rates of property turnover and thus for South Shore's increasingly large black population.

Residential Choice as a Moral Act

The recounting of one important incident can perhaps serve to illustrate the heightened sensitivity which South Shore leaders had to the issue of whites' placing their homes on the market. As a result of the high school incident, a plea was made to parents of eye witnesses to allow their children to identify the guilty in order to insure their incarceration. A high-ranking officer of the commission, one who had played a leading role in the series of meetings and events which followed the school fracas, implored the board of directors at its monthly meeting to find parents who would "have the guts to stand up and fight these punks." In a highly melodramatic climax to his speech, he exclaimed that if no one would be found to come forth, "I'm putting my house up for sale, I'm telling you that."

A hush fell over the audience; there was no other possible statement which could have had greater significance or carried with it more shock. A resolute symbol of South Shore's hope for stability had spoken words considered taboo in such a setting. In the end the threat turned out to be an empty one; no one testified and like so many of his neighbors with similar stated intentions, the officer remained in South Shore. But his choice of threat and the response to it was instructive. For just as moving out was a symbol of "throwing in the towel," simply remaining was taken as a symbol of positive action to help the community. That is, South Shore leaders viewed remaining in the area as something extraordinary— something which one did either because of devotion to his community, because it was "the right thing" or because "you can't just run away." Although they generally viewed other South Shore people as remaining because of community amenities and the costs inherent in relocating, for them remaining assumed a moral imperative. Such persons were proud that they were remaining, and the commission setting provided a source of mutual confirmation that each had followed the proper course. As one very active South Shore woman put it: "We're working for our community to make it a good one, and meanwhile we'll just have to hold each other up."

MAKING TALK

Everyday Conversations

In settings other than commission meetings, South Shore residents who were not community leaders did not allude to such ideals when discussing—generally, in a more open way—the issue of people moving. In any urban area, it is normal for many people to move in the course of a given year and it is also normal for a much larger number of persons to be *thinking about moving*. In the context of a racially changing area, any thought about moving becomes fused with the racial change issue, first because it is the most salient community issue extant, and second because it is the one reason for moving which potentially, at least, applies equally to all. Thus when one white South Shore resident tells another he is going to move, or is considering a move, the second party will raise the race issue, if only in a subtle way, for it is the most commonly appropriate response.

Such a frequent juxtaposition in thought and conversation of moving and race would reasonably be expected to lead to a melding of the two issues even in the mind of a person whose intended departure had, at least when he first considered moving, nothing whatever to do with racial change. For those who, under different neighborhood circumstances would not even be considering moving, the possibility becomes a live option—one which is weighed, considered, discussed, and often, if only through inertia, rejected. Thus for those who move and those who don't move, racial change becomes the reason why "people are leaving South Shore."

Perhaps this is why residents so frequently spoke about moving but so infrequently did and why so many seem to have thought that so many others were fleeing from blacks. Moving and race are the big issues in South Shore, and they are talked about, like the weather and national politics, much more than they are acted upon. Perhaps it is for this reason that participant observers, whether an academic investigator or a resident trying to understand his environment, could so easily have come to what appears to be a false conclusion.

Ideology and Action

The content of everyday talk is not only a distortion of ecological reality, it is also of limited utility in predicting the behavior of the speaker. The disparity between stated intention and action following the South Shore High School fracas has already been noted. Fulton,[19] in his 1960 study of the predominantly middle-class Jewish area of Russel Woods in Detroit, interviewed the same sample of white residents at the beginning of that neighborhood's transition process as he did two years later. He found that although there was a high correlation between anti-Negro prejudice and *stated intention to move,* the same relationship did not hold between prejudice and *actual* movement from this rapidly changing area two years later. Fulton interprets this to be due to the fact that so many of those who intended to move remained, whereas so many of those who expressed an intention to remain had later, in fact, moved. In absolute numbers, more of the latter group than of the former moved during the study period.

Other studies provide additional evidence that articulated ideology and residential integration have less to do with one another than is ordinarily supposed. Rapkin and Grigsby, in interviewing white Philadelphia purchasers of homes in changing areas, found that buyers appeared to be about as liberal or conservative regarding integration as most Philadelphians. These buyers were generally

19. Robert L. Fulton. "Russel Woods: A Study of a Neighborhood's Initial Response to Negro Invasion" (unpublished Ph.D. dissertation, Dept. of Sociology, Wayne State University, 1960).

prejudiced enough not to relish the idea of a black living next door, but they purchased in a changing area anyway because of attributes of the house or the convenience of its location to work or other family members.[20]

Results consistent with these were obtained by Grier and Grier[21] in their interviews with developers and salesmen of fifty racially mixed housing developments throughout the United States, including the deep South. In no instance was the "liberality" of any portion of the local white market considered important to success of integration and in several instances developers reported that attempts to sell houses to members of liberal political and religious groups on the basis of "integration" were failures. Instead, whites who purchased did so for the mundane reasons involving housing value or convenience to work. Further, the Griers found successfully integrated projects inhabited by whites of all socioeconomic classes and of varying ethnicity; there was no tendency for the well-educated or for Jews (often considered the most "liberal" of ethnic groups) to be disproportionately represented in integrated housing.[22]

Finally, Gans[23] in his study of Levittown, New Jersey, reports that white purchasers in that town bought homes next door to blacks because blacks were given the choicest lots in the community. It was whites who wanted lots with the same amenities who bought next door to blacks, rather than whites who were particularly liberal or committed to integration. The success of integration in this lower middle-class community contrasts sharply with failures in other areas, including other Levitt developments, where integration became an ideological issue.

20. See Rapkin and Grigsby, *The Demand for Housing.* That the attributes of the house, such as "more house for the money," is the paramount consideration of home seekers (and not considerations of community conditions) was the conclusion of a recent study of Philadelphia suburbanites. See Herbert Gans, *The Levittowners* (New York: Pantheon, 1967).

21. Eunice Grier and George Grier, *Privately Developed Interracial Housing: An Analysis of Experience* (Berkeley: University of California Press, 1960).

22. Some conclusions of the Griers' study: "Jews are seldom evident in interracial developments to a degree greatly exceeding their proportion in the local population. . . . There is no indication that inclinations of whites to accept interracial housing increases with income and financial security. . . . White families with children do not necessarily shun interracial communities; the average number of children per white family in several interracial developments exceeds the national average. White families average more children than Negro families in developments for which data are available." *Ibid.,* pp. 24, 25.

23. Gans, *The Levittowners.*

THE HYDE PARK CASE

The example of successful racial integration which looms largest in the literature is that of Hyde Park in Chicago; any general explanation of racial change ought to be able to make sense of that major case in point. The success of integration in that area is often credited primarily (although not completely) to the attitudes of the local population and to the presence of an ideologically liberal community organization—the Hyde Park-Kenwood Community Conference.[24] An alternative interpretation is possible. The presence in Hyde Park of the University of Chicago generates a strong demand for housing by persons who are associated with that institution or who desire to live in a community characterized by the intellectual atmosphere of a prestigious university. Because persons falling within these categories in Chicago are generally white, the demand for Hyde Park housing among whites is higher than it would otherwise be. The original black in-migration into the area in the late 1940s, it is argued, was made possible not by the liberality of the white residents but by the extraordinary demand for housing within the black community created by the rapid growth of the city's black population during the wartime period and to a less than concomitant growth of the Chicago housing stock available to blacks.

This pressure, together with the increasing physical deterioration of the area owing to age and obsolescence, created an increasingly great disparity between the worth of Hyde Park housing to blacks and to whites. Finally, at some point this disparity became great enough to facilitate the transfer of housing (in that portion of the community adjoining black areas) from the white to the Negro market. As the black population continued to increase, white demand continued to decline and black demand continued to rise. Even so, the presence of the university generated a white demand greater than would otherwise have been present, thus preserving the whiteness—especially those parts of it closest to the university campus—for a longer period of time than would have otherwise

24. See, for example, Abrahamson, *A Neighborhood Finds Itself*; James V. Cunningham, *The Resurgent Neighborhood* (Notre Dame, Indiana: Fides Publishers, Inc., 1965); Marshall B. Clinard, *Slums and Community Development* (New York: The Free Press, 1966), pp. 316, 323; Leonard Broom and Philip Selznick, *Sociology,* fourth edition, pp. 459–461.

occurred. In the end, the community was "saved" by a clearance of much housing occupied by blacks and its replacement by subsidized upper-income housing, and by extraordinary efforts at building-code enforcement and police surveillance. Further, expansion of the univertsity and establishment of new institutions in the area also inflated white demand for proximate housing.

These measures were successful in that crime was reduced and amenities were created which made residence in the area *tenable* for whites who wished to live there *for reasons involving (primarily) the presence of the university*. The point is not that whites chose to live in Hyde Park because of amenities made possible by urban renewal; rather they wished to live in Hyde Park for other reasons, and the presence of amenities, the removal of honky-tonk "bowery" strips, and the lowering of crime rates made it *possible for their choice of Hyde Park to be acted upon*. Many blacks remained in the community after clearance was over and some blacks—those who could afford and cared for the newly built upper-income housing—moved in. These blacks then, together with the university white community, came to constitute an at least partially integrated area.[25]

Accompanying this success of "stable integration" was a rather sharp increase in land values and rents paid by whites.[26] This is often interpreted to be a *result* of integration's success. In terms of the present argument, however, the higher rents paid by whites are taken to be a *requisite* for successful integration. That is, in Hyde Park the transfer of increasing numbers of housing units from the white to the Negro market was stopped by a decrease in the disparity between the two markets—a decrease made possible, on the one hand, by an increasing supply of black housing in other Chicago

25. Many local observers in Hyde Park consider their community to be imperfectly integrated. The black population lives primarily in the northwestern quadrant of the community; the easternmost portions of the area remain overwhelmingly white. I call it an integrated community in the text because transition, once begun, has been halted and a large proportion (approximately 50 percent) of its population remains black. In addition, there are many blocks in the community (probably the entire central third) in which both blacks and whites have lived for several years.

26. This increase in Hyde Park land values was mentioned frequently by real estate dealers interviewed in Hyde Park as well as in other areas of Chicago. Documentation of rising land values is also contained in Jack Meltzer *et al.*, "Selected Aspects of Urban Renewal in Chicago: An Annotated Statistical Summary" (a report prepared for the Metropolitan Housing and Planning Council [Chicago] by the Center for Urban Studies, University of Chicago, August, 1965).

areas relative to the growth of the black population, and, on the other hand, by a growth in white demand made possible by an increase in the size of the university and the creation in the area of an environment in which middle-class whites, drawn there by the university, considered it possible to live.

In short, integration "works" in Hyde Park because *everyone pays black prices*. Integration may continue there even if housing is offered to blacks and whites in the community on an equal footing (as it often is not), because in this one area of Chicago, the two housing markets are close to being in equilibrium. It is thus mistaken to view good housing values to whites as a sign that long-term integration is possible (as was frequently done in South Shore and as is done in the professional literature.)[27] Depressed prices to whites are instead a symptom of the very mechanism which inhibits long-term integration.

THE DUAL MARKET IN SOUTH SHORE

An explanation of racial change in South Shore thus follows the same line of logic. Vacancies in South Shore were worth more to blacks than to whites because of different characteristics of the general supply-demand ratios within the Negro and white markets. Perhaps the lack of white demand reflected a reluctance on the part of whites to locate or relocate in a biracial area. But such factors, based on racial attitudes of mobile whites, are not *necessary* to explain transition; variations in demand due to differentials in population growth and available supplies of substantial housing alone suffice to explain the continuing growth of South Shore's black population.

A community can experience relatively rapid transition without there being any extraordinary tendency for resident whites to move —either within or out of their community. In the year 1960, at the beginning of the black influx into South Shore, 54.6 percent of community area residents were living in a household location dif-

27. Mayer, for example, considers the bargain prices which whites could pay for housing in the changing Russel Woods area of Detroit as a factor which could potentially create stability in that area. See: Albert J. Mayer, "Russel Woods: Change Without Conflict," in Nathan Glazer and Davis McEntire (eds.), *Studies in Housing and Minority Groups* (Berkeley: University of California Press, 1960), pp. 298–320.

ferent from the one they occupied in 1955 (almost the city-wide norm).[28] With such high rates of mobility, it is conceivable that the entire population of a typical community could replace itself through normal market mechanisms within a period of ten or fifteen years. It should not be surprising, therefore, that a complete racial transition over what would be a longer period of time could occur without there being any signs of flight or extraordinary mobility.

As in the case of Hyde Park, it is not likely that South Shore's pattern of racial change was due to its community organization. For all of its activity and ambition, the commission could not make either the speed or the pattern of black migration in South Shore substantially different from that of other changing areas. Even the slow rates of property turnover were likely not a result of commission effort. For if the commission had been responsible for the slow rate of property turnover, one would expect that fewer units on the Negro market would have resulted in fewer units becoming Negro-occupied. Effective intervention in mobility patterns should have resulted, perforce, in distinguishing South Shore's racial replacement rate. But it did not.

Therefore we can say that racial change patterns are determined by ecological forces beyond the local community. Variations in residential patterning are more parsimoniously explained in terms of those forces (and the dual market in which they become manifest) than in terms of the articulated racial ideologies of resident whites or the actions of organizations which attempt to intervene on their behalf.

It may well be that anti-Negro prejudice prompted some South Shore residents to move and to leave their community (who would not otherwise have done so) and that measures used in the present study were not sufficiently sensitive to tap such mobility. Despite the high mobility rates common to urban areas, there are some persons who tend to remain for all their lives in the same dwelling.[29] This minority might have been "forced" to move as various South Shore sub-areas became predominantly or completely black. But it

28. Evelyn M. Kitagawa and Karl Taeuber (eds.), *Local Community Factbook, Chicago Metropolitan Area, 1960* (Chicago Community Inventory, University of Chicago, 1963).
29. See: Florence E. Jay, "Those Who Stay: A Sociological Study of the Stability of a Community" (unpublished Ph.D. dissertation, Department of Sociology, University of Pittsburgh, 1956).

does seem that the existence of such individuals cannot be a significant determinant of a community's racial fate. *A large number of persons would have changed their residence no matter what racial conditions existed in South Shore* (and perhaps a similar number of movers would have relocated in other communities). The rates of racial change characteristic of South Shore may seem at first glance so high as to indicate that only a flight of white residents could make them possible. But when viewed in the context of the high mobility rate of the urban population in general, it becomes perfectly reasonable for such a racial change process to occur within the context of a market characterized by normal turnover. Normal mobility makes neighborhood racial change *possible;* when markets are structured in such manner that blacks continuously constitute the bulk of those who move into the resulting vacancies, racial change is *inevitable.*

9
Patterns of Black-White Interaction

ALTHOUGH South Shore was becoming virtually an all-black community, it is possible that during the transition period, geographical propinquity may have led to some degree of racial integration. Three forms of integration are possible during the transition process: *demographic* integration, whereby a given setting contains both blacks and whites in some specified proportions; *biracial interaction*, whereby non-antagonistic social interaction is occurring between blacks and whites to some specific extent; *transracial solidarity*, defined as conditions in which whites and blacks interact freely and without constraint, so that race ceases to function as an important source of social cleavage or as a criterion for friendship and primary group selection. This chapter describes the extent, form, and most common contexts of these kinds of integration in South Shore. With the data gathered, I will try to explain the more general processes which, in the context of black-white propinquity, inhibit or promote the cross-racial sharing of social life. Interpersonal racial integration was not a salient goal of the South Shore Commission, but it is possible that, under certain circumstances, it nevertheless came into being.

GENERAL STRATEGY

We have many descriptions of communities striving for integration, yet seldom does information on the subject of actual interracial contact go beyond the anecdotal level. Many community studies cheerfully recount instances when whites and blacks serve on the same committee or come together in a constructive joint

174

enterprise.[1] No precise information indicates the frequency of the contacts, the contexts in which they most often occur, or the dynamics of their development. The absence of such information inhibits the development of a sound theory of cross-racial interaction and, at a more practical level, precludes rigorous comparative analysis or evaluation of various forms of intervention which have integration as their goal.

In this study, counts were made of blacks and whites participating in given community settings. Although it is not a direct measure of all possible kinds of biracial interaction occurring in the area, much can be learned by an examination of racial patterns in various community public and quasi-public locales. Various loci of community activity in South Shore were investigated including schools, churches, recreational facilities, retail shops, and voluntary organizations. The basic technique was simply to take head-counts of blacks and whites participating in given organizations or observed in specific settings. In some instances I used reports of organizational chairmen and presidents; in others, I inspected organizational group photographs appearing in the community newspaper. In most instances, however, I was present to count the numbers of whites and blacks in the setting.

Although data gathered in this manner do not directly measure the degree of *neighboring* across racial lines, it is perhaps safe to assume that if people routinely neighbor across racial lines they also go to places such as stores, parks, and churches with one another and will appear at least occasionally in the same community settings. It is also assumed that if whites and blacks are participating together in the same community institutions, they will, as a minimum criterion, be present in the same settings at the same time.

ORDERED SEGMENTATION IN SOUTH SHORE

The inhibitions to integration in an area like South Shore cannot be properly understood by reliance upon such concepts as "prejudiced attitudes," "bigotry," or white "status anxiety," as these terms are ordinarily employed to explain interracial avoidance be-

1. See Philip A. Johnson, *Call Me Neighbor, Call Me Friend* (New York: Doubleday, 1965); William Biddle and Loureide Biddle, *The Community Development Process: The Rediscovery of Local Initiative* (New York: Holt, Rinehart and Winston, 1965).

havior. We can assume that what Suttles[2] refers to as "ordered segmentation" is natural to any community; the fact that South Shore blacks differed from South Shore whites in religion (few black Catholics, no Jews), ethnicity, economic status (blacks lower),[3] stage of life cycle (blacks younger with more children), and length of residency in the area would all act to deter biracial contact. That is, racial distinctions coincided with other common bases for social differentiation.

Urban settings have as their critical social characteristic the fact that intimate relationships between all parties are precluded by sheer vastness of the numbers of people.[4] Selection is thus necessary. In South Shore, as everywhere else in American society, people are "uptight" in the presence of persons who are unknown, unproven, and thus, to them, undependable. The genuine psychic (and occasionally, physical) risks which accompany encounters with strangers, lead local residents to develop certain techniques for "gaining associates, avoiding enemies and establishing each other's intentions."[5] These techniques evolve in the search for cues which bespeak similarity, or existence of some other form of personal tie (e.g., mutual friendship, blood relationship), which would imply dependability and trustworthiness. Where such cues are not forthcoming, mutual avoidance behavior (or outright hostility) results.

In South Shore not only do authentic social and demographic differences exist between the black and white populations, but there are also more subtle differences in virtually all black-white confrontations. A few examples may be cited. Whites and blacks in South Shore *sound* different; among whites, speech varies with length of residence in Chicago, family status background, and ethnicity. Blacks have an analogous internal pattern of speech differentiation—in addition to a common touch of Southern Negro

2. Gerald D. Suttles, *The Social Order of the Slum: Ethnicity and Territory in the Inner City* (University of Chicago Press, 1968).

3. Changes in South Shore's welfare case loads and crime rates add some evidence for this point (see Chapter Three). Although differences in net income between black and white family units is generally small (or nonexistent) in changing areas, the fact that black households are more likely to have multiple breadwinners and that black males are more likely to hold blue-collar jobs, constitute real status differences. See Karl Taeuber and Alma Taeuber, *Negroes in Cities* (Chicago: Aldine, 1965), p. 159 and Chapters 7 and 8.

4. See Louis Wirth, "Urbanism as a way of life," in Albert Reiss, Jr., ed., *Louis Wirth on Cities and Social Life* (University of Chicago Press, 1964), pp. 61–83.

5. Suttles, *The Social Order of the Slum*.

dialect, not quite absent even among many middle-class Chicago-born blacks. Young blacks *walk differently* from young whites; many, boys especially, use a swagger which sets them apart from their white schoolmates.[6] Without carrying out a complete inventory of black and white habits and folkways, we know these differences exist, and that, whether they speak of them or not, both blacks and whites in South Shore were sensitive to them.

PUBLIC PLACES AND PRIVATE BEHAVIOR

These distinctions, some obvious and some subtle, are more or less problematic for the persons involved, depending upon the public place in which whites and blacks happen to come together. Public places are defined, for this discussion, as settings in which no *explicit* criteria exist for the exclusion of any person or group. Yet public places vary in the degree to which they tend to actually exclude certain types of persons or social groups. Given the inhibitions to random intimacy which exist in urban settings, public places can be viewed as exclusive insofar as they serve as arenas for the kinds of informal, intimate, and uninhibited sorts of behaviors ordinarily associated with peer group activity. In contrast, public places are inclusive insofar as they act as settings in which formalized roles are routinely attended to by participants, who expect that others will also attend to the performance of prescribed activity and behavior. Thus, public places may be differentiated according to the degree to which they serve as arenas for public as opposed to more private behavior.

RETAIL STORES

An example of a relatively *public* place for *public* behavior is the local retail store. In South Shore they are rather formal; patrons arrive to purchase merchandise and then exit. Although various forms of informal activity occur, including chats between owners and customers, the usual undirected patter and diffuse banter evident in some lower-class business settings[7] tend to be absent.

6. *Ibid.* See also Harold Finestone, "Cats, kicks, and color," *Social Problems,* V (July 1957), 3–13.
7. Suttles, *The Social Order of the Slum.*

Yet despite the relatively formal nature of shopping in South Shore (relative both to shopping in other kinds of areas and to other South Shore public settings), it is indeed a social activity as well as a utilitarian one. Shopping is the social activity which most frequently takes adult residents out of their homes and into the community. An examination of racial compositions of shopping settings may, in addition to providing benchmark data on the status of demographic integration in this important social setting, also indicate something of the extent to which a significant opportunity context exists for the promotion of other kinds of integration.

South Shore has two major internal shopping strips (71st and 79th Streets) both of which run east-west traversing black, mixed, and white residential areas. The streets are shown in Figure 10

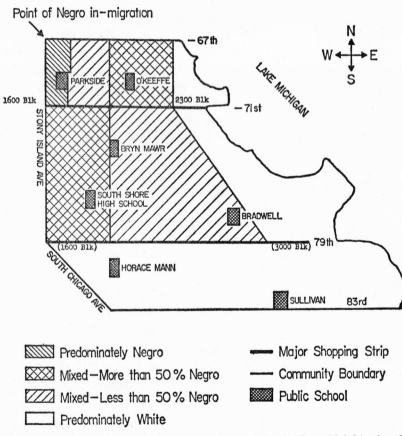

FIGURE 10: Approximate Racial Composition of South Shore Neighborhoods and Adjacent Shopping Strips

TABLE 21

RACIAL COMPOSITION OF SOUTH SHORE SHOPPING AREAS*

Street and Hundred Block[a]	Number of Black Patrons in Shops	Number of White Patrons in Shops	Total Both Races	Percent of All Patrons White
71st Street				
1600, 1700	35	6	41	15
1800, 1900	67	36	103	35
2000, 2100	74	142	216	66
2200, 2300	19	148	167	89
79th Street				
1600, 1700	49	3	52	6
1800, 1900	33	40	73	55
2000, 2100	2	29	31	94
2200, 2300	5	36	41	88
2400, 2500	0	41	41	100
2600, 2700	8	211	219	96
2800, 2900	5	92	97	95
3000	1	93	94	99

* Based on a single visit, daytime weekday count, April 1967.
[a] Each row represents two sides of two shopping blocks.

along with a portrayal of the approximate racial composition of the surrounding neighborhoods. I visited each of the shopping strips during business hours on shopping days, and made racial head-counts for all street-level retail establishments (including restaurants and taverns) on both streets.[8]

Racial retail shopping patterns were found generally to coincide with racial residential patterns. That is, individual stores and business blocks surrounded by predominantly black residents were patronized almost exclusively by blacks; those in white areas, by whites; those in mixed areas, by members of both races. Table 21 presents the results of head counts taken of shopping blocks; Table 22 presents results of the same operation in terms of composition of individual stores.

If a setting is arbitrarily considered to be demographically integrated if at least 10 percent of its population consists of members

8. For some establishments, such as beauty shops, there was no way to make a complete count unobtrusively; in such instances, only those patrons visible through plate glass windows were counted. Employees, detectable by uniforms, positions behind counters, or general demeanor, were excluded from the counts.

TABLE 22

RACIAL COMPOSITION OF INDIVIDUAL STORES ON TWO SHOPPING STRIPS, DAYTIME SOUTH SHORE*

Shopping Street	Number of White Stores[a]	Number of Persons in White Stores	Number of Black Stores[a]	Number of Persons in Black Stores	Number of Integrated Stores[a]	Number of Persons in Integrated Stores	Percent of All Stores Integrated	Percent of All Persons Integrated
71st Street	4	85	2	16	14	235	70	70
79th Street	12	212	2	21	4	67	22	22

* Consideration was given only to shops serving eight or more persons.
[a] Stores classified White or Black were those in which at least 90 percent of persons on the premises were of the same race. "Integrated" stores were those in which fewer than 90 percent of persons on the premises were of the same race.

of each race, then it can be said that the 71st Street area is integrated for its entire length and that 70 percent of its shops are integrated. However, 79th Street is generally segregated in its entire length with only 22 percent of its shops integrated. The congruence of this pattern with the nature of the surrounding residential areas indicates that the factor of distance outweighs other possible considerations (for example, the desire for psychically safe shopping territory) in determining shopping patterns.

Certain interesting exceptions to the pattern are provided by those establishments which by their nature or traditional neighborhood usage render personal services or which serve as settings for informal, more intimate interaction. All barber and beauty shops, regardless of location, were segregated. Establishments catering to recreational and social needs were often segregated; three of seven restaurants on otherwise integrated 71st Street were serving only whites, whereas all six supermarkets on the street were integrated. Perhaps consistent with its attraction for customers of a particular ethnicity and with its function as a social setting, the kosher butcher shop was the only food store not serving a biracial clientele.

SATURDAY NIGHT RACIAL PATTERNS

This tendency toward greater segregation of social and recreational settings is confirmed by analogous data collected on a Saturday night during the same time period. Americans typically reserve Saturday night as a social, festive occasion and almost all activities during those hours partake of a heightened air of sociability.[9] With many retail stores closed, but with bars and restaurants open and catering to large numbers of persons, both 71st and 79th Streets were more segregated at night than during the day.[10] Table 23 presents the results of a head-count made of business establishments open on a Saturday night.

The integrated types of settings on Saturday night included

9. For persons excluded from social activity on Saturday night, these hours are, as the lyrics of the popular song imply, "the loneliest night of the week."

10. For example, the 71st Street daytime count included only one segregated bar whereas the night count included six segregated bars. Because many retail shops are closed at night, the prevalence of open bars has the consequence of dramatically increasing the *proportion* of segregated establishments and the absolute number of segregated establishments.

TABLE 23

RACIAL COMPOSITION OF SOUTH SHORE SHOPPING AREAS, SATURDAY NIGHT*

Shopping Street	Number of White Stores[a]	Number of Persons in White Stores	Number of Black Stores[a]	Number of Persons in Black Stores	Number of Integrated Stores[a]	Number of Persons in Integrated Stores	Percent of All Stores Integrated	Percent of All Persons Integrated
71st Street	4	120	10	300	10	141	42	34
79th Street	14	359	7	272	2	19	9	3

* Consideration was given only to establishments observed to be serving eight or more persons.
[a] Stores classified as White or Black were those in which at least 90 percent of persons on the premises were of the same race. Integrated stores were those in which fewer than 90 percent of persons on the premises were of the same race.

motion picture theaters (a leisure setting, ordinarily with minimal interaction), several restaurants, and those grocery stores and super-markets keeping late hours. Yet even in the case of restaurants and groceries, there was a tendency toward increased segregation on Saturday night, as compared to weekdays. South Shore's two bowling alleys, integrated by day, become all-black at night.

The tendency toward Saturday night segregation (including a significant increase in the numbers of blacks over whites on the streets) may be explained in various ways. It may be due to a white fear of being in a black setting at night when "crime in the streets" is a more salient concern. Or whites may simply be ex-periencing different forms of recreation than blacks—forms which are only available outside of South Shore (as in the Loop area). The increased segregation of non-recreation settings may simply re-flect that these are the hours in which black housewives, more likely to be working during the day, are shopping for household goods. Such factors notwithstanding, the fact that South Shore's business district is integrated by day but segregated (and heavily black) at night, is consistent with the observation that intimate contexts tend to inhibit integration. It is reasonable to find that during the hours reserved for intimacy, segregation increases.

Special scrutiny of one sort of segregated leisure setting, the neighborhood tavern, can provide some insight into explaining the metamorphosis of places from white to black status. There was al-most total racial segregation in taverns with, in certain places, *alter-nating* black and white establishments along a given block.[11] Tavern owners can themselves influence racial patterns by, in the words of one bartender-owner, "give them (blacks) the big hello." But the several tavern owners who were interviewed felt that although the owner can influence the racial process, he cannot determine it. A bar "just becomes colored" as blacks patronize it with increasing frequency. For white tavern patrons, it is a matter of "the colored took the place over" or "the colored forced everybody out." These phrases were used again and again to explain "what happened" to a particular establishment which once was frequented by whites but eventually became a black setting.

11. Except for one bar I observed that had one black patron and nine white patrons, all twenty-one South Shore taverns were completely segregated on Saturday night.

To make sense of this "explanation" of tavern change, it must be noted that of all public settings in South Shore, probably none was more private than the neighborhood tavern. Although the tavern is officially open to the public, it is in fact (at least in South Shore) an intimate setting frequented by a small and stable group of regulars who use the establishment as a focal point of their social lives.[12] For the few middle-class taverns in South Shore (which also were segregated) this characterization is likely less accurate than for working-class establishments. But even here, the tavern is a place where people let their hair down, where backstage and on-stage behavioral routines[13] tend to merge and thus where increased social vulnerability makes for anxiety in the presence of persons who fail to give satisfactory signals of trustworthiness and forgiving acceptance of what may be transgressions of various normative codes. Thus blacks, who share mannerisms, clothing tastes, musical preferences and other tavern-specific behavior habits at variance with white cultural counterparts are outsiders in the white environment. Their very presence serves to inhibit the kind of interactions for which the tavern is sought out by neighborhood whites; they can thus "take over" an establishment by simply being in it.[14]

OUTDOOR RECREATION

Parks are a day-time setting in which informal social activity is routine.[15] Sports activities, especially for unathletic adults, carry potential for awkward displays of poor coordination, falls, and other evidence of incompetence and indignity. For some, parks are places where psychic vulnerability runs high.

A head-count was made at South Shore's largest park (Rainbow

12. Gans (1962) has confirmed that this is also the pattern for Italian-American working-class males.

13. See Erving Goffman, *The Presentation of Self in Everyday Life* (New York: Doubleday, 1959).

14. The same pheonomenon can be observed in the case of houseguests' "taking over" a home by simply being in it for a period longer than that desired by the hosts. Guests, who often cannot "understand" if confronted with such an accusation, can avoid the problem by either "becoming just like a member of the family" (that is, host accepts guest as an intimate) or by devising schemes whereby extensive absences from the scene can be gracefully arranged.

15. The situation is not strictly comparable to taverns, for the relative expansiveness of space may permit a greater degree of insularity to an intimate gathering.

Beach), which provides facilities available nowhere else in South Shore—for example, tennis, beach bathing, formal gardens, and field houses. On a sunny Sunday in May 1967, only two of the several thousand persons at the park were black, and these were small children in the company of white adults. Rainbow Beach Park, in 1962, was the scene of a nonviolent civil rights "wade-in," protesting the racial segregation of some of the city's beaches (including Rainbow). Ironically, this much publicized event and the accompanying acrimonious remarks by whites may have served to dramatize Rainbow Beach's *de facto* status as a white public place, thus deterring blacks from risking the cost of a subsequent spontaneous visit. That Rainbow Beach was also a place where individuals routinely appear in abbreviated costume (bathing suits, tennis clothes, etc.), and thus routinely expose body areas ordinarily considered private, would act to increase anxieties stemming from interpersonal vulnerability.

Yet the special circumstances of Rainbow Beach were not significant because almost all of South Shore's parks were racially segregated—including those inside the community area and without any known history of incidents. I inspected seven smaller parks and playlots on the same warm Sunday; almost all were catering exclusively to small children with a few parents supervising. The only park catering to adult passive recreation (located on South Shore Drive at 68th Street) was occupied by thirteen white adults and three white children, all of whom sat on benches, and one black child who sat with his dog on the grass at an opposite end of the small greensward.

South Shore's six remaining parks were all scenes of active recreation. In those parks located in segregated areas (either all black or all white), participation was limited to persons of the same race as the surrounding area. At a soccer field at Phillips and 82nd, all game participants and spectators (approximately 200) were white; only black children were present at two playlots (one at Parkside School, 69th at East End, and one at O'Keeffe School, 69th at Merrill) in predominately (although not exclusively) black areas.

One park in a racially mixed residential area (69th at Oglesby) served only black children. The playlot at Bryn Mawr School (74th at Chappel), also in a biracial residential area, was used by approximately fifty black children and forty white children. One ball game was in progress; all players were white. Of the various play-groups, only one—a dyad—was racially mixed, although the two playlots were serving equal numbers of white and black children.

Rosenblum Park, at 76th Street and Bennett, stands contiguous to both black and white residential areas. Seven ball games were in simultaneous progress while I observed, all being played by ado-lescent boys. Four games were all-black; two were all white; one was racially mixed. The two tot lots in the park are situated in diagonally opposite corners of the recreation area, with clear visibility from one to the other. The tot lot in the northwest corner was used by approximately thirty-five black children, one white child, and seven supervising black adult women. The tot lot in the southwest corner of the park showed an opposite racial pattern; it was being utilized by twenty white children, one black child and four white supervisors. It it noteworthy that two such playlots in the same park situated at a distance of no more than 200 feet from one another should be almost completely racially segregated.

The lack of evidence of demographic integration leads to the suspicion that South Shore residents, when taking outdoor recrea-tion as well as public indoor recreation, do not lead integrated social lives. Members of different races do not accompany one another to parks and do not mingle once they arrive in parks. For children, some limited cross-racial contact seems to occur; for adults, there seems to be none whatsoever.

SCHOOLS

Schools in a community are a crucial determinant of the social lives of children; they provide settings for intimate inter-action and their attendance boundaries tend to circumscribe a child's opportunities for friendship formation.[16] For some parents, schools are also a social setting (for example, PTA, volunteer work), but because of parents' more numerous alternative sources of social interaction, and because of the relative small propor-tion of their time spent in school contexts, the school is of much less social significance.

The racial composition of South Shore's public schools from 1963

16. Marion Roper, "The City and the Primary Group" (unpublished Ph.D. dissertation, University of Chicago, 1934).

TABLE 24

RACIAL COMPOSITION OF SOUTH SHORE PUBLIC SCHOOLS

1963, 1964, 1965, 1966

School	Proportion of Student Body Black			
	1963	1964	1965	1966
Parkside	90.3	96.6	97.8	99.1
O'Keeffe	39.8	67.3	85.4	93.9
Bryn Mawr	16.3	37.2	55.2	66.1
Mann	7.0	26.6	43.0	55.1
Bradwell	0.1	0.2	0.7	3.7
Sullivan	0.0	0.0	0.0	2.3
South Shore High[a]	1.5	7.0	24.8	41.8

SOURCES: 1963 data, *Chicago Sun-Times*, October 24, 1963; 1964, 1965 data, *Southeast Economist* (Chicago), October 17, 1965; 1966 data, *Southeast Economist* (Chicago), October 23, 1966.

[a] High school boundary zone was modified between 1964 and 1965 with the inclusion of Parkside and O'Keeffe and the exclusion of a larger all-black elementary school as "feeder" schools in the fall of 1965. The net effect of this change on the high school's racial composition was negligible.

through 1966 is presented in Table 24. In 1966, two of the community's six elementary schools were demographically integrated (using the 10 percent convention). The South Shore High School and one of the three Catholic schools also were demographically integrated.[17]

PTA meetings held in 1966 at the three integrated public schools (Mann, Bryn Mawr, and the high school) were attended by members of both races and so were PTA meetings at the predominantly black O'Keeffe school which drew an approximately equal number of whites and blacks to its meetings, although its student body was 74 percent black. In general, whites participated most in South Shore's school affairs, including in its biracial schools. In all schools in which any appreciable number of white children were enrolled, whites dominated the adult organizations. All newly elected officers of the high school PTA were white despite the fact that over 42 percent of the school's student body was black at the time of the 1967 PTA Spring elections. In other biracial schools, as in almost all of South Shore's biracial settings, blacks were always underrepresented in top leadership positions.

17. No intensive observations were made of student life within schools.

RELIGIOUS INSTITUTIONS

South Shore's religious organizations provide settings which are a mix of formality and informality. During worship services individuals find themselves in a situation where every move of every participant, including gestures and signs of affect, is determined either by explicit ritual, tradition, or local habit. In other church activities, such as funerals, weddings, bowling games, and club meetings, social interaction is more spontaneous, intense, and intimate.

It is thus not surprising to find that whatever integration existed in church organizations existed primarily in terms of worship activity and not in terms of church parareligious social life. Four of South Shore's sixteen Protestant churches hold integrated (again, by the 10 percent criterion) church services; one had an integrated *membership* list. Table 25 presents a detailed summary of the racial composition of South Shore's churches and church-related schools.[18]

Church life, outside of worship services, was virtually completely segregated and completely white. Two church membership screening committees had a black member (to help find the "good element," according to the white chairman); several churches had black Sunday school teachers and one church had two black women helping to establish a youth program. These active blacks (as was true of most black church members in South Shore), were all women.

Another important variation in church racial patterns, one strikingly revealed in Table 25, was the difference in the degree to which black children, compared to black adults, were being served by South Shore churches. Eight church Sunday schools were at least 10 percent black; in one case a church with only 10 percent black membership had a Sunday school which was 98 percent black. Fully 48 percent of Protestant Sunday school attenders were black; 11 percent of those enrolled in Catholic day schools were black.

18. Interviews with local clergy were carried out during the summer of 1965 and spring of 1966. I personally interviewed twelve clergymen; additional interview material was provided by E. Maynard Moore, III, who based part of his interview schedule on mine, thus generating a total of twenty-three comparable cases. Respondents interviewed by both investigators generally gave identical responses to the two researchers. (See Moore, 1966.)

TABLE 25

RACIAL COMPOSITION OF SOUTH SHORE'S CHRISTIAN CHURCHES AND CHURCH-RELATED SCHOOLS

Denomination of Church	Number of Church Members	Number of Blacks in Member-ship	Percent of Membership Black	Number Sunday Attenders	Number Black Sunday Attenders	Percent Sunday Attenders Black	Number Enrolled in Sunday School	Number of Blacks in Sunday School	Percent of Sunday School Black
Protestant									
Community	1,775	14	0.8	625	27	4.3	350	160	45.0
Episcopal	450	30	6.6	250	25	10.0	87	20	23.0
Lutheran	305	25	8.0	113	10	8.8	45	25	55.0
Methodist	650	25	3.8	200	30	15.0	390	250	64.0
Methodist	210	21	10.0	90	9	10.0	159	157	99.0
Christian Science	250	1	0.4	250	7	2.8	160	12	7.5
Bible Church	75	5	6.6	65	35	53.0	150	100	66.0
Sub-Totals	3,715	121	3.3	1,593	143	8.9	1,360	724	53.0
Nine Other Protestant Churches	2,285	0	0	994	0	0	140	0	0
Protestant Totals	6,000	121	2.0	2,587	143	5.5	1,500	724	48.0
Catholic[a]									
(1) Catholic	1,200[b]	70[b]	5.0	4,000	100	2.5	485	110	23.0
(2) Catholic	1,900[b]	1[b]	0.5	3,000	0	0	200	10	5.0
(3) Catholic	2,700[b]	325[b]	12.0	9,000	477	53.0	732	40	5.5
Catholic Totals	5,800[b]	396[b]	6.8	16,000	577	3.6	1,417	160	11.0

[a] Catholic school data refer to day school enrollments, not Sunday school. Except for Church No. 3, attendance data based on actual head counts on a Sunday, Spring 1966.

[b] Refers to number of families rather than individuals.

Other sources: Reports of clergymen to the writer and to E. Maynard Moore, III. See Maynard Moore, III, "The Church and Racial Change in South Shore" (unpublished paper, The Divinity School, University of Chicago, 1966).

The contrast between adult and child integration in church settings is again suggestive of the significance of interpersonal vulnerability as a determinant of racial patterns. Parents of both races were willing to place their children in racially mixed settings because such settings provided no psychic difficulties for *them* (the parents). Children, perhaps having different criteria for mutual identification and for establishing boundaries of community (such as sex, age, territory, athletic standing), were possibly less likely to find the settings painful, although the segregation patterns at play, as well as evidence presented by Suttles,[19] would suggest otherwise. In any event, children are not as free as their parents to pick and choose their social settings, regardless of the inconvenience or personal discomfort they might experience.

This lack of widespread adult black participation in South Shore church life may simply be due to black inhibitions, to black preferences for the ecclesiastical style of all-black congregations, or perhaps to black hostility toward whites. But in some cases, it is clear that blacks were deliberately excluded from South Shore church activities. In one instance, revealed with dismay by the pastor of the church (and confirmed subsequently in an interview with the victim), a black woman was invited by the pastor's wife to join an all-white church bowling team. The other bowlers' subsequent demand that the black woman be excluded from the team was resisted by the clergyman. The issue was resolved by the bowlers who, rather than accept the black as a team member, severed formal ties between the church and the bowling league. The church was in a biracial residential area and the exclusionist bowlers had been praying in an integrated sanctuary for many months before the incident occurred.

Perhaps because of such events, one South Shore black woman was prompted to remark: "The church people here feel like the churches belong to them and we are coming to take it away from them. That's just how they feel. . . . They tolerate us, because it's their Christian duty to tolerate us, but not to love us or have us join in their fellowship." Another black woman, when asked what churches in the community could be doing to help the situation, remarked: "They could invite all the members to take part in the various church organizations. As it is, the women's groups meet in

19. Suttles, *The Social Order of the Slum*, Chapters 9, 10.

people's homes so that they can refuse you, and they have said that they will refuse you. Mrs. X asked me to come to one, but another lady told me that we weren't welcome."

Both of the women quoted were members of the church where the bowling incident occurred. The church minister was outspokenly liberal in his racial views, active in the community, and committed to an "open church." His was one of the first South Shore churches to take in a black member. He told me: "Generally we try to use the church as a setting for new forms of social interaction. When the whites meet the Negroes within the church, they see what fine people they are and their fears are allayed. I think this adds to the stability of the area; the people say 'Well, if the people moving into South Shore are like these people, I see no reason to move.' I think that is the effect we are having." Yet in light of the exclusionist practices of the church's social institutions and the black responses to them, as quoted above, it would seem that the effects upon whites have been less than dramatic, and that the embittered feelings of exclusion among blacks may be among the significant results of the "new forms of social interaction."

Pastoral Role Conflict

In order to understand the general racial patterns among South Shore's churches, one must consider the strain which neighborhood change places upon the clergyman's role. The pastor is under pressure from his flock to exclude blacks—if not from Sunday morning pews, at least from church social activities. If the clergyman defies his congregation, he risks an institutional setback like the one experienced by the pastor whose church lost its bowling league —a major social activity. Most clergymen reported that at least a few of the members had threatened to withdraw from the church if a black was ever admitted to worship—although significantly, all clergyment were surprised to learn that no resignations were ever forthcoming even in those instances in which a large number of blacks became church members. Even so, such threats were taken seriously by many clergymen.

On the other hand, only increased black participation could prevent the loss of a self-supporting church for the denomination. One South Shore minister analyzed the situation this way:

In the past the church has generally handled racial change in an unintelligent manner: total exclusion of Negroes. This meant that

Negroes entered the area but not the church; the opportunity of the church to render service to these newcomers was lost; the opportunity to render stability to their lives and to the community was lost. . . . Finally, the church was left with ten or twenty white members and could no longer maintain itself financially. So it would have to be turned into a mission and draw upon funds from the hierarchy for maintenance. The policy here, however, is to avoid this mistake. This is not a new policy; I like to think of it rather as the continuation of the old policy: the ready acceptance of newcomers. We do this from the standpoint of financial need and also of Christian morality.

It was characteristic of South Shore Christian clergymen to perceive the moral and financial imperatives of integrating blacks into the church. Some clergy stated that they thought there were not going to be enough denominational blacks to go around and that only those churches which aggressively proselytized among the newcomers were going to survive. Still, most clergymen were reluctant to push their people too far.

A common method of handling this conflicting set of expecta-tions—one from the white flock to whom one is responsible, the other from one's professional and institutional duty—was to com-promise. Blacks were not sought, but when they appeared at the church door they were welcomed. Lay members could be con-fronted with explicit policies handed down by denomination au-thorities and with the clear-cut moral imperative that, at least, for purposes of praying, blacks should not be excluded from white environments. But the clergy left the church's social institutions in the hands of laymen to manage on an exclusionist basis—though in their Sunday sermons included references to "brotherly love" and appropriate quotes from the Bible in the hope that communicants would "make the connection."

Meanwhile, the clergy hoped that as whites left the community, blacks could be assimilated fast enough (although *only* fast enough) to keep operations solvent. Many South Shore ministers, judged from the rather sturdy financial condition of their churches,[20] seemed to be accomplishing their goal. And while following that policy, they could view their black members as evidence that theirs was an in-tegrated church in which blacks had been accepted. The dictates of an urban ministry were being obeyed; new forms of social interac-

20. See E. Maynard Moore, III, "The Church and Racial Change in South Shore" (unpublished paper, The Divinity School, University of Chicago, 1966).

tion and fellowship were being created. The actual results were sanctuaries which were biracial on Sunday mornings but located in churches which, as institutions, remained largely segregated. This "compromise" rested on the formality and unstrained behavior characteristic of the church service (which included blacks), in contrast to the more informal and intimate nature of church "social life" (from which blacks were excluded).

An Exception: The Baptist Church

A fundamentalist Baptist church, located in a predominantly black area, stood apart from all other religious institutions in South Shore in that equal numbers of whites and blacks attended services; it was, in other respects as well, the most completely integrated of all South Shore religious institutions.[21] It was also distinct in that worship services were a more basic part of the life of the church than in other denominations. Worship was a time of spontaneity and much animated social interaction. Members were working class and lower-middle class; it was among the poorer churches in South Shore—both in terms of its worshippers' income and its annual institutional budget. Among South Shore clergy, its minister was least familiar with the liberal conventional wisdom concerning the role of the urban ministry and the "crisis in the city"—utterances which permeated interview responses from most other area clergy. This fundamentalist minister was the only South Shore clergyman to ever indicate a past history of "prejudice" toward blacks.

That such conditions gave rise to the only case of trans-racial solidarity in a church context is perhaps surprising; for this reason I will later discuss the Baptist church and several other such "deviant" cases. For the moment, it should be noted that the conditions of spontaneity and intimacy characteristic of fundamentalist religion could lead *only* to one of two states: either complete racial exclusion *or* complete racial integration with concomitant total acceptance. If blacks were to be present at all, their presence would have to be unreservedly accepted; otherwise, the resultant inhibitions would have destroyed the nature of the religious experience and thus the very reason for the coming together.

---

21. The divergence in this church between the number of black *attenders* and number of black *members* (as indicated by data in Table 25) was due to the fact that a personal revelation was a requisite for formal membership; many blacks were in the situation of having formal induction pending such a revelation.

VOLUNTARY ASSOCIATIONS

The many national charity and service organizations (such as Lions, American Legion, Veterans of Foreign Wars, B'nai B'rith) serving South Shore, were all exclusively white.[22] None of the more than fifty organizational group photographs of South Shore residents published in the *Southeast Economist*[23] included blacks. The South Shore Country Club, the boards and officer corps of two local hospitals and of the Chamber of Commerce were also without black participants.

There was in South Shore a pervading theme in the manner in which residents discussed the possible "integration" of their local institutions: a tendency to demarcate certain institutions in the community as "white" and others (few in number), as "Negro," "nigger," or "colored." White South Shore residents spoke of "our church," and "our neighborhood." The major characteristic of the collectivity being spoken of was that members were similar to the speaker—and in South Shore that meant (among other things) that members were white. In the face of the rather ambiguous legal ownership status of most churches, clubs, and associations, long-term community residents truly regarded the institutions as their *own;* institutions which their funds and efforts had created and maintained, and which were seen to exist for the perpetual use of themselves and persons like themselves. It is likely that many blacks moving into the community shared this perspective—at least to some degree—and except for a few militants or pioneers, they believed white South Shore institutions "belonged" to other kinds of people. Several blacks interviewed seemed surprised and awed (and somewhat uncomfortable) by the fact that they were actually being welcomed into some white institutions. Only slowly and often with a good deal of organizational in-fighting, soul-searching, and,

22. I was informed that a tutoring center at the South Shore YMCA was racially integrated. Pressures of time did not permit a first-hand investigation of its program.

23. The *Southeast Economist* serves South Shore as well as a much larger region of the South Side as a community newspaper. An organization was considered to be located in South Shore if at least half of all addresses of those photographed were within the study area.

for blacks, a summoning of confidence, was such a perspective being slightly modified.

The South Shore Commission

The most prominent exception to the general pattern of black exclusion (or omission) from the ranks of important community groups was the South Shore Commission, which at least after 1964 was biracial in its leadership and membership. Although blacks remained greatly underrepresented in commission leadership positions during the study period, several on the board of directors and one of six officers were black. Many commission sub-groups were also biracial, including several committees and various block club organizations. But it is safe to say, because only a small proportion of South Shore's residents involved themselves in any block club or other commission activity, that its effectiveness in creating biracial contacts was probably limited to a small leadership group in the community.

From its very inception, the commission was not an informal social organization; as an association of Protestants, Catholics, and Jews, it had from the beginning brought together persons who were less than completely at ease in each other's presence. As blacks were brought into membership it continued to function primarily as an instrumental organization, not as a setting for intimate socializing. The commission provided a series of public meetings, outings, and fund-raising entertainments wherein public behavior was the accepted norm.

In the context of commission activity, as in the case of other biracial voluntary organizations in South Shore, cross-racial interaction was more formal and guarded than were interactions (also quite formal) between members of the same race. Because of the uniqueness of biracial interaction in American society, blacks and whites were in the difficult situation of having to create *de novo* a formal mode for social interaction, given the obvious and subtle differences between blacks and whites and the lack of mutual knowledge of what the other party might consider appropriate talking behavior. Thus there was a need to avoid the unknown transgressions which might occur if spontaneous behavior were to run its course. It was accomplished by both blacks and whites resorting to a zealous interpersonal courtesy (to ward off any conceivable slight or "misunderstanding"), unrelenting pleasantness, and a well-understood, tacit, mutual agreement to limit the subject of all conversation to small talk. Behavior was carefully guarded; words and expressions were selected with extraordinary care.

For blacks, the heightened self-consciousness generally resulted in deferential postures toward their white colleagues, and an ongoing monitoring of behavior to avoid any possible controversy which might set them in opposition to policies favored by any significant number of whites. I recall several substantive examples: The commission was known by black members to be cooperating through its tenant referral service with landlords who refused to rent housing to non-whites. The actions entailed in such cooperation were probably illegal under the Chicago Fair Housing Ordinance and were a source of distress to black commission members. Yet they preferred, in the words of one, not to "make a fuss" against a policy which they indicated (to me) that they found obnoxious. Similarly, black commission members assented to quota systems for maintaining whites in buildings and blocks which otherwise would have become predominantly black. Again, there was public acquiescence in spite of privately held feelings that such policies were improper and also in violation of the housing ordinance.

When blacks volunteered to speak, as at commission board meetings, their comments were sometimes irrelevant to the topics under discussion and not presented in a manner under which action could easily be taken. Rather than make motions, blacks tentatively *expressed* themselves—resulting in statements which, when not acted upon by others, simply died—even when a majority in the room seemed in sympathy with the point being made. In committee work, blacks were not, in local parlance, "take charge people." Black participants in South Shore activities seemed to be self-conscious to the point where forthright expression of opinion and resultant effective action was inhibited.

That this effect of biracial interaction was most pronounced in the case of blacks, and not whites, is perhaps explicable (at least in part) in terms of another important feature of biracial interaction in South Shore: blacks and whites seldom come together as equals. This fact adds an additional dimension to the vulnerability of the alien persons who were not only in a numerical minority but, because of status differences, were especially vulnerable to the sanctions of those who possessed so disproportionate an amount of wealth, power, and expertise.

These status differences were pervasive. In general, blacks moving into South Shore were of lower socioeconomic status than the whites they replaced.[24] The same status differentiation was reflected within organizational contexts such as the commission. White males of the commission's governing board were almost all proprietors, lawyers, physicians, and stock brokers, and black members were generally salesmen, schoolteachers, and low-level supervisors.

Unlike white leaders, blacks did not find their way to the board because of their personal wealth, power, or expertise, but instead because of their race and an acceptance of commission goals. Blacks were originally "brought in" the commission for fear that without some black "representation" on the board of directors, the organization could be accused of being segregationist and thus lose black constituents to the Woodlawn Organization on the north. After one black became active in the commission, other blacks were recruited into the organization—in a way described in an interview with a white commission leader who shared responsibility for nominating new board members:

There has been a great need to get Negro leaders involved in the commission; that's extremely important. We need to get Negroes and whites who will work together without resorting to special, selfish interests. We need strong Negro leadership in the area and it's best if we can do it through the commission.

We asked Mr. X [the first black to be active in the commission] to recommend some Negroes for us for the board. He came up with four and we said how about six. So six it was; hell, we took them all.

Thus, as is evidenced by the means by which they came into the organization, commission blacks were largely interchangeable with any number of other blacks, with the consequence that their status vis-à-vis their white colleagues could only suffer. Several black members were viewed approvingly by whites as "real work horses" who make a "fine contribution," but none had the contacts with the political, religious, and business leaders of Chicago which were seen to be the really important determinants of South Shore's future. A good work horse may be hard to find, but a member of the Chicago

24. See note 3.

School Board or the editor of a Chicago daily newspaper is impossible to replace. Such differences in the degree to which people are important to an organization's goals do not bode well for parity in interpersonal relationships.

The case of biracial interaction in the Commission would seem to provide an explanation for the findings generated by tests of the contact hypothesis. A large body of literature suggests that more favorable white attitudes toward blacks result from biracial interaction in which whites and blacks share the same status, are in mutually dependent roles, and where contact is intimate rather than superficial.[25] These are the conditions in which social vulnerability to alien and unknown individuals is minimized for members of both races. Where the conditions are not present, the contact hypothesis suggests that biracial interaction is expected to yield either no effects or an increased amount of "negative" white evaluation of blacks.

Indeed, the latter results were the consequences in such groups as the commission. For whites, participation with blacks led to the observation that they (blacks) "aren't real leaders." The middle-class analogue of the lazy colored boy remained the dominant white stereotype. For blacks, interaction in such settings would seem to debilitate energies as whites come to be seen as the real makers of decisions and holders of power.[26] The really crucial organizational

25. Various studies have yielded somewhat conflicting evidence on the validity of the contact hypothesis. Three classic studies which indicate a positive relationship between "improvement" in white attitudes toward blacks with increasing contact are Morton Deutsch and Mary Collins, *Interracial Housing: A Psychological Evaluation of a Social Experiment* (Minneapolis: University of Minnesota Press, 1951); Shirley Star, Robin M. Williams, Jr., and Samuel A. Stouffer, "Negro Soldiers," in Samuel Stouffer *et al., The American Soldier: Adjustment During Army Life,* Vol. I (Princeton University Press, 1949); and Robert K. Merton *et al.,* "Social facts and social fictions: the dynamics of race relations in Milltown" (New York: Columbia University Bureau of Applied Social Research, 1949). Three reports providing evidence for the opposite conclusion are Gordon Allport and Bernard Kramer, "Some roots of prejudice," *Journal of Psychology,* XXI (Fall, 1946), 9–39; Bernard M. Kramer "Residential Contact as a Determinant of Attitudes Toward Negroes" (unpublished Ph.d dissertation, Harvard University, 1950); and Alvin Winder, "White Attitudes Towards Negro-White Interaction in an Area of Changing Racial Composition" (unpublished Ph.D dissertation, Committee on Human Development, University of Chicago, 1952). A synthesis of these mixed findings, consistent with the criteria for effective positive attitude change as specified in the above text, appears in Daniel Wilner, Rosabelle Walkley and Stuart Cook, *Human Relations in Interracial Housing: A Study of the Contact Hypothesis* (Minneapolis: University of Minnesota Press, 1955).

26. Francis Fox Piven and Richard Cloward, "The case against racial integration," *Social Work,* XII (January, 1967), 12–21.

skills which blacks observed were those involving the use of contacts (such as friends in high places) and resources (such as personal fortunes) which they neither possessed nor stood a good chance of ever possessing.

"Marginal Groups": Instances of Transracial Solidarity

In addition to the Baptist church, there were three other contexts in South Shore in which transracial solidarity seemed to exist. These were marginal organizations—marginal in that meetings were held only on an irregular basis and in that they were organizations founded on premises of dissent and protest which limited their appeal to only a small number of participants. One such group was a local branch of Veterans for Peace in Vietnam, an organization with leftist political orientations (including several persons of Marxist ideology) which held occasional meetings above a South Shore store during the study period. Another group was the O'Keeffe Area Council—technically a part of the South Shore Commission but with an active leadership which, because of its rather "pro-Negro," "anti-establishment" orientation, was often independent of the commission in spirit and in action.

Finally, there was the South Shore Organization for Human Rights, a group active in fostering open occupancy and other civil rights goals in South Shore and metropolitan Chicago. This group was indigenous to South Shore, having been stimulated by a young clergyman during his rather brief association with a South Shore Protestant church. Like Veterans for Peace and the O'Keeffe Area Council, its active membership consisted of only a handful of persons; it carried out independent programs such as "testing" the racial practices of local real estate firms and the commision's Tenant Referral Service.

These three organizations differed from other South Shore institutions not only in terms of their marginality, but also in terms of the "tone" of biracial interactions shared by members. In all of these contexts, as in the case of the Baptist church, interaction across racial lines seemed to come easily; interaction was unstilted, informal and direct. Except possibly for the Veterans for Peace, these were all informal social organizations, with blacks and whites living out shared social as well as shared institutional lives. Race largely disappeared as a source of cleavage or a determinant of institutional roles.

In other respects, these groups were quite diverse. The Baptist church was largely working class with many recent migrants from the South and Appalachia. The O'Keeffe Council consisted of young well-educated professionals; to a lesser extent, the same was true of the Organization for Human Rights. Veterans for Peace was an extremely diverse group of blue-collar workers, small businessmen, and a few professionals. Parishioners of the Baptist church were apolitical, religious fundamentalists; members of the other groups were identified with secular, left-leaning ideologies.[27]

Within each of these groups, race and status differences were not obviously correlated; businessmen or professionals within each were as likely to be black as white. In addition, these groups were alike in that each was in an alien environment. The church was surrounded by more stolid, richer congregations; Veterans for Peace, the Organization for Human Rights, and the O'Keeffe Council existed in the shadow of the powerful South Shore Commission and other "moderate" or conservative institutions which supported Chicago's and the nation's existing political arrangements. The various deviant traits of these groups' members thus created a situation in which organizational alternatives within the South Shore area were lacking. The result may have been an organizational commitment of sufficient strength to overcome any inhibitions which racial differences might have created. Finally, members of these groups

27. These findings are consistent with other studies which have uncovered the extremely diverse conditions under which racial integration occurs and the seeming irrelevance of "prejudice" or racial "attitude" in determining when and where integration exists. George Grier and Eunice Grier, *Privately Developed Interracial Housing: An Analysis of Experience* (Berkeley: University of California Press, 1960), found integrated housing developments to be heterogeneous in terms of the income, education, ethnicity, stage of life cycle, and geographical origin of residents. Supporting findings are also reported in Chester Rapkin and William Grigsby, *The Demand for Housing in Racially Mixed Areas* (Berkeley: University of California Press, 1960), and Albert Mayer, "Russel Woods: change without conflict, a case study of neighborhood racial change in Detroit" in Nathan Glazer and Davis McEntire, eds., *Studies in Housing and Minority Groups* (Berkeley: University of California Press, 1960).

Membership status of the Baptist church was relatively homogeneous. Veterans for Peace was led by a well-to-do black funeral director and several of his black business colleagues, whereas whites included in their ranks (along with a few professionals) a TV repairman and a sign painter. The O'Keeffe Council included in its top leadership cadre a black businessman and a black lawyer along with a white businessman and a white engineer. The Organization for Human Rights was dominated by a white clergyman and a group of black and white women who were either white-collar workers or had lower-middle class husbands.

were similar in that most were either new to the South Shore area, or, because of their youth, new to South Shore organizational life. A lack of previous ties to existing structures may thus similarly facilitate commitments to organizations which, in that they are biracial, operate with new kinds of *modus vivendi*.

CONCLUSIONS

Although South Shore's total racial composition provided initial evidence of some forms of racial integration in the area, social life is essentially segregated. The nature of the contexts in which varying forms of integration are found suggests that fear of exposure and mutual suspiciousness between members of the two races inhibit biracial sharing of public places which serve as loci of private behavior. Thus some degree of demographic integration and a slight amount of biracial interaction can occur in public places in which public behavior traditionally ensues. That is, extensive integration (primarily by demographic indices) occurs in places like retail shops, church chapels, and formal organizations oriented toward the accomplishment of instrumental goals. In such settings, social interaction across racial lines is not reflective of transracial solidarity. Nor can the results of such interaction be assumed to promote eventual solidarity, given the problematic power disparities which are general concomitants of such black-white interaction. Presumably because of the greater psychic and practical dilemmas it would create, integration of any sort is absent from informal settings like church socials, service clubs, taverns, Saturday night bowling, and parks.

Because their activities and commitments tend to be local, women are more likely than men to find themselves in biracial circumstances. Protestants are more likely than are Catholics or Jews, and children—perhaps because they are less free to vary their milieu according to preference—are likely to have the most experience of biracial contact.

Although both blacks and whites face common problems under conditions of biracial propinquity and contact, the consequences on the two groups are not identical. In South Shore, as in the rest of the society, the integration experiment opens with the most important and useful institutions, organizations and settings as white, and the "challengers" or "invaders" as black. *The circumstances are thus not parallel.* The widely shared community conceptions so generated of intruders versus preservers, applied to blacks and whites respectively, provide still another distinction consistent with the status and power disparities widely observed to exist between blacks and whites. Not only is the development of transracial solidarity made more difficult as a result, but, in addition, the psychic difficulties which blacks must face when entering the alien white context are further intensified.[28] That is, biracial interaction challenges members of both races to overcome certain fears of the dissimilar, the unproven, and the threatening. But for blacks, there is the added problem of knowing that in presenting oneself in a biracial setting, one is challenging and pushing to gain something otherwise unavailable. The modal black response would seem to be either hostility (as in some manifestations of the civil rights movement) or, as was common in South Shore, a show of deference and total capitulation to white preferences.

Integration of a thoroughgoing type, what has been termed transracial solidarity, occurred in South Shore in only a few settings. These were instances in which there were cross-racial communalities of a shared and deviant ideology (mutual recognition of which provided bases for the development of needed social alternatives); an equality in occupational status and organizational usefulness (providing cross-racial parity in interpersonal vulnerability); and, among both blacks and whites, a lack of previously constituted local organizational ties (precluding habit or social pressures from inhibiting affiliation with groups which have integration as one of their innovative features).

All settings observed in South Shore (I attempted to be exhaustive) which shared these characteristics were found to approximate the circumstance of transracial solidarity; no other instances of this form of integration were found. If other possible contingencies to racial integration are to be uncovered, or if those observed in South Shore are to be confirmed as determinant (either singly, or in some value-added combination), additional case studies and eventual comparative analysis will be necessary. But for the present, it is well

28. Charles J. Levy, *Voluntary Servitude: Whites in the Negro Movement* (New York: Appleton-Century-Crofts, 1968) provides a description of an instance (whites in the southern civil rights movement) in which the tables are turned, that is, where biracial interaction occurs in a black dominated context (with analogous intensification of difficulties for whites).

to note that the conditions cited as concomitants of transracial solidarity in South Shore are precisely those which are likely to provide the overarching cues of similarity, reliability, and trust which would seem requisite for the building and maintenance of racially integrated associations, institutions, and community.

Perhaps if given enough years (years for which the commission was fighting), South Shore would be transformed into a community in which transracial solidarity (or at least biracial interaction) was a routine part of social life. Seven years after large-scale black in-migration had begun, a few signs of such a transformation were in evidence, although not nearly enough to alter the conclusion that South Shore would pass through its transition without a major alteration of the racially segregated lives of the blacks and whites who temporarily shared its neighborhoods, schools, and some of its churches and associations.

10
Summary:
Dilemmas
of Doing Good
in the City

THE efforts of the South Shore Commission and the public resources allocated to "save" South Shore were, in terms of the primary goals for this one community, wasted. Chicago whites were indeed giving up South Shore for the "greener pastures" unseen by Homer Hoyt twenty years earlier; they were leaving it to a black population which evidently found South Shore's pastures green enough to justify spending more money to live there than the whites whose aspirations, tastes, and opportunities were taking them to other areas. South Shore was simply in transition—moving toward resegregation at approximately the speed which would be expected of a changing middle-class community in the mid-1960s.

During the transition, the area was biracial and this circumstance provided opportunities for interaction between blacks and whites ordinarily lacking in urban communities. But as the racial line continued its movement across the community, additional elaboration of biracial interaction was inhibited. Blacks and whites came to share certain kinds of public places in which formalized public behaviors were played out. But private settings for private behavior— places shared with those who are trusted—generally remained segregated.

Some whites may continue to live in South Shore: a cluster of transient University of Chicago graduate students on the northern boundary, a scatter here and there of those too poor or too old to move, and a high-rise wall of those who are rich enough to live, shop, and park their cars within the confines of the "gold coast" high-rise apartment structures on the lakeshore. But this will constitute a white minority living on the edge of a black community.

204

South Shore's failures were not due to unscrupulous real estate dealers exploiting the ignorant, nor to a bigoted population, nor to the machinations of dark political forces—although each of these received some blame in various South Shore quarters. South Shore's transition was orderly; there were no violent responses from whites and they did not flee. South Shore was likely as stable during its transition as any comparable middle-class community not experiencing racial change (where, as we have seen, property changes hands at much the same rate)—but this degree of stability was simply not sufficient to accomplish commission goals. People still moved frequently, and with each move, another housing unit was likely to fall upon the Negro market. Because of the efforts of the South Shore Commission, some of these units which became available to blacks remained on the white market as well. But because of a complex set of market forces, and despite all efforts, such units were more likely to become occupied by blacks than by whites.

The commission made many attempts to compensate for the disparity between the white and Negro housing markets. From the standpoint of the organization's leaders, they had "tried almost everything" and had exhausted themselves to "preserve" their community. They succeeded in building one of the more powerful community organizations in the United States—one with hundreds of volunteer workers, an annual budget which neared $100,000, and goals enthusiastically supported by the city's political, religious, and business elite. They had the sophistication to devote extensive effort in programs which intervened directly in local real estate markets.

IMPEDIMENTS TO ACTION

Although much was done in South Shore, more could have been done, or at least done sooner. The commission was founded in advance of racial change, but most of its important programs were not established until long after transition had begun. Possibly, had a tenant referral service (primarily for whites), a fair housing center (exclusively for blacks), and the host of other commission programs been as fully developed in 1960 as they were in 1966, another outcome could have resulted.

But it would have been difficult for the commission to have moved any faster than it did. It simply takes time to conceive of new techniques and strategies, and more time to have them instituted. Yet several programs, some of which later became official organizational policies, were rejected years earlier as either too ambitious or too radical. A plan for a central tenant screening service had been advanced by the commission's first executive director well before his resignation in 1963 and was similar to the plan finally instituted in the spring of 1967. It had been rejected, in part, because it was seen by local real estate management firms to involve a usurpation of one of their key functions.

That the commission made no attempt to force realtors into accepting this scheme was due to a lack of commission power and prestige (at that time), and also to the conviction of many commission leaders that theirs was an organization devoted to moderation and never to pressure. This moderation was not, however, a basis for dealing with certain categories of persons—"block-busters," black juvenile delinquents, welfare mothers, and criminals.

Commission leaders were upper middle-class businessmen and professionals; they were disposed to "talk things over like gentlemen" with those whom they opposed, but with whom they had certain communalities in status, life-style, and ethnicity and upon whose financial and moral support their organization rested. The increasing propensity of the commission to get tough, even with some such persons, came with increasing organizational power and with growing desperation. More people became more willing to "try anything" as the alternatives to the more distasteful actions became fewer. The result is that some categories of action were continuously dependent upon a perception of crisis. Thus the general unity of purpose which existed in white South Shore may not be enough; unity of strategy is also important—especially in cases where racial change makes time a community's most precious resource.

The real question, however, is whether any community action could have worked—no matter how fast or how big. Most commission schemes rested on the dubious assumption that black people are not as attracted as whites to a community which is clean, well-maintained, safe, and filled with physical and social amenities. To the extent that this assumption is false, improvement programs have no consequence on black migration—except, perhaps, to accelerate its rate and to improve the facilities blacks inherit. Even the most ambitious program, the Tenant Referral Service, which aimed at direct intervention in housing markets, may have had little consequence—and not because it lacked proper scale. Making transition more efficient may be a legitimate social goal, but it was not the goal of the South Shore Commission.

For the racial change process to be halted, a community must have some important resource *peculiarly* attractive to whites. Late in the study period, South Shore leaders began to press for a research park or college which would fill that function. Lacking such a resource, the only alternative is to gain control of the housing market and dictate racial composition by the fiat of a quota system.[1] Such a scheme was afoot in South Shore in the plan to transfer management of contiguous blocks of South Shore apartment structures into the hands of a single management firm. A real estate company which could be trusted to maintain property at a high level and under a specified racial quota would be compensated for its sacrifice of premium black rents by an expanded volume of management business and the increased efficiencies and ease of control which management of all buildings in a single territory would facilitate. Further, a cooperative stance by a powerful and prestigious community organization would facilitate a firm's gaining zoning variations and governmental subsidies which can be enormously profitable to a developer able to exploit such opportunities.[2] This would seem to be a practical strategy for many of the parties involved. Whether the results would benefit Chicago's black community is a different question—one to be taken up shortly. But such a scheme might well be feasible; it could be institutionalized in the form of a semi-public authority consisting of community leaders, politicians, and real estate dealers. Similar arrangements have been made for other purposes in the past.

LATENT ORGANIZATIONAL GOALS: SUCCESS

The commission had one clear success: it grew. Organizations have, besides their formal or manifest goals, the latent goals

1. For discussions of quotas and stability which take a different perspective than mine, see James Tillman, "In Defense of Neighborhood Stabilization," *The Journal of Intergroup Relations,* III (Autumn 1962), 238–251; Peter Marcuse, "Benign Quotas Reexamined," *Journal of Intergroup Relations,* III (Spring, 1962), 101–116; Downs, "Metropolitan Growth and Future Political Problems," *Land Economics,* XXXVII (November 1961), 311–320.

2. See: Charles Abrams, *The City Is the Frontier* (New York: Macmillan, 1966).

of maintaining and enhancing themselves.[3] In the commission's case, these latent goals were somewhat manifest ones as well. That is, the growth and development of the commission was explicitly regarded as something to be desired and worked for. The justification was first that the commission's growth reflected a movement toward solution of South Shore's problems, and second that community organization was *in itself* something ennobling both for participants and for the general society. Participation in an organization like the commission reflected, it was said over and over again in South Shore, "taking an interest in one's community," not "being a sheep," and "doing some good in the world."

The idea is widely accepted in American society that communities should have strong community organizations and that participation in them is socially and personally rewarding. Unless they are particularly mischievous, what the groups actually *do* is less important than that they grow and prosper. This view is widely held among students of community life who often argue that voluntary groups provide participants with an enhanced self-image and act as a bulwark against extremist political activity, personal alienation, and other dangers of "mass society."[4] Among lay persons, support for community organization rests on more diffuse bases, but seems related to the general belief that such groups represent a manifestation of participatory democracy, with people deciding and creating for themselves the kind of community in which they are to live.

South Shore's leaders certainly held this view and thought virtually all others held it as well. Thus community leaders were *surprised* and *offended* when receiving any sign that their techniques or goals were being questioned. South Shore's residents expected their community to be rewarded by various civic and political agencies on the basis that "here is a community that is *organized*," and, in the words of a commission president (addressed to an audience containing public dignitaries), a community "which has decided we're tired of having things happen to us . . . we are going to de-

---

3. David Sills, *The Volunteers* (New York: The Free Press, 1957). See also: Sheldon L. Messinger, "Organizational Transformation," *American Sociological Review*, XX (Fall 1955), 3–10; Philip Selznick, *TVA and the Grass Roots* (Berkeley and Los Angeles: University of California Press, 1949); Robert Merton, *Social Theory and Social Structure* (New York: The Free Press, 1957), Chapter 1.

4. For examples, see: James S. Coleman, *Community Conflict* (New York: The Free Press, 1957), pp. 21–23; William Kornhauser, *The Politics of Mass Society* (New York: The Free Press, 1959).

termine what happens in this community." Many of the appeals for goods and services which went out to city and religious agencies were based, in part, upon the premise that communities which "do things for themselves" should receive priority treatment.

The pride in "what South Shore is doing" rested on a knowledge of the impressive growth in the scale of commission activities: the ever-expanding numbers of persons served by Tenant Referral Service, the steeply-rising budget, the larger and larger numbers of commission programs. Although the organizational growth may not have accomplished the commission's primary manifest goal, the commission itself was "doing a real job." In this, commission participants took pride, and unlike such pride in some other types of organizations (such as a public welfare agency or a spy ring) it could be outspoken and even used strategically to further other commission goals.

Commission growth was strategically functional in still another way; it helped to sustain the energies of people who were losing.[5] The commission appealed explicitly for financial support, membership, and participation on the grounds that its latent goals were legitimate. People were asked directly to help the commission grow, and growth was taken as a sign that money and effort invested had been well spent. Commission workers generally received no personal economic gain for their efforts. Rewards were primarily derived from a sense that something was being accomplished for South Shore and its commission.

This feeling of accomplishment persisted even in the face of important signs of organizational failure which were well known to all commission leaders. The most dramatic evidence was the rapidly changing racial composition of the schools, something which was front-page news in the community newspaper. Similarly, increased gang activity, the decline in quality of merchandise, and increased shop vacancy rates on the shopping strips,[6] and the increasingly frequent acts of vandalism and crime were all well known.

5. That energetic participation in voluntary associations is difficult to generate and harder still to sustain over a long period of time are points explained in: Bernard Barber, "Participation and Mass Apathy in Associations," in Alvin Gouldner (ed.), *Studies in Leadership* (New York: Harper, 1950); pp. 447–504; Martin Lipset *et al.*, *Union Democracy* (New York: The Free Press, 1956), pp. 261, 262.

6. For a comparison of retail business turnover in South Shore with that in three other Chicago communities, see: Brian J. L. Berry, "Comparative Mortality Experience of Small Business in Four Chicago Communities" (Background Paper

Yet there was a conviction, which during the study period showed few signs of flagging, that much was being accomplished, that success was within reach—that with another new program the commission would finally be on the road to success. The organization and the community were always described by commission leaders as being at the crossroads; if a strategic action were taken or a new program mounted, the tide would be turned. There were always developments that could be cited to obscure both to speaker and listener the reality of continuing failure.[7] But failure was in the area of manifest goals only; the continuing vitality of the commission was in part facilitated by the ability of its leaders to focus on what in other kinds of organizations would clearly be latent goals—a sphere in which South Shore's success was dramatic and could not be denied.

Making Demands, Celebrating Results

There is another reason for this unflagging organizational energy in the face of what otherwise would have been discouraging information. The fact was that the commission's constant barrage of demands and requests brought with them concrete results. The new high school, a new park fieldhouse, a city code enforcement center, a modest urban renewal program, a new school district plan—all represented payoff for community efforts. There were also expectations that other gains would follow: Project 71, a new college, additional clearance of blighted areas, still another school plan.[8] Commission requests were always sympathetically received. As a commission official remarked: "We have the ear of the mayor; he has our community's interests at heart."

In almost all significant commission programs, the key ingredient to success was action by an external public or quasi-public body

---

No. 4, Small Business Relocation Study, Center for Urban Studies, University of Chicago, November 1966).

7. See Leon Festinger, Henry W. Riecken, Jr., and Stanley Schachter, *When Prophecy Fails* (Minneapolis: University of Minnesota Press, 1956).

8. In a dramatic move in August, 1967, the School Board approved a busing scheme proposed by the new superintendent of Chicago schools. This plan, still being hotly contested, was designed (according to the new integration plan): "to anchor the whites that still reside in the city." South Shore leaders praised the plan with great enthusiasm. See *Chicago Daily News*, August 25, 1967, pp. 6, 10; *Chicago Sun-Times*, August 27, 1967, pp. 3, 4.

which would result in a gain for South Shore. Whether the issue was urban renewal, classroom size, gang control, or garbage collection, there was an ongoing attempt to generate priority treatment for the community—and frequently such priority treatment resulted. No one in South Shore complained that their community was getting something less than an equal share; rather the problem was seen in terms of South Shore's need for *more* than an equal share. Among South Shore leaders there was a feeling of power, of self-efficacy, a confidence in one's ability to achieve results. It was less significant that the gains were not having their intended effect; victories in the battle to influence public decisions were important in themselves.

Most organizational effort (other than routine staff operations) consisted in generating demands upon public and quasi-public bodies which would result in such victories. People had to be mobilized to attend school board hearings; staff members had to be dispatched to courtrooms to be certain that South Shore cases were appropriately handled; and residents had to be encouraged to demand a gun control law in the Illinois legislature. Most important, the top officers and most powerful commission leaders spent their time in closed meetings with the mayor, the superintendent of schools, high-ranking police and court officials, and with officers of Chicago civic organizations, generating the kinds of policies and programs felt to be needed by South Shore. Even the commission's Tenant Referral Service, which of all commission programs depended least upon outside assistance, could function only with the cooperative stance of the Chicago Commission on Human Relations and Board of Realtors.

South Shore and "Self-Help"

It would thus follow that one of the key distinctions which is sometimes made between a community organization like the South Shore Commission and more conflict-oriented organizations such as those formed by Alinsky's Industrial Areas Foundation is not valid. Clinard,[9] for example, has argued that the essence of what he

9. Clinard argues that community development "as a form of social and economic development . . . uses self-help, with technical assistance only to implement this self-help." See: Marshal Clinard, *Slums and Community Development* (New York: The Free Press, 1966), p. 127. In Clinard's view the role of government is limited to providing professional expertise, "stimulation," and "coordination."

refers to as "community development" is "self-help"—with the implication that groups like the early Woodlawn Organization in Chicago fail to meet the criterion completely because so much of their organizational effort is expended in making demands and asking other groups to "give" them things. The South Shore Commission, an organization which bears all the external characteristics of a "self-help" group according to Clinard's definition,[10] upon closer scrutiny seems also to be dependent for its growth and vigor upon the making of demands and having those demands met. Clearly, the case of the South Shore Commission does not provide evidence that vigorous community organization can ordinarily be created and sustained on any other basis.

The main distinction between the Commission and such "protest groups," *in this regard,* are the *techniques* used to generate support for demands. The commission attempted to "persuade" and "educate." Unlike protest groups, there was *never* any picketing or name-calling directed against those (among the legitimate) whose response was not favorable to commission demands. In the main, the commission depended upon the personal contacts of its leaders together with a general sympathy for commission goals among Chicago's political, economic, and religious elite. Needless to say, these kinds of contacts generally are not available to residents of neighborhoods in which protest organizations are usually formed.

That such a political style was appropriate to these kinds of people in this kind of a community is demonstrated in the painful awkwardness of those blacks who, somewhat inadvertently, became colleagues in an organization like the commission. They lacked the contacts, the clout and powerful people's sympathetic understanding for South Shore's problems as black people saw them. The result was a pervasive power asymmetry in relations between blacks and whites. Participating blacks were not helped by the fact that they also were, by dint of circumstances endemic to integration processes, the outsiders pushing in against white preservers. The net result was uncomfortable for all, but perhaps especially for the blacks who were, in a real sense, out of their place.

10. Clinard states: "Urban community development involves democratic action, stressing citizen participation, self-help, and self-determination through group action, in meeting the problems created by city life." A more detailed list of community development characteristics is provided in his work. *Ibid.,* p. 126.

IMPLICATIONS OF COMMUNITY AUTONOMY

For commission whites, however, their community organization provided a meaningful link between themselves and the larger society, and an outlet for their creativity and a confirmation of self-worth. Community organization brings control of the environment closer to the grass roots—or at least provides that impression to the participants. These effects of community organization have received widespread attention in the literature and, in fact, form the basis of research and practice in the field of community development.[11]

But bringing power closer to the local level also implies more efficient means of controlling people's lives—especially the lives of those individuals who, either because they are deviant or are in some way considered undesirable, depend on anonymity and distance from control centers for freedom from harassment. The success of an organization like the commission in gaining power in a community poses the question of how much of the resultant social control is desirable in American society—at least as the society is presently constituted.

In South Shore, for example, various commission activities were injurious to individuals who would likely have escaped reprisals had they been living in a less well-organized community. Cooperative arrangements between schools, police, real estate firms, and commission officials made it possible for action to be taken against persons living in communal or "overcrowded" housing arrangements, persons with prison records, families with delinquent children, and individuals, and marginal businessmen maintaining property in ways not desired by the community organization. Of course, such persons were seen as a threat to the community's preservation and, in this sense, the commission would have been remiss in its duties and would have defined itself as an ineffective body had it not taken action against them. Attempts were sometimes made to help such

11. See *Ibid.*; William Biddle and Loureide Biddle, *The Community Development Process* (New York: Holt, Rinehart, Winston, 1965); Carl C. Taylor, "Community Development Programs and Methods," *Community Development Review*, III (December 1956), 37–39; Roland L. Warren, *The Community in America* (Chicago: Rand McNally and Co., 1963).

individuals (if they were young) rather than to remove them from the community. But it is probably unrealistic to expect any community organization to take responsibility for solving problems created by the general plight of the American black—problems which have proven too difficult for rather substantial government programs and for sophisticated social scientists. To be an effective organization, the commission had to be "tough"—despite the fact that several commission leaders took these steps reluctantly with much soul-searching to determine that their ends did, in fact, justify their means.

Compared to many other governing bodies with power to influence the allocation of public resources and to deliver sanctions for undesired conduct, a community organization like the South Shore Commission is unregulated by other public bodies and operates through processes largely invisible even to the specific public that supports it. The advantages of community control of local institutions, raised most frequently in reference to low-income minority communities, have been widely broadcast and are sometimes accepted as a panacea for urban ills. Some of those advantages cannot easily be denied. But South Shore was also a community and its ambitious attempt to achieve autonomy raises dilemmas of accountability and control which are of general relevance. Closer proximity of power to the controlled may make institutions more responsive to the needs of local people, but it also makes social control that much more efficient. The challenge of making such institutions rational and humane thus continues, no matter at what level power resides. There may indeed be solutions, and those solutions may lie in the direction of local autonomy, but the community organization model does not, in itself, provide all the answers. Perhaps it is the nature of the context in which power is exercised—and not the *level* at which it is exercised—that is ultimately most crucial.

THE COMPETITION FOR RESOURCES: TOWARD A
MORE HUMAN HUMAN ECOLOGY

The case of South Shore autonomy raises the possibility that the autonomy of one community may be inconsistent with the autonomy of another. Completely independent action on the part of different communities which are part of the same urban system is an impossibility. A community organization will always be limited in its achievements by its competing counterparts elsewhere. It may well have a success, but that success will, by its very nature, delimit the possibilities for autonomous action in some other community.

My argument is that the growth, in numbers and in power of community organizations (along with other complementary developments), suggests the emergence of what may be termed a new ecological reality. Classic human ecological theory explains urban growth and change in terms of a competition among land users for certain strategic urban spaces—for reasons relating to topography, centrality, or proximity to another strategic element.[12] But the South Shore case suggests that there is a second system of competition—a competition among already situated land users to attract to their area a kind of land user who is seen as one who will enhance the condition of the shared territory.

In the South Shore instance the scarce commodities in the competitive process are middle-class whites and the other competing parties are, most directly, the community organizations which surround the Chicago ghetto, also struggling to attract middle-class whites. Indirectly, all other white middle-class or potential white middle-class areas in metropolitan Chicago are involved in the same competition. To achieve victory in this competitive struggle, South Shore attempted to gain the public facilities and services that were seen as necessary for creating the environmental conditions which would attract the scarce commodity. Integration provided an appropriate line of talk for negotiating the delivery of these resources.

Although the level of priority received by South Shore did not alter the community's future, examples do exist whereby success is facilitated by commitments of public funds. The case of Hyde Park, discussed frequently in this work, was an instance in which massive infusion of urban renewal money provided an important ingredient in that area's success in the competitive process. That is, Hyde Park's physical renewal remade the environment into one in which middle-class whites who wished to live near the University of Chicago could fulfill their desires. Similarly, any urban renewal project brings to an area the amenities and facilities which allow it to compete successfully for the kinds of persons who, having wide

12. See Robert Park, *Human Communities* (New York: The Free Press, 1952); Amos Hawley, *Human Ecology* (New York: The Ronald Press, 1950).

housing options, would otherwise not live there. The deployment of persons over an urban area is, in part, a result of the competition between "land areas" for a scarce type of land user.

This struggle between communities to attract middle-class whites is only one form of a more general competition among land areas for certain kinds of land users. Wherever there is a land parcel, there are persons who have a self-conscious interest in its future, perhaps because they own a portion or all of it (and their very livelihood depends upon its future); or, perhaps, as in the South Shore instance, they associate a specific land area with a way of life which they cherish and are anxious that the area have a future consonant with their values. For other kinds of land and attachments to land, the process is the same: chambers of commerce, shopping strip associations, state governors, or investors in virgin lands, all attempt to bring to their area the kinds of conditions which will attract the desired land users, thus enhancing the parcel in question. In each instance there is a competition with other similarly situated land parcels to attract the particular sought-after land users.

This competition system is obviously different from that usually described by the classical ecologists and their followers. True, people and land users continue to compete for scarce, desirable, or peculiarly strategic urban spaces. But more and more, urban spaces are competing for certain kinds of people and land users. People compete for areas—and areas compete for people. Thus there are two competitive processes occurring simultaneously and interacting with one another.

The second form of competition is becoming relatively more important than it was in the past in urban areas. Certainly land speculators, developers, chambers of commerce, and other "land interest groups" are not new on the American scene. But the possibilities for effecting basic changes in the conditions of the competition have been greatly enlarged by new technologies and the increasing scale of governmental intervention. Public interventions have remade sections of the urban environment by harnessing newly found public resources and technologies to effect an area goal. The future promises more of the same. The intervention may not be exclusively physical; the South Shore school-community cooperation plan is a "social" case in point. Even when efforts are modest and all that is required is a zoning variance or road improvement, the result is similar: areas are modified with the effect of placing them in a more strategic position vis-à-vis the kinds of land users they are attempting to attract. Thus areas are becoming strategic because of man-made capital and social improvements—and not because of certain characteristics related to natural topography or centrality. Meanwhile, human migration patterns are shaped, individual life chances are determined and patterns of social relationships molded.

Any such activities which significantly affect the desirability of certain land areas require at least the cooperation of governmental authorities, even in cases where there is no commitment of public funds. Therefore, public policy would be well guided by the fact that investments made in a certain area are likely to affect not only that area but all other areas which are in competition with it. It is not appropriate to view a single community as though it functioned in a vacuum apart from other areas. Taking neighborhood quality (as the term is often used by planners and laymen alike) to refer primarily to the "quality" of the neighborhood land user, and not to the quality of the land and environment,[13] it becomes apparent that a single area has no natural process of degeneration or regeneration apart from simultaneous occurrences in other parts of the same urban system.

Public planners delude themselves if in "regenerating" one area, they fail to take into account the consequences for other areas which are likely to be "degenerated" as a result. By bringing one area to middle-class status, the planner is relegating a competing area to working-class status. This then, is one more reason for comprehensive as opposed to piecemeal planning and for the creation of an objective rationale for the allocation of public resources between competing areas and parcels. Given the lack of such rationale in the American urban system, the distribution of environmental resources is determined by the outcome of power struggles among the stewards of competing land areas. Community organizations are, in themselves, probably insignificant competitors compared to chambers of commerce and large land-owners and developers. Regardless of the outcomes of the struggle, the point is that politics and planning are indistinguishable—with land use patterns determined by

13. See Herbert Gans, *The Urban Villagers* (New York: The Free Press, 1962), p. 308.

the elites and sub-elites who together constitute a given urban political economy.[14]

Public Participation in Planning

A corollary of this general argument is that although the wishes of indigenous citizens and community leaders may be relevant to planning decisions, the enthusiasm felt in some planning circles for giving the people what they want needs to be tempered by the realization that the goals of various community groups and organized landholders may be mutually exclusive. The problem is not just the limited financial resources of public coffers, but dilemmas of a more subtle sort.

Again, returning to the South Shore example, requests were frequently made to civic agencies for various amenities, which are not desired because they will enhance the quality of life *per se* but because they are perceived to be important to the goal of attracting certain kinds of persons to the area. Because other Chicago communities have the same goal as South Shore, they make similar requests. Even if public resources were great enough to permit the granting of all such requests, no one community would be any closer to its goals as a result, because the goal of each is a *relative* advantage over the others rather than the achievement of an absolute level of environmental quality. The point, in the South Shore case, is that not *all* communities that wish to be white and middle class can succeed in being white and middle class. Some will succeed and some will not; the question becomes one of determining by what process the resources are to be distributed, for this will ultimately determine the deployment of economic and social groups within the metropolitan area.

Planning Criteria

It follows, then, that public intervention should be based on an understanding of the processes inherent in the urban system. In the South Shore case, the commission received the cooperation of various external authorities and some degree of priority treatment because it was engaged in an attempt to make South Shore "an

14. See Martin Meyerson and Edward C. Banfield, *Politics, Planning and the Public Interest* (New York: The Free Press, 1955); Scott Greer, *Urban Renewal and American Cities* (New York: Bobbs Merrill, 1965).

integrated community of high standards." Even if one grants that it is worthwhile to create as many such communities in the city as possible (or simply to create as many *white* areas as possible), the question is still whether South Shore represented the best place to attempt to develop such a community. It might have been more strategic to give other competing areas the priorities given South Shore so that the chances for success in any one area could be maximized. Although South Shore was not a particularly poor place to strive for such a goal, I simply want to indicate the kinds of considerations which should have been made in deciding which city area was the most strategic—considerations which may or may not have been made by the various officials involved.

It may have been more appropriate, for example, for South Shore—an outlying area near a job-rich heavy industrial region— to be allowed or even *induced* to serve a black working-class population with relocation of its present middle-class residents to a different competing area, perhaps to a close-in community convenient to Chicago's Loop. In any event, it would not seem appropriate to compound the power advantages which a community like South Shore has by legitimizing its goals as appropriate *public* goals purely on the basis that it is good for a community to remain high quality (middle class) or that it is good to give people what they want, or even that it is good to have integration. In terms of the goals of the larger metropolis, the more rational strategy may be a completely different one.

Resources used to improve a community (or a given land parcel), by providing it with a *relative* advantage over a competing area, are largely wasted resources. Such expenditures represent *public* outlays for *private* benefits. This is of course not unusual in the United States; it is the way most public resources are spent which effect land use.[15] With present arrangements, resource allocation will perhaps always be determined by power struggles among competing land interests. The competition of land stewards for resources and potential land users is simply the geographical manifestation of the American political economy as it generally operates. The powerful use government resources to maximize opportunity for further ex-

---

15. See Grant McConnell, *Private Power and American Democracy* (New York: Knopf, 1966); Milton Mankoff, *The Poverty of Progress* (New York: Holt, Rinehart, Winston, 1972).

ploitation. In land use policy, as in other arenas, an understanding of this system might lay the groundwork for a more rational resource distribution process.

If residential racial integration was to become an authentic social goal in the context of such a reformed resource allocation system, the policy directive would be two-pronged: build more housing; and banish racial discrimination through policed enforcement of fair housing laws. A more direct solution would simply be to assign people to housing in a racially random matter by government edict; the two less drastic measures are more feasible.

In the short-term, new housing opportunities—especially housing available to blacks—would satiate black demand, thus causing parity between the Negro and white housing markets. Eventually, with normal turnover of the existing housing stock, the dual market would tend to wither away—especially if blacks made parallel gains in employment, income, and political power. Integration would thus be facilitated without the need to hold housing off the Negro market. Housing prices to blacks would fall, rather than rise, and the size of the total American housing stock would undergo a concomitant net increase.

The alternatives of managed integration involve either massive intervention like urban renewal, which subsidizes the desired and taxes the undesired, or less dramatically visible interventions which implement other forms of quota systems—thereby penalizing those blacks who were the potential occupants of superior housing in the otherwise expanding ghetto. A "success" at integration in either such instance, given a lack of compensatory expansion of black housing opportunities elsewhere, exacerbates the disequilibrium between the two markets, making it all the more difficult for the next border area to achieve a similar success. Thus, even as an "experiment" such instances of integration fail, because they make more difficult, not less difficult, the generalization of the very circumstance they were supposed to "demonstrate."

Improving the *quality and quantity* of black people's housing and achieving the spatial integration of American blacks are not sepaarte or contradictory goals. To question which is more important is to raise a false issue. They are inseparable and, significantly, the solution to the integration problem is through the solution to the quality-quantity problem. Public policy recognizing this principle would be a step in the right direction. By providing enough good housing to blacks, the major requisite condition for residential integration would be achieved.

FINAL SPECULATIONS

Compared to other mechanisms through which large numbers of persons manage to gain a higher level of living, racial succession is *relatively* painless.[16] Whites move on to better options and blacks inherit housing superior to that otherwise available. For many, this process is imperfect and even tragic; it "spoils" a community for people like those in the South Shore Commission and others who share their interests.

But racial succession accomplishes something *within present contexts*. It is the means by which the benefits of an expanding and improving housing supply[17] are delivered to consumers. It is a mechanism which establishes land use priorities in a manner reflecting the general social priorities of the U.S. system: the well-to-do receive the best, the poor and the black receive the worst. It is a system which works well to accomplish land-use deployment appropriate to a stratified caste-ridden society. Given these larger structural features, amelioration is systemically unable to ameliorate.

Intervention for integration, as typically practiced, represents an attempt to manipulate the mechanism without changing the nature of the machine. It thereby becomes a strategy capable of much mischief and little benefit. It aims at interrupting the natural flow of housing to people otherwise generated by the pull of superior housing for whites and the push of black population growth. It gives rise to all manner of tactics justified in terms of an enlightened goal,

16. For perspective, compare with mobility costs in other contexts: Barrington Moore, *Social Origins of Dictatorship and Democracy* (Boston: Beacon Press, 1966); Donald Cressey, *Theft of the Nation* (New York: Harper and Row, 1969); Ida Tarbell, *The History of the Standard Oil Company* (New York: Macmillan, 1937); Bernard Fall, *The Two Viet-Nams* (New York: Praeger, 1963); Herbert Gans, *The Urban Villagers*.

17. Bernard J. Frieden, "Housing and National Urban Goals" in James Q. Wilson, ed., *The Metropolitan Enigma* (Cambridge: Harvard University Press, 1968; Bernard J. Frieden, *The Future of Old Neighborhoods* (Cambridge: MIT Press, 1964).

but which cause higher housing prices for blacks, increased difficulties for long-term integration generally, and a loss of personal autonomy for those on the margins. The nobility of its stated goal is lost in the reality of the motivations which make its strategies.

The process of integration, when it does occur, takes place not between races, but between people. That is, integration can occur only when the circumstances are appropriate for individuals. That circumstance is one of biracial equality and a measure of trust and sharing rooted in mutual dependence. In purely spatial terms, large-scale racial integration will most likely result when arbitrary discrimination ends the dual market and when blacks achieve income parity with whites sufficient to compete for housing in areas presently beyond their means.

In the case of residence and race, as perhaps in all the others, integration before equality is putting the cart before the horse. The high people are brought together with the low people and within a context of formal equality, some are more equal than others.[18] The unwholesome ecological and social-psychological consequences appear endemic to the circumstance. If so, intervention of this sort not only does not succeed, it is dangerous. At a minimum, it appears to be a lot of work for nothing.

18. There exists a large literature with the opposite implication: See for example, Marion Radke et al., "Social Perceptions and Attitudes of Children," Genetic Psychology Monographs, XL (1949), 327–447; Max Deutscher and Isador Chein, "The Psychological Effects of Enforced Segregation: A Survey of Social Science Opinion," Journal of Psychology, XXVI (Fall 1948), 259–287; John Cottrel, "The Effects of Segregation and the Consequences of Desegregation: A Social Science Statement," Minnesota Law Review, XXXVII (Spring 1953), 427–439; Warren Haggstrom, "Self Esteem and Other Characteristics of Residentially Desegregated Negroes" (unpublished Ph.D. dissertation, Department of Sociology, University of Michigan, 1962). James S. Coleman, et. al., Equality of Educational Opportunity (Washington, D.C.: U.S. Government Printing Office). A perspective paralleling my own and influential to my thinking is contained in: Richard Cloward and Francis Fox Piven, "The Case Against Urban Desegregation," Social Work, XII (January 1967), 12–21.

Postscript

In the spring of 1970, I made a brief return visit to South Shore and found conditions there very different than when I had last seen the community three years before. Almost all the differences stemmed from the fact that South Shore had moved closer to becoming an all-black community, and its commission had undergone changes consistent with that circumstance.

The commission still exists, and has offices in the same building. The executive director I had known had left for employment with a Jewish service organization in the West. His job was now filled with an Alinsky-trained community organizer who talks tough and spends his nights mixing with "the people." The man who was president of the commission when I first came to South Shore had moved to a northern suburb; his replacement was a veteran commission worker who, during my study, had always been seen as the most "left-wing" of all commission participants.

Although both of these new men are white, as were their predecessors, their ascendancy marks more than a personnel change. The commission has dropped managed integration (or any other kind of integration) as its goal and no longer speaks of community improvement in racial terms. The stated commission goal is now to make South Shore simply a "good community," and that has generally meant that many of the activities of the old commission continue under the new order. Thus housing code enforcement, anti-crime street patrols, school-community cooperation, gang control, urban renewal, and aesthetic improvement remain important commission priorities. The Tenant Referral Service continues and the tenant screening system is seen as a "gut issue" by the new leaders.

Its most recent battles (both successful) were against the establishment of a Mahalia Jackson chicken stand in a residential area and the blocking of a half-way house in the O'Keeffe neighborhood. The commission still fights "deviant" landlords but now threatens them with commission-sponsored tenants' unions instead of using the strategy of persuasion which had previously been favored. The programs are thus similar to past operations, but with the difference that the action policy-base has shifted from race to class (or life-style). The South Shore Commission still exists, in large measure, to fight off the "undesirables," but gone is the idea that such a battle ipso-facto has a racial component.

Any other policy, in the context of South Shore's 1970 racial composition, would have been absurd. Commission membership is now mostly black, and of its major working committees four of five are headed by black persons (all college-educated, middle-class). The commission office, which at the time of the study was a model of business-like decorum, had become more informal, with various volunteers and staff members pleasantly moving about with a good bit of friendly chatter. Most striking, the all-white cast of 1966–67 had become almost all black in 1970.

The commission's director of tenant referral had resigned her position and had taken her contacts with her to begin a competitive referral service under the aegis of the South Shore Chamber of Commerce. Another commission staffer also resigned and a third was fired during a heated controversy. The exit of almost the entire executive staff was seen as a clear ratification of the "new commission"—one which had shifted from an integrationist goal to that of resignation to (or even enthusiasm for) South Shore's black future. The politics of the new leadership was generally quite leftist, perhaps militant, compared to the old South Shore. Whereas the old commission did not feel it could go so far as to endorse open-occupancy legislation, the new commission went on record as favoring an investigation of police harassment of the Black Panther Party. It should not be surprising that many of the veteran white commission members were upset with this turn of events.

A conservative South Side newspaper, never widely read in South Shore (*The Daily Calumet*), ran a long exposé on the so-called radical takeover of the commission.[1] Some Board members, in agree-

1. *The Southeast Economist,* always a commission booster, remained loyal and defended the organization. In language no doubt offensive to some of the

ment with the article (which others accused them of planting), resigned in protest. The local community bank withdrew part of its
support and other donors also held back. The new commission president defended the changes and publicly accused his adversaries of
"a concerted campaign to destroy the people's community organization by cutting off traditional sources of money . . . and spreading vicious lies, rumors, and distortions about the commission and
its activities; these attacks have included personal mudslinging and
character assassination." [2] Such language was not used in the old
commission; the style as well as the substance must have marked
a turning point in the tenor of organizational life.

The commission leadership was beyond the point of compromise
with the old exclusionists and their successors; the new mission was
to reconstruct the commission on a broad base of support through
expanded block-club organization and community service activity.
Contacts with the elite and large donations from single donors had
to be replaced by mass organization and mass dues. Public relations ceased minimizing the number of blacks in the community and
began touting the "new commission," which, in the new president's
words to his constituents, "means relevance—relevance to the
people of South Shore—relevance to the needs of South Shore." [3]

Racial head-counts of South Shore's 1970 school population reveal quite clearly that nothing would have been more irrelevant
than a continuation of the former integration policy. The data contained in Table 26 seems to indicate that community transition was
well into its final phase. The speed of racial change was likely as
rapid after the study period as it was in the previous years. In the
period 1963–1966 black enrollments of three schools (O'Keeffe,
Bryn Mawr, Mann) increased approximately 50 percent; in the

commission's new leaders, the paper editorialized, in part: "Thanks to a tremendous
amount of work and dedication of residents, the South Shore Commission accomplished many fine things. Today, by and large, South Shore is still a highly
desirable place to live. It has been estimated that about 1400 new families
bought in South Shore last year. Many of these are college professors and
graduate students. However, over the years—especially the last few—there has
been an influx of people of other types and colors. They were different. They
were not necessarily 'inferior.' One who comes to mind is a union secretary,
a black lady, whose efforts on behalf of the O'Keeffe community caused her to
be commended in the City Council. Her number is legion." See the *Southeast
Economist* (Chicago), Jan. 15, 1970.

2. *South Shore Scene* (Chicago), Volume II, No. 1, Feb. 1970.
3. Undated letter to the community, South Shore Commission.

TABLE 26
RACIAL COMPOSITION OF SOUTH SHORE'S PUBLIC SCHOOLS,
1963, 1966, 1969, 1970

School	Percent of Enrollment Black			
	1963	1966	1969	1970
Parkside	90.3	99.1	99.8	100.0
O'Keeffe	39.8	93.9	97.5	98.3
Bryn Mawr	16.3	66.1	93.1	96.8
Bryn Mawr Annex[a]	0	0	95.3	96.1
Mann	7.0	55.1	95.6	97.1
Bradwell	0.1	3.7	68.7	86.5
Sullivan	0	2.3	3.2	4.1
South Shore High	1.5	41.8	90.0	97.7

SOURCE: Chicago Board of Education.
[a] Added to the district after 1966 to relieve overcrowding at Bryn Mawr school.

next three-year interval, two schools (Mann and Bradwell) experienced a similar change, and racial change in a third school (Bryn-Mawr) was extremely rapid. Similarly, South Shore High School, something of an overall measure of racial composition of the school district, experienced more rapid change after the study period than before.

As we have noted, these data on school racial composition overstate the degree of black occupancy; it is likely that the 1970 high school racial composition of 97.7 percent black does not correspond to the community's overall racial composition. The whites on the lakefront are too old to have children in school; the scatter of graduate students in O'Keeffe are too young to have school-age children. But it is not difficult to conclude that, for all intents and purposes, whites with school-age children are no longer moving into South Shore and that most who once lived there are now gone.[4] Thus, South Shore's historical position as the home of middle-class child-rearing whites is over.

A series of 1970 community hearings, held by Commission Area Councils to air common problems, came up with these priority concerns, as listed in the *South Shore Scene*:[5]

4. Data was not gathered which could determine if there was a white "flight" during this period, or if South Shore property turnover remained stable.
5. *South Shore Scene*, Vol. II, No. 2, March 1970, p. 1.

RAINBOW NEIGHBORS
1. Bryn Mawr School: poor quality education, lack of discipline, substitute teachers and overcrowding
2. Bradwell School: discipline problems
3. Burglaries in residential and commercial areas
4. Undesirables, crime and vice reportedly emanating from the Bellereve Hotel at 73rd & Yates
5. Poor street and building maintenance
6. Increase in radio patrol

JEFFERY-YATES
1. Crime on 79th Street
2. Better discipline and overcrowding at Horace Mann School
3. Buildings converted to provide illegal apartments
4. More block-clubs needed
5. Increase in radio patrol

PARKSIDE
1. Broken windows and poor lighting at Parkside Elementary
2. Need radio patrol units
3. 67th Street—Stony Island Urban Renewal Project needs drastic acceleration and priority treatment
4. Need more blocks organized
5. 71st Street merchants reducing maintenance and quality

O'KEEFFE
1. Reject request for halfway house on Jefferey
2. Need full-time recreation program at O'Keeffe School
3. Get rid of all abandoned cars
4. Overcrowding and poor quality education at O'Keeffe School
5. Improve conditions at South Shore High School
6. Dirty and inadequate commercial strips, especially 71st Street
7. Poor building maintenance

Those familiar with black communities will recognize in this list conditions typically complained of in black areas. South Shore's heartland, Bryn Mawr, is served by a school almost completely black. Where once the specialty of Byrn Mawr School, the pride of South Shore's middle-class, was its program of enrichment for the gifted, its current thrust is, like almost all of South Shore's schools, the maintenance of discipline. Bryn Mawr School parents demanded and received a replacement for the white principal who had formerly been esteemed by area residents. The poor performance of children in school was seen as caused by failures in the school system rather than, as it previously was, to the changing clientele of the schools. Demands were thus made for smaller classes, better teachers and more responsive administrators. Similarly, higher crime rates were not explained by racial change, but were seen as due to inadequate police protection. The commission executive director fought for more police and citizens asked for "stepped up" law enforcement. South Shore residents demanded that "police quit referring to South Shore as a 'changing community' as a reason for crime . . . and that police stop suggesting that merchants put iron grills on their windows." [6]

The changes which have come to South Shore were anticipated all along by at least some community residents—people who were popular neither with the commission nor with the enemies of the commission. Little attention was payed to them during the study period; perhaps more should have been. They probably found the abstract arguments of the "community-minded" on the values of self-determination and viable urban living to be as meaningless as the speeches of local sociologists who talked of voluntarism and turning the tide of urban decay. For them, the end was inevitable and you didn't have to be a sociologist to know which way the social wind was blowing. One was a South Shore real estate man, an owner of much commercial property in the area, who never took much interest in the South Shore Commission. During the study, I came into contact with such people only by accident or when sampling real estate dealers as part of the larger survey. In a 1969 newspaper interview, this man spoke in the same tone (referred to as negative in commission circles) that he and some others had used at the beginning of the study period. He spoke of the difficulties faced by white merchants when racial change began, but observed that those difficulties had been since resolved: "When the merchants got over the hump, and decided they had to recognize that South Shore would be either white or black, things began to stabilize. The merchants realize that we are black now." He concluded on a more general note: "You know, when the Irish came to South Shore, the English thought the end of the world had come. When the Jews came, the

6. *Ibid.*, p. 2.

Irish thought the end of the world was here. Then when the blacks started coming in, there was the end of the world again. The world is always coming to an end in South Shore." [7]

7. *Chicago Daily News,* Feb. 26, 1969, p. 4.

Appendix

Survey
Methods

THE basic methodology for the research findings reported in Chapter Two was an analysis of structured interviews held with representatives of a sample of Chicago real estate firms which owned or managed apartment buildings. Interviews were carried out, in the main, during the last half of 1966.

The universe. Preliminary interviews suggested that real-estate dealers who rent apartments almost daily would hold rather clear-cut positions concerning the behavior of rents, maintenance costs, vacancy rates, and profits which accrue to the holders of property in areas of racial change or potential racial change. The firms of such individuals constituted the universe from which the sample was drawn. It is recognized that others also play an important role in real-estate market processes (such as financial institutions, home-owners), but such parties were not included in the study universe.

The sample. It was considered important to generate enough cases within sampled areas to facilitate inter-neighborhood comparisons. For this reason, an attempt was made to interview *all* professional landlords operating within five quite different types of market areas.

The first important criterion for choice of areas was that there be a significant number of apartment units within the area. Three areas within the city of Chicago and two suburban towns were selected as appropriate for the present study. These areas were considered appropriate because each had a large number of structures containing ten or more apartment units and because each was regarded as a more or less cohesive "market region" by various real estate informants.

Taken together, these market regions (as described in Chapter Two) represent a variety of racial conditions and thus permit comparisons between areas along this dimension. In addition to comparisons along racial variables, the choice of sample areas also permits a comparison of communities of differing socioeconomic status; the inclusion of two suburbs permits a comparison of independently incorporated areas (with independent real-estate boards) with non-autonomous Chicago communities (which lack such independent boards).

The president or an owner of each real-estate firm with an office in the selected market regions was asked to participate. In those instances where local real-estate offices were branch offices of larger firms, the manager of the local branch as well as the president of the firm was included in the sample.

Sampling procedure. Every business operating an office phone has the option of a free listing in the "yellow pages" of an appropriate neighborhood Illinois Bell Telephone Directory. For this reason, the neighborhood directory listings were taken to constitute a complete listing of professional landlords from which samples could be drawn. Those firms listed under the heading "Real Estate" which were not engaged in renting apartments were eliminated from the sample.

Interviewing procedures. The initial sample included 327 real-estate firms. A letter explaining the study but not its precise purpose was mailed to each firm. This letter solicited the cooperation of the respondent and indicated that a staff member would phone to arrange an interview. In those instances where respondents expressed reluctance to be interviewed (but not an out-and-out refusal) or in cases where respondents repeatedly postponed or delayed appointments, interviewers stopped in for interviews. This tactic was found to be effective in gaining additional interviews and only twice elicited hostile responses.

The interviewing staff consisted primarily of University of Chicago graduate students working under my supervision (I also participated in data gathering). The intent of the questions on the interview schedule was explained to interviewers and they were encouraged to probe respondents when replies seemed ambiguous or when there was reluctance to answer. Interviews lasted approximately seventy minutes. In most instances respondents were cooperative and seemed favorably disposed toward the interview situation. Where this was not the case, the interviewer noted on the interview schedule that there was hostility or suspicion.

The survey instrument. The interview schedule aimed primarily at tapping the cognitive set with which real-estate agents and owners could be expected to anticipate racial change in buildings they operated. The attempt was to learn what a real estate dealer thinks happens as a building goes through various kinds of racial experiences.

For purposes of description, the interview schedule can be divided into eight sections. Questions 1–4 consist of introductory remarks and a group of questions which, on the basis of trial interviews, were felt to be "rapport building." Questions 5–12 investigate the conditions under which buildings and neighborhoods undergo racial change.

Questions 13–18 elicit the attitudes of respondents toward the behavior of *rents* under various racial conditions. Respondents were shown a card listing five different rent levels and were asked to specify which rental level best approximated the rent which would be collected under specified neighborhood and building racial conditions. The use of five rental levels facilitated the gathering of relatively specific responses and at the same time made it possible to learn the perceived magnitude of changes in rental income as well as their *direction*. It was found during trial interviews that posing questions in this manner led to minimal confusion on the part of respondents.

Questions 19–22 represent an attempt to learn how professional landlords view the effects of various racial conditions upon maintenance expenses involved in operating a structure. Here the respondent was shown a card listing various kinds of racial conditions and was asked to indicate at which points maintenance costs were least or greatest.

Questions 23–32 request respondents to specify the effects of various stages of racial change upon the general profitability of operating a structure. It was found during trial interviews that respondents could be expected to differentiate profits accruing to *agents* (those who manage property but do not own) from profits accruing to *owners*. For this reason, both circumstances were investigated.

Questions 33–43 seek to gather specific information regarding the size, type of operation, area served, and racial experience of the firm represented by the respondent.

Questions 44–63 investigate the social and educational background of respondents, their organizational and friendship affiliations, professional activities, and certain other experiences thought likely to affect perceptions of the racial change process.

Questions 64–70 tap the interviewer's observations of the respondent's race, the atmosphere and location of his office, his general attitude toward Negroes and toward the interviewing situation.

Generally, there was an attempt made to have questions follow one another in a reasonable way in order to facilitate comprehension by the respondent. Additionally, there was an attempt to alternate open-ended questions with precoded ones to enable the interviewer to continue writing while the respondent considered a subsequent question which did not require lengthy reporting. Still another guide for structuring the schedules was to disperse the most "threatening" questions throughout the interview schedule to avoid alienating the respondent. Finally, the two questions which were regarded as most likely to upset respondents (62 and 63) were placed at the very end of the schedule in order to preclude their contamination of answers to other questions.

The response rate. A total of 177 interviews were successfully completed. In the course of contacting and interviewing these persons, 64 other individuals were dropped from consideration as not being part of the universe. These were individuals who were deceased, retired, or otherwise out of business or who were members of other firms which were already represented in the sample. There were individuals within the sampled universe who refused to grant interviews. Reasons cited by such persons included lack of time, hostility toward the University of Chicago, and the feeling that their answers would not be useful. The total response rate is 68 percent. A breakdown of response data by area is contained in the following table.

Problems and biases. Civil rights activities regarding open-occupancy in Chicago (led by Martin Luther King) were frequent during the spring and summer of 1966. The resultant disputes received much attention and were often referred to by respondents. The exact effect of such events upon responses given is difficult to assess; they may have created resistance which increased the number

TABLE 27

RESPONSE PATTERN BY SAMPLE AREA

Neighborhood Type by Racial Condition	Number of Successful Interviews	Number of Unsuccessful Interviews	Number of Refusals	Response Rate	Adjusted Sample Size[a]	Number Dropped from Sample	Unadjusted Sample Size
Northeast Chicago (white)	59	4	26	.663	89	15	104
Suburbs (predominantly white)	33	7	12	.635	52	7	59
South Shore (in transition)	31	1	11	.721	43	27	70
Southeast Chicago (black)	39	3	15	.684	57	13	70
Hyde Park (integrated)	8	0	4	.666	12	2	14
Loop (city-wide)	7	0	0	1.000	7	0	7
Total	177	15	68	4.369	260	64	324

[a] Respondents considered not to be a part of the universe were dropped from consideration and not interviewed.

of persons who refused to be interviewed or who continuously indicated no variation in rents or profits with changes in neighborhood
racial composition.

Women were underrepresented among the respondents. In the
three instances where it was known that women were the heads of
real-estate firms, there were refusals.

Because professional landlords could only enter the sample by
having an office within one of the study areas, many firms which
operated buildings within the study areas but from offices located
elsewhere were not represented. Among these are financial institutions holding temporary or permanent control of structures which
came into their hands through mortgage defaults or receivership
arrangements. The degree to which such landlords have different
perceptions of market processes from the sampled persons cannot
be known on the basis of data collected.

Index

Abrahamson, Julia, 8
Agents, real estate, 190, 205; profits in changing area, 29–33
Alinsky, Saul, 211, 223
Apartment listings, 115, 116
Apartments vs. single-family units, 16–20
Armour Square, 190
Asymmetry in integration, 201, 202, 212
Auburn-Gresham, 140, 142
Autonomy. *See* Community control

Baptist Church, 193, 195
Biracial interaction, 174
Black in-migration: restraints upon, 117–118; speed of, 131–147
Blacklists, 122
Black Panther Party, 224
Black-white rent differences. *See* Color tax; Dual market; Housing values and race
Blacks, interchangeability of, 197, 198
Block busters, 36, 123–125, 200
Block clubs, 80
Boundaries of South Shore, 45–50
Bradwell, 54, 226
Bryn Mawr East, 53, 225
Bryn Mawr Plan, 93–94, 110
Bryn Mawr West, 53, 225
Bunche, Ralph, 98
Burgess, Ernest, 7, 48

Chamber of Commerce, 88, 224
Chauffeur service, 113
Chel-Win area, 54
Chel-Win Association, 54, 75, 76
Chicago Board of Realtors, 211
Chicago Commission on Human Relations, 124, 211
Chicago Daily News, 12
Chicago Dwellings Association, 102
Chicago Sun Times, 12
Chicago, University of, 12, 82, 87, 115, 126, 169, 204, 215
Christian duty, 190
Christian Science Monitor, 80
Church role, 63, 64, 111

City, 80
City politics, 107–109
Civil rights marches, 233
Clinard, Marshall, 211
Code enforcement, 101–103
Color tax, 15, 19, 28, 29
Community control, 81, 213
Community improvement associations, 4, 7, 208, 213, 214
Competition among land areas, 214–218
Crime: in South Shore, 83–89; newspaper reports of, 86
Cross-Racial parity, 202, 222

Daily Calumet, 224
Daley, Richard, 67, 108
Demographic integration, 174
Dentler, Robert, 8, 103
Discrimination: landlords practice of, 23; tests of, 116, 117; commission complicity in, 117, 118; effects of, 221, 222
Downs, Anthony, 81, 117
Dual market, 19–40, 101, 109, 220, 222
Duncan, Otis Dudley, 5, 6, 7, 144

Ecological forces, 3, 4, 10, 12
Elites and land use, 218
End, world coming to, 228
Ethnic cues, 176
Euphemisms, function of, 72–74
Evanston, 21–27
Exclusionists-integrationists, 66–69
Executive sessions, 67

Factbook. *See* Local community areas
Fair Housing Center, 125, 126
Fair Housing Ordinance, 23, 34, 118, 192
Fulton, Robert, 167

Gans, Herbert, 168
Gold Coast, 204
"Good Negroes," 98
Grey areas, 9
Grier, Eunice and George, 168

237